Passion, Power, and Promise

Passion, Power, and Promise

Introducing the Holy Spirit

ROBERT C. FENNELL

WIPF & STOCK · Eugene, Oregon

PASSION, POWER, AND PROMISE
Introducing the Holy Spirit

Wipf & Stock
An Imprint of Wipf and Stock Publishers
199 W. 8th Ave., Suite 3
Eugene, OR 97401

www.wipfandstock.com

PAPERBACK ISBN: 979-8-3852-6565-7
HARDCOVER ISBN: 979-8-3852-6566-4
EBOOK ISBN: 979-8-3852-6567-1

VERSION NUMBER 041326

Dedicated to all who seek the Holy Spirit

Contents

Acknowledgments

ANY PROJECT WORTH ITS salt is the result of many collaborations and relationships. I am sincerely grateful, first, to the dozens of United and Uniting Church colleagues around the world (and their academic institutions) who generously assisted me in finding and understanding the expressions of doctrine that their denominations embrace. The United Church of Canada Foundation deserves a special mention for its generous and important support for researchers through the McGeachy Senior Scholarship, which I was most fortunate to receive. The McGeachy funds permitted research and writing time I would not otherwise have had. I am grateful to Atlantic School of Theology (AST) and my colleagues there for their support of this project. Leave funded by the McGeachy Scholarship enabled AST to engage Morgan Bell as our visiting resident scholar in theology in winter 2024. Thanks go out to Morgan as well for his willingness to teach in my stead and to engage with AST's students on new and important theological themes. The McGeachy Scholarship also provided funding for research assistance from Desdemona Shaw, proofreading expertise from Sarah Grondin (who saved me from many errors), and support in bringing the book to publication. I thank Pine Hill Divinity Hall for funding another much-needed research assistant, Ben Kinsey. Warm thanks to Jun-Hyok Chon, Ruibiao Li, and Chuan Xu who provided expert translation services. Special thanks to Kate Jones, who wrote the thoughtful discussion questions for each chapter.

Professors David Deane, Pamela McCarroll, Geoff Thompson, Veli-Matti Kärkäinnen, Vahan H. Tootikian, and Michael Welker offered congenial and insightful advice to my research queries. Simon LeSieur kindly shared his doctoral research with me. Notes from the readers of manuscript drafts—Harold Wells and Evan Smith—put me on a better footing in several aspects of this study, in matters great and small. I sincerely thank them all. My students in the Holy Spirit in International Perspective course helped me to see things that I would have missed on my own—my thanks to them.

I am also grateful to the Annual Ecumenical Mission of Strathcona County (2024) and the Cork Lectures at Vancouver School of Theology and St. Andrew's Hall (2025) for their respective invitations to deliver lectures and studies in person, which gave me crucial opportunities to sharpen what I wanted to say in these pages.

Matthew Wimer and the team at Wipf and Stock have once again been wonderful partners in bringing this book to press.

As always, I am tremendously grateful to my spouse, Sally Shaw, who takes a lively interest and offers important challenges and affirmations to my thinking. Last but not least, I am indeed thankful that I have felt the guidance and presence of the Holy Spirit throughout this project. Thanks be to God.

Introduction

In approaching the theme of the Holy Spirit the reader need not expect a neat systematics.

—Brendan Leahy, "Hiding Behind the Works"

[A] theologian should resist all attempts to over systematize a topic
[pneumatology]
that by its very nature is dynamic, lively, and elusive.

—Veli-Matti Kärkäinnen, The Holy Spirit

In these pages you will discover the sublime and the absurd, the joyful and the sombre, the profound and the everyday. All this is entirely in keeping with the nature and work of the Holy Spirit. My goal has been to bring both clear language and theological insight to the surface of my own and others' awareness of the Holy Spirit, not to diminish the Mystery of it all but as a celebration of the Spirit's splendid presence and work throughout creation.

The permission suggested by the two quotations above to offer an ad hoc work of theology was no small relief in the writing of this book. While there is always in me a desire for order and coherence, the effervescent profusion of the Holy Spirit's diverse life and work can scarcely be confined to a few marks on a page. We shouldn't necessarily expect that our understanding of the Holy Spirit will be altogether tidy and neat. The Holy Spirit is by nature an uncontrollable reality. All theological work in relation to the Holy Spirit is also prone to being untidy. We might like to be able to say something coherent, concise, and comprehensive in our systematic work with respect to the Holy Spirit, but that is often difficult, just by nature of the subject matter.

Here, I have only been able to capture a glimpse of the doctrine of pneumatology and to note down my observations. From the theologians of antiquity, to the Reformers, to the contemporary efforts of United and Uniting Church denominations all over the world, we find a rich and delightful feast for both the theologically curious and those earnestly searching spiritual renewal or enlightenment.

The Purpose of This Book

This book aims to do three things:

1. The first purpose is to offer a meaningful and robust introductory account of the Holy Spirit, illuminated when possible by insights from the United and Uniting Churches of the world. This purpose arises from my observations over many years that this branch of Christian thought (pneumatology) is often overlooked or underdeveloped in many United and Uniting Churches, including my own (The United Church of Canada).[1] A careful search is needed to find what these denominations have to offer.
2. The second objective is to set the United and Uniting Churches' teaching about the Holy Spirit within the context of Scripture and alongside the creeds and doctrinal formulations of both the ancient church and the Protestant Reformations. The heart of this objective is the task of locating the United and Uniting witness in relation to the shared ecumenical and historical contexts that these "younger" churches still consider essential.
3. The third and final purpose of this book is to describe, briefly, the nature of theology as it is done within the United and Uniting Church denominations of the world.

Eugene Rogers laments "the continual lip service and equally continual lack of substance accorded the Holy Spirit in modern Christian thought. Committed to talk of the Spirit by multiple traditions, modern Christian thought has less and less to say about it."[2] With the exception of the im-

1. "The denomination's theological reservoirs would be deepened by further research and sustained reflection on the doctrine of the Holy Spirit." Schweitzer et al., "Conclusion," 341. *Hope Peace Unrest*, by Schweitzer and Kwon, is an important recent contribution.

2. Rogers, *After the Spirit*, 1.

portant testimony of Pentecostal thought, which is growing in significance every year, I would agree with Rogers that this is largely true. The understanding of the Holy Spirit in mainline churches has been called "anemic,"[3] but the extent of teaching and clear expression about the Spirit in Western theology as a whole is limited. This circumstance is not altogether new. Even the ancient Christian theologian, Ephrem the Syrian, who in other passages clearly had a high regard for the Spirit, slights her with near-indifference in one place:

> Praise to the unlimited Father.
> Praise to the inscrutable Son,
> Together with the Holy Spirit.[4]

Ephrem's benign neglect in this stanza of his hymn is emblematic of the way that pneumatology is sometimes left out in the cold as an afterthought of Christian theology. After the ancient church settled the question of the Holy Spirit's divine status within the Trinity, pneumatology has typically taken a back seat. Just as often, the Spirit has not even been invited along on many theological journeys. For example, neither the Westminster Confession (1646), which is so important in Reformed theology, nor the Lutheran Augsburg Confession (1530), has a separate article on the Holy Spirit. At the congregational/parish level, it might not be uncommon to see what Simon LeSieur notices: "In the absence of pneumatological clarity, the presence of the Holy Spirit is generally assumed, [but] rarely taught."[5]

It is not that Christians dislike the Spirit. Indeed, the role and presence of the Holy Spirit is deeply valued in the Christian life. There is consistent, worldwide longing for the Spirit's presence, gifts, and blessings throughout Christian history, right up to the present moment. But there seems to be a gap in many traditions in terms of speaking clearly and systematically about who the Holy Spirit is and what the Holy Spirit does. This is evidently not a new development, if Augustine is to be believed:

> With respect to the Holy Spirit . . . there has not been as yet, on the part of learned and distinguished investigators of the Scriptures, a discussion of the subject full enough or careful enough to make it possible for us to obtain an intelligent conception of what also constitutes His special individuality.[6]

3. LeSieur, *Come, Holy Spirit*, 5.
4. Ephrem, *Hymns* 67.24.
5. LeSieur, *Come, Holy Spirit*, 29–30.
6. Augustine, *Of Faith and the Creed* 9.19.

Robert Jenson notices something similar about the ancient Christian era: "Even the Nicene Creed devotes comparatively little space to the Spirit in comparison with the Father and the Son."[7] In more recent days, the same sentiment is heard: "At times the church has veered toward silence in matters of the Spirit."[8] This gap or negligence in studying or speaking of the Holy Spirit seems to be especially true within the mainline or liberal denominations, including the United and Uniting Churches of the world. A good example of this is the otherwise excellent *Leuenberg Agreement*, which in 1973 articulated an ecumenically significant theological consensus among European Protestant Churches. Yet here we find only a small handful of mentions of the Holy Spirit, and at that, the Spirit is mostly an adjunctive helper of Jesus Christ, who is the truly active agent.[9]

The other side of the coin is that in major anthologies of pneumatology, contributions from United or Uniting Church sources are extremely rare. Some might suggest that this is because United and Uniting Churches tend to emphasize Christian practices, or practical theology, in contrast to doctrinal theology and written statements. There is probably some truth to this. Without delving far into *why* the United and Uniting Churches (and some other traditions) sometimes neglect the Spirit as a theological subject worthy of written reflection, I simply want to begin by noting that this is the case.

To the extent that Swiss-German theologian Karl Barth (1886–1968) has influenced the United and Uniting Churches—and his influence has been significant throughout contemporary Protestantism—the pneumatology of these denominations has been impoverished. Despite his many vital contributions, Barth did not provide a satisfying account of the Holy Spirit, except insofar as indicating that the Spirit was a kind of helpmate or shadow to the Son, Jesus Christ. As Eugene Rogers has put it, Barth's practice was "never to speak of the Spirit apart from the Son."[10] To be sure, Spirit and Son are indeed one in the Trinity, but Christian thought also holds them to be distinctive in important ways. Barth, like many others, focused his work on Christology, making Jesus Christ the most important subject for theological reflection. Much of Western Christian thought (both Protestant and Roman Catholic) from the Reformations era onward has done the same, as have many of the denominations that arose in response to Western missionary

7. Jenson, "Introduction," xiii.

8. Jenson, "Introduction," xiii.

9. Community of Protestant Churches in Europe, *Leuenburg Agreement*, 2.10, 2.13, 2.14.

10. Rogers, *After the Spirit*, 30–31.

activity in various regions of Africa and Asia. Again, Christology has predominated in most theological work: It is "theology's gold standard."[11] As a result, pneumatology has suffered from benign neglect, or at least fallen behind. But it is surely pointless to pit the Persons of the Trinity against each other, as though one were more important than another. All we can aim to do now is to address the gap and grow in our understanding of the Holy Spirit.

This book, then, is directed toward responding to that gap. The specific way I will do this is by drawing upon the written materials of many United and Uniting Churches, their theologians, the Bible, and other theological resources, ancient and contemporary, aiming to answer those two vital questions:

- *Who* is the Holy Spirit? (Part One)
- *What* does the Holy Spirit do? (Part Two)

I hope that addressing these questions will provide helpful theological resources to Christian believers, the curious, the committed, preachers, teachers, students, and others interested in the spiritual life and in the theological grounding of the Christian faith.

The Scope and Limits of This Book

Even as I have sought to accomplish the three goals noted above, I am mindful of the caution of Ephrem the Syrian. Ephrem cannily noted that there will always remain a mystery to the Holy Spirit: "Who can depict the Holy Spirit with discussions?"[12] Or writing? Or singing? All human efforts will be incomplete. Reverence for the divine mystery and indeed silence before the ineffable One are always appropriate stances. Respect for lived experience of the Holy Spirit (spirituality) is also uppermost, including those experiences that cannot truly be expressed through words. Even so, we shall endeavor to say a few things that might be helpful in theological terms. I have looked across history to retrieve many of the expressions of faith regarding the Holy Spirit present in the First and Second Testaments (or Old and New Testaments) of the Bible, as well as the first centuries of the ancient church. Given the importance of the Reformers to the United and Uniting Churches, I have also consulted three key figures: Martin Luther, John Calvin, and John Wesley. Although Wesley is significantly separated in time from the first

11. Rogers, *After the Spirit*, 38.
12. Ephrem, *Hymns* 33.7.

two, the legacies of all three continue to resonate for twenty-first-century Protestants. Lastly, I have included the witness of many of the approximately forty United and Uniting Churches that currently exist around the world. Despite my best efforts, I was not able to find sufficient written materials from all forty to be able to claim that I consulted the complete United and Uniting family. I was able to locate contributions from about three-quarters of them. It is important to note also that some of the United and Uniting Churches identify no doctrinal statements at all, apart from the ancient creeds, as meaningful to them.

Overview

The book begins by diving into the heart of the matter, by asking in Part One, *Who is the Holy Spirit?* The significance of language, names, images, and terms for the Holy Spirit is the first step. We consider the Spirit's place and relations within the Trinity, and how the vital principle of *appropriation* functions. This focus on the immanent, "interior" nature of the Spirit is then turned outwardly to consider how She interacts with creation, including humankind. Part One concludes by exploring how pneumatology is always bound up with Christology.

In Part Two, we turn to the action of the Spirit, to respond to the question, *What does the Holy Spirit do?* The keynote of *transformation* is at the heart of this section, as we focus on the work of the Holy Spirit toward creation, for the sake of individuals, and for the common good, both within and beyond the church.

Part Three is a brief foray into the approaches that are distinctive to United and Uniting denominations as they go about the work of theological writing about pneumatology and other doctrinal themes. The last chapter ("Postlude") rounds out the book by providing a glimpse into some unresolved issues and future prospects.

Passion, Power, and Promise

The *passion* of the Holy Spirit is to enact, in and with all creation, the fulfillment of God's purposes in the realm (kingdom) of God.

The *power* of the Holy Spirit is revealed in the giving of gifts, inspiration, and guidance to all human creatures, helping and urging them to align with God's purposes.

The *promise* of the Holy Spirit is that, in the end, no sin or trouble will prevent the triune God from bringing about the loving redemption, joy, and transformation of all creation.

PART ONE

Who Is the Holy Spirit?

Chapter 1

Prelude: Silence

There is great value in beginning any study of a theological subject with a period of silence. Much, or most, of the reality of God and God's ways remain hidden in mystery, beyond speech and even adequate thought. Silence, an ancient friend of all spiritual seekers, is welcome at any stage of reading, as it has been in the writing of this book. With this in mind, I invite you, the reader, to pause now for a moment of silent reflection.

~

After we have kept silence, what shall we say? How can we begin to speak of the person—the "who"—of the Holy Spirit? The next five chapters offer a study of the way that the Holy Spirit is properly considered as one with the Trinity, the triune God—not a piece or part, nor an instrument nor a tool of God. The Trinity itself is a mystery, and no less so when Christian theology endeavors to speak of the three triune Persons. But we will make an attempt nonetheless. Closely connected to this is the principle or doctrine of *appropriation*, which suggests that certain aspects, characteristics, or actions of the divine Three-in-One can be helpfully thought of as distinctively descriptive of just one of the three Persons. In this case, what is "appropriated" or attributed to the Spirit will be of special interest.

Next, we turn to a series of reflections on the language, names, images, and terms that Christians use to speak of the Holy Spirit. Most of these are drawn from the First and Second Testaments of the Bible, the most ancient source for Christian thought. These linguistic expressions have proven to be fruitful and durable, even if they are sometimes perplexing or culturally unfamiliar in the present day. This in turn leads to a discussion of how the

Holy Spirit is Someone not only within the Trinity, but also Someone turned toward creation and humankind. Finally, I will present a short account of how speaking of the Holy Spirit (pneumatology) invariably involves thinking about the Person of Jesus Christ (Christology), and vice versa.

FOR REFLECTION OR DISCUSSION

1. "Much, or most, of the reality of God and God's ways remain hidden in mystery, beyond speech and even adequate thought." What are some of the mysteries of God or questions about God that you ponder in silence, rather than put into concrete thoughts or words?

Chapter 2

Who Is the Holy Spirit Within the Trinity?

For look: one is three and three is one.
They are mingled, yet not fastened [to one another].
They are divided, yet not cut.
This marvel silences us entirely.
—Ephrem the Syrian, The Hymns on Faith

ONE WOULD THINK AFTER reading these words of Ephrem the Syrian (c. 306–73) that even the briefest contemplation of the Trinity should render us speechless. As noted in chapter 1 ("Prelude"), there is indeed good reason to begin with silent wonder when bringing such a mystery to mind. Even so, neither Ephrem nor countless other Christian thinkers have fully embraced that injunction to refrain from words!

What then to say about God the Trinity, if we resolve not to keep silent?

The inward life of the Trinity, the relations of the three Persons toward each other, undoubtedly lies shrouded in mystery. Still, there are some clues offered by the Bible and Christian teaching down through the ages. The inward-facing aspect of the Trinity's life and reality (God "within" God, so to speak) is often called the *immanent* Trinity. In contrast, other aspects of God seem to us human creatures to be turned outwardly toward creation and human beings. These aspects reflect the *economic* Trinity. This has nothing to do with trade, markets, or the exchange of money. "Economic" here is rooted in the Greek word *oikoumene*, suggesting something like *the ordering of a household*. By extension and a refined use of the term, the economic Trinity has to do with the way that God acts toward humankind and creation as a whole. In this section, we will look at the *immanent* Trinity—the inward life of the Three Divine Persons who are One.

"One Is Enough"

But first, a short story. As legend has it, seven-year-old Erin, with her bright red hair and shining green eyes, was asked one morning in her Irish catechism class why there is only one God. She thought for a moment, then replied confidently, "Because one is enough."

Erin is not wrong. A central, indispensable faith claim of Christian theology and belief is that *God is One.* There is only one God. Yet Christian theology also affirms that there is a "threeness" to God. God is *triune.* God is Trinity. Yet God is also One. There is only One God, not three gods: "Hear, O Israel: the Lord our God, the Lord is One."[1] For someone committed to religious or philosophical monotheism, or to ancient Greek monadism, this apparent contradiction between threeness and oneness is a bridge too far, and they cannot agree. God is One, plain and simple, so why confuse things with tripleness? To others, to assert that God is triune, or Three-in-One, is outright heresy. How can there be three gods? Can there be three gods? *No,* reply Christians, *there is only One God.* As Basil the Great of Caesarea (c. 329–79) says, "Let no one think that I am saying that there are three persons."[2] Yet the one God is also Triune—a Trinity. Or, in another manner of speaking, the Trinity is a single, plural reality.

At this point, more than a few persons have thrown up their hands and left the conversation. It sounds, at one level, like an unsolvable riddle. Even so, it is not a math problem, as the numbers seem to suggest.

The Christian conviction that God is triune, a Triunity, is extremely ancient. From almost the beginning of the Christian movement, following the resurrection and ascension of Jesus, Christians have worshiped the one God who exists in threeness. Beyond the apparent mental gymnastics this might demand, Christian theology has gone on to say that God is not like any other thing, entity, or person that exists. God is not a *something* that can be scrutinized in the way that one might study a *thing,* dissect it, categorize it, or understand it in relation to similar things that are *things.* God is not that. At best, we could say that God is a Someone, but not a human someone; and not a person like we are persons; and certainly not a creature like other creatures. At this point, there is wisdom again in retreating into

1. Deut 6:4 NIV.
2. Basil, *On the Holy Spirit* 16.38.

silence and wondering at this great mystery. Such silence would not be misplaced, and silence at this point might be good for our spirituality as well as our peace of mind.

When Christians do resolve, however, to say something about God, there is at least a gesture toward certain key affirmations: one God in Three, Three in one God, Triunity, a Trinity. There is no perfect way of expressing this. But in Christian thought, God is not "God" at all if God is *not* Three in One. This is crucial: God is *not* God if "God" is not triune. This belief in the triune God is finally a faith claim made by the faithful. It is not the result of evidence, testing, analysis, and conclusions in the way that most modern sciences like to proceed. Drawing upon the biblical witness, learning from the testimony of ancestors in faith, and reflecting on Christian experiences, the affirmation of the Trinity—a single, plural reality—is a faith claim, not a theorem, a theory, or an empirically proven fact over which human beings can exert control. The threeness of God is especially grounded in how God self-reveals—"outwardly," so to speak—in God's actions in the world. This sense of the outward or *economic* Trinity is something to which we'll return in chapter 5.

Allowing for Mystery

Eugene Rogers is correct in noting that in modern theology (since about 1750), the focus on the human subject within Christian thought has resulted in theology tending to view "the Persons of the Trinity [as] centers of consciousness—rather than agents of a single activity."[3] There is a modern tilt toward supposing that the language of "three persons" implies three minds, three selves, or three personalities inside God. But this is not true to Christian tradition at its best. Premodern theologies and convictions were better able, on the whole, to hold together the Oneness of the Threeness of God without contradiction. For God to be a mystery was not in itself a problem for them. In contrast, modernity and the shift to a preference for scientific materialism have damaged most Western persons' capacity for mystery, wonder, paradox, and awe. Most Westerners in this era prefer the flat and explainable, the dissectible and the provable, the material and the rational. Much Christian teaching is, in that sense, disappointing to modernity—or possibly incoherent.

Even so, Christian theology and belief stubbornly persist in affirming the Trinity and God's Triunity. Indeed, it is *constitutive* of Christian theology that it remain trinitarian. One could certainly hold other views and speak of

3. Rogers, *After the Spirit*, 5.

a god or many gods in other ways, but at that point it immediately ceases to be a *Christian* account of God. God is One in Three: Father, Son, and Holy Spirit. Sometimes this traditional language is helpfully made less gender-specific with formulations such as Creator, Christ, and Spirit; or Creator, Redeemer, Sustainer. However it is phrased, Christian theology always needs to preserve a measure of humility and admit that names and terms alone cannot capture and contain the fullness of the reality of God. "The Spirit is vast and wild," testifies The United Church of Canada, and so "we recognize that our understanding of the Holy is always partial and limited."[4] God is beyond our language and concepts—yet desires to be known. Any language we use will ultimately fail and be inadequate. But it is not wrong to try to get as close as possible.

Within this context, the focus of this book is the Holy Spirit, who is *one with* the Trinity and fully divine. I am careful here *not* to say, "one of the Trinity" nor "part of the Trinity," as if the Trinity were divisible or had parts, like a machine. Neither is true, for God is One—always One. Within the fullness of Christian teaching about the mystery that is the Trinity, and together with ("one with") the fullness of the triune God, the Spirit exceeds our full understanding. What we say will ultimately be inadequate. However, we are given glimpses. This book tries to catch some of these glimpses and reflect on them.

Hierarchy or Equality?

One of the questions that has faced Christian thought from the beginning is how to imagine or think about the relations among the three Persons of the Trinity. Most often, a hierarchical relationship has been claimed. Specifically, the Father is thought or presumed to be at the "top" of a triad, or a pyramid or ladder, followed by the Son, then the Spirit. It is a commonplace in theology to refer to them as the First, Second, and Third Persons (Father, Son, and Holy Spirit). Without a doubt, there are certain passages in the Bible that gesture in the direction of such a hierarchy. For example, in John 16:13, Jesus says, "When the Spirit of truth comes, he will guide you into all the truth; *for he will not speak on his own, but will speak whatever he hears,* and he will declare to you the things that are to come" (emphasis added). The idea that the Spirit does not speak in the Spirit's own right could suggest a kind of subordination of the Spirit to the Son or to the Father.

To the ancient Christian writers, this was perhaps indeed the intention in their treatment of the question. Augustine of Hippo (354–430) suggested a

4. United Church of Canada, "Song of Faith."

few metaphors for the Spirit. His terms—the "bond," "communion," "friendship," or "love" between Father and Son—implies a kind of status for the Spirit that is lesser than the other two.[5] In Augustine's terms, the Father and the Son are the primary divine actors. The Spirit has a role, but is more like a lively linking "energy" than a Person. As important as *love* and *communion* truly are (such as when we think of the connections between human beings), there is a subtle demotion of that "third" reality (the Spirit). The Holy Spirit is portrayed, subtly, as subservient and subordinate to the main actors in the relationship. While Augustine has been and remains influential in Christian theology, I fear that these linguistic turns influence our seeing the Holy Spirit as a relational dynamic between *other* Someones (the Important Ones), rather than a fully formed Divine Person who *is one with* the other Persons. As Helen Bergin writes, the concern "is the constant placement of the Spirit as the third-mentioned yet equal divine person. Such positioning can suggest the Spirit as being derivative *from* or *through* the Father and the Son, and barely distinct in the Spirit's own right."[6]

The subtle demotion of the Holy Spirit's status was already indicated by Irenaeus of Lyon (c. 125–200), two centuries before Augustine. Irenaeus offered an analogy of the Word and Spirit as functioning like the two hands of God the Father. Irenaeus writes, "For with Him [the Father] were always present the Word and Wisdom, the Son and the Spirit, by whom and in whom, freely and spontaneously, He made all things.[7]" And again, he says, "For by the hands of the Father, that is, by the Son and the Holy Spirit, man . . . was made in the likeness of God."[8] Perhaps Irenaeus was thinking of Ps 33:6—"By the word of the Lord the heavens were made, and all their host by the breath [Hebrew: *ruach*, also translated as *spirit*] of his mouth." In any case, Irenaeus doesn't develop the analogy further. It might have been for him a brief stroke of the pen as he tried out another metaphor for the way that the economic Trinity operates *ad extra*—toward creation. Unfortunately, the impression remained for many generations that the triune God has "parts," or that the Father is the "real God" and the Son and Spirit are merely agents or instruments of the Father, rather than *one with* the Father.

Much later, in the sixteenth century, we find John Calvin (1509–64) speaking in hierarchical terms about the three Persons. To be sure, Calvin is careful to note that the three Persons are one: "It is quite clear that in God's essence reside three persons in whom one God is known . . . [and]

5. Augustine, *Trinity* 5.3.12; 6.1.7.
6. Bergin, "Feminist Pneumatology," 189.
7. Irenaeus, *Against Heresies* 4.20.1.
8. Irenaeus, *Against Heresies* 5.6.1.

we conclude that Word and Spirit are nothing else than the very essence of God."[9] Still, Calvin tilts the theological imagination toward an instrumental view, something like Irenaeus and Augustine did, centuries before: "The Holy Spirit is the bond by which Christ effectually unites us to himself."[10] Calvin also exemplifies a common theological claim that the Spirit's purpose is mainly to glorify the Son, perhaps drawing on John 16:14—"He will glorify me because he will take what is mine and declare it to you." In this vein, Calvin writes, "God the Father gives us the Holy Spirit for his Son's sake."[11] It is curious that the Spirit is not working for the sake of the Spirit, nor the sake of the whole Trinity, but sounds here like a representative of the Son. In a similar vein, the Uniting Presbyterian Church of Southern Africa (UPCSA) testifies that "all outward action of the Godhead begins with the Father and proceeds through the Son in the Spirit."[12] While some moderating language follows, the UPCSA is not alone in inheriting hierarchical assumptions about the Triune Someones.

These notes are not meant to condemn Calvin, other writers, the UPCSA, nor any Christian tradition, but only to demonstrate how theological writing can bend (or perhaps distort) the dynamic of full coequality among the Persons of the Trinity by implying a subordinate status for the Spirit. Such language raises doubts about the equality and coeternity of the three divine Persons. Similarly, it was commonplace in ancient Christian thought to speak of the Holy Spirit as facilitating human beings' approach to Jesus Christ, who then leads them to God the Father through a ladder-like progression. Irenaeus writes: "In the Church was deposited communion with Christ, that is, the Holy Spirit, pledge of incorruptibility, confirmation of our faith, and ladder of our ascent towards God."[13] In the next generation, Origen (c. 185–253) concurs, speaking of advancing "to higher degrees of perfection."[14] As Lewis Ayres notes, according to Origen, "it is through participation in the Spirit that we participate in Christ and thus ascend to the Father."[15] Several decades after Origen, Basil echoes the thought: "Thus the way of the knowledge of God lies from the One Spirit, through the One Son, to the One Father."[16] The same hierarchical chain, but in reverse (from

9. Calvin, *Institutes* 1.13.16.

10. Calvin, *Institutes* 3.1.1.

11. Calvin, *Institutes* 3.1.2.

12. Uniting Presbyterian Church of Southern Africa, *Manual*, 27.

13. Irenaeus, *Against Heresies* 3.24.1.

14. Origen, *De Principiis* 1.3.8.

15. Ayres, "Holy Spirit as the 'Undiminished Giver,'" 62.

16. Basil, *Holy Spirit* 18.47.

Father to Son to Spirit to human beings), provides us with goodness, holiness, and dignity. The subtext of these constructions is that the Spirit functions as a kind of courier or helper to the Son and the Father. The important goal is to get to the Father, via the Spirit and the Son.

All this begs the question: If all three Persons of the Trinity are one, is this sequential, "laddered" encounter necessary? If each Person is truly God—as the ancient creeds and these very theologians profess—can we not say that to encounter the Spirit is truly to encounter God? The ancient conviction that the fullness of God is fully present and active in each Person of the Trinity seems to testify in that direction. I have no doubt and no illusions that Irenaeus, Augustine, Calvin, and countless others who use hierarchical language for the Trinity were much wiser than I am as a theologian, but the demotion of the Spirit's importance in the divine hierarchy remains a problem for understanding the Spirit in fully coequal terms with the Father and Son. I suppose we can give Augustine some reprieve, in that he did offer this corrective: "Let it not be supposed that in this Trinity there is any separation in respect of time or place, but that these Three are equal and co-eternal, and absolutely of one nature. . . . [No one] is saved by the Father without the Son and the Holy Spirit."[17] Yet a great deal of trinitarian theology (as well as Christology and pneumatology)—indeed, perhaps most of it—has taken for granted and repeated the hierarchical norm with little or no critique. In contrast, twentieth- and twenty-first-century theologians, especially feminist and liberation theologians, have been more critical of this implied or explicitly stated hierarchy.

There is good reason to be critical. One of the arguments against a fixed hierarchy within the Trinity is the problematic habit of drawing a parallel between the nature of human creatures and the nature of God. In other words, it is common to reflect on how God is *like* us, or how we are (or should be) *like* God. This is called the *analogia entis*—the "analogy of being." A possible outcome of that comparison is to identify, even if subconsciously and unintentionally, God the Father and God the Son as being "above" God the Spirit. Worse still, since Father and Son are exclusively male terms, does this imply that maleness is "above" femaleness? A second concern arises with the implication or assertion of any hierarchy at all. Why should one Person be "above" any of the others? Does this mean that it is right and good that some kinds of human beings should naturally be above other kinds? Should one race or nation be superior over another? Faithful and exacting critique and alternatives to these damaging and erroneous constructions,

17. Augustine, "Letter 169" 2.5 .

such as male dominance or racial superiority rooted in a hierarchical view of God, are called for. We need alternatives.

Another Option

Despite the powerful, persistent, and historical habit of identifying a hierarchy within the triune God, there is another and better option: equality. If we look closely, that model is indeed present in older Christian traditions, as well as in modern and postmodern theologies. A formal (and ancient) term for the equality and mutuality of the three Persons of the Trinity is *perichoresis* (Greek) or *circumincession* (Latin). Both terms suggest something like a circle dance, or a circle of singers blending their voices toward the center. No dancer or singer is above or more important than the others. All are equal in status and importance. So also, in a perichoretic model of the Trinity, all the divine Persons are equal: none stands over or governs the others. Ambrose of Milan (c. 339–97) teaches that in the One and triune God, "oneness knows no order, equality knows no gradation[.]"[18] Augustine, despite his language of "communion" and "bond" to indicate the Spirit's place between the Father and Son, boldly stated that the Holy Spirit is "also true God; therefore absolutely equal to the Father and the Son, and consubstantial and co-eternal in the oneness of the three."[19] Without directly addressing the question of hierarchy (which he does favor elsewhere in his writing), Augustine famously offers the analogy of a human being's memory, understanding, and will: "Each name refers to a single thing, and yet each of these single name is the product of all three"—none of which is prior to or superior to the others.[20] All are vital, interdependent parts of the same mind. Ambrose suggests that within the Trinity, "there is no affront of subjection, but a community of power."[21] Again, the idea of a "single, plural reality" is helpful.

In what is called the Eastern tradition or the Orthodox Church, few theologians were insistent on hierarchical models. Suggesting that the Trinity can be compared to the sun (the Father), its shining (the Son), and its heat (the Spirit), Ephrem lays out in poetic fashion how all three are intermingled and yet distinctive:

18. Ambrose, *Holy Spirit* 3.16.
19. Augustine, *Trinity* 1.2.13.
20. Augustine, *Trinity* 4.5.30; see also 10.4.18.
21. Ambrose, *Holy Spirit* 3.2.

> Who could investigate how and where
> [The sun's] ray is joined, [and where] its heat
> Is joined and dwells?
> They are neither separate nor confused.
> They are distinct [yet] mingled, joined and dwelling together [and equal],
> Great marvel![22]

Gregory Nazianzen (c. 329–90) of Constantinople offered further analogies for the Trinity as "spring, stream, and river" or "sun, ray, and light."[23] Similarly, Gregory's contemporary, Basil, suggested (like Ephrem) "sun, light, and heat." These are attractive, nature-based, non-gendered, and (almost) non-hierarchical metaphors. I say "almost" because *sun* and *source* still have some primacy in the relationship among the elements. For example, there would be no *ray* or *light* without the sun.[24] But these Eastern theologians point us in a helpful direction. Basil provides something of a corrective when he notes, "In truth, he [the Spirit] existed, and pre-existed, and co-existed with the Father and the Son before the ages."[25] There is no "before and after" among the divine Persons, then. Neither do we need to think of them as "higher and lower." Calvin is helpful here: "In each hypostasis [divine expression or Person] the whole divine nature is understood."[26]

Hierarchical models for the Trinity are less pronounced or even ignored in United and Uniting Church perspectives. They are typically anti-hierarchical, or at least post-hierarchical. The United Church of Canada suggests terms such as "Creator, Redeemer, and Sustainer . . . Mother, Friend, and Comforter."[27] Many years earlier, this same denomination used more traditional language, but still without specifically hierarchical overtones: "Knowing God thus, as Creator and Father, as Redeemer in Christ, and as Holy Spirit working in us, we confess our faith in the Holy Trinity."[28] In the straightforward terms of the United Church in Papua New Guinea and the Solomon Islands, the presence of the Holy Spirit "is the presence of God."[29] No mention is made of one Person having a lesser status.

22. Ephrem, *Hymns* 73.7.

23. Gregory Nazianzen, *Fifth Theological Oration* §31, §32.

24. It is worth noting that both Ephrem's and Gregory's analogies are still modalistic.

25. Basil, *On the Holy Spirit* 19.48.

26. Calvin, *Institutes* 1.18.19.

27. United Church of Canada, "Song of Faith."

28. United Church of Canada, "Statement of Faith."

29. United Church in Papua New Guinea and the Solomon Islands, *Basis for the Union*, art. 4.

The Spirit Is Truly God

The Holy Spirit's coequality with the Father and the Son was settled, finally, at the Council of Constantinople in 381. Various factions across the Christian world had been bickering about the status of the Holy Spirit. Was She a creature, or the Creator? Was She a special envoy of the Father and Son, but not divine herself? The Council took the Nicene Creed (from the Council of Nicaea, 325) and expanded it with some crucial language. In 325, the consensus of the Council had been merely to state, in the sparest of terms, "We believe in the Holy Spirit." This left rather a lot open to interpretation. One of the factions, the *Pneumatomachoi*, or "Spirit-fighters," claimed that the Holy Spirit was *not* divine. What Christians and Jews had called the "Spirit" was, to these contrarians, a created being, a *something*, but not divine; and it was certainly lesser than God. The Spirit might be an agent or emissary of God in this way of thinking, but not coequal and coeternal with God. Thus whatever the Nicene Creed's term "Spirit" pointed toward as a linguistic referent was strictly *of this world*, and not intrinsic to the divine nature. So the argument ran.

Like the Arians (who denied the divinity of Jesus Christ) before them, the Pneumatomachoi battled with their theological and ecclesial counterparts, but in the end did not carry the day in terms of broad Christian consensus. The 381 Council of Constantinople updated the creed by adding the following (in italics):

> We believe in the Holy Spirit, *the Lord and Giver of life, who proceeds from the Father, who with the Father and the Son together is worshiped and glorified, who spoke by the prophets.*

This is a potent corrective. Notice the range of divine attributes identified here as properly of the Spirit: *Lord* (like the Lord God, Yahweh); *Giver of life* (as in Creator, not a created creature); *who is . . . worshiped and glorified* (one doesn't worship a created thing, but God alone); *who spoke by the prophets* (this is the One whose voice the prophets overheard and passed along—the voice of God alone). The Council declared publicly and definitively, *Let there be no doubt, dear Pneumatomachoi, the Holy Spirit is divine, and One with the triune God.* That is the message of the Council in 381.[30] The Athanasian Creed (probably composed in the fifth century CE) continues the theme, naming the Holy Spirit as fully coequal with the Father and the Son: all are

30. It's rather a good thing that more was said at this Council about the Holy Spirit, especially since the other main creed of Christianity, the Apostles' Creed, says exceptionally little.

"uncreated, boundless, eternal, omnipotent, Lord." John Wesley (1703–91) considered this treatment of the Trinity "the best I ever saw."[31]

Since then, the consensus of Christian theology has been to continue to affirm that the Spirit is not "part" of creation, nor a created something. The Holy Spirit is One with the Creator; or in other words, *is* the Creator, just as the Father *is* the Creator and the Son *is* the Creator. The considerable energy and ink expended by the Pneumatomachoi and others to argue that the Holy Spirit was a creature, among the created things of heaven and earth, has been swept aside. Again, Basil's pithy phrase is instructive: "In truth, [the Spirit] existed, and pre-existed, and co-existed with the Father and the Son before the ages."[32] In the contemporary era, United Church of Christ [USA] theologian Roger Shinn echoes this teaching in a clear way: "The Holy Spirit is not someone other than God, not some deputy God sends when busy with other things. The Holy Spirit is God, the Spirit of God, the same Spirit who is mentioned in the second verse of the Bible."[33] Accordingly, Christianity asserts that the Spirit is not only Creator, but also Maker and Hope and Divine Power, for "in everything the Holy Spirit is indivisible and inseparable from the Father and the Son,"[34] as Basil puts it. Every work of the Father and the Son is unified with the Spirit. If we used a strictly human analogy (which will inevitably be inadequate), we could say that the Persons of the triune God are "of one mind" at all times. They are united in will and united in purpose. There are lingering hierarchical perspectives in Christian theology, but the divine status of the Spirit is no longer contested.

It is entirely right, then, to speak of the Holy Spirit *as* God. Jesus seems to have spoken in these terms: "God is spirit [Greek: *pneuma*], and those who worship him must worship in spirit and truth" (John 4:24). As the United Church of Christ [USA] prays, "We believe in you, O God, Eternal Spirit."[35] Centuries earlier, Basil notes with care that "sins against God and against the Holy Spirit are the same thing."[36] It is wrong, in contrast, to suppose that "God" and "God the Holy Spirit" are not one and the same. Ambrose proclaims, "If you say the Spirit, you have named also God the Father . . . and the Son[.]"[37] The attributes and powers of the triune God are true of

31. Wesley, "On the Trinity," 377.
32. Basil, *On the Holy Spirit* 19.48.
33. Shinn, *Confessing Our Faith*, 77.
34. Basil, *On the Holy Spirit* 16.37.
35. United Church of Christ [USA], "Statement of Faith (1981)."
36. Basil, *On the Holy Spirit* 16.27.
37. Ambrose, *Holy Spirit* 1.3.

each and all triune Persons. Within that single, plural reality, exist only "one and the same will, one calling, and one giving of commands."[38] This unity is attested throughout the witness of the United and Uniting Churches.

The attributes and characteristics of the Holy Spirit are, consequently, the same as the attributes and characteristics associated with God. Basil tells us that the Holy Spirit is "infinite in power, unlimited in greatness, immeasurable by time of ages, and generous with the goods that it has."[39] The Holy Spirit is worthy of praise, worship, and adoration: "Should we not exalt him who is divine in nature, unbounded in greatness, powerful in his energies, and good in his deeds?"[40] The highest attributes of mercy, holiness, and goodness reside in the Spirit. To the extent that we can imagine God having human-like qualities and emotions, the Spirit "is described as speaking, warning, grieving, weeping, rejoicing, consoling."[41] These personal characteristics are important to note, in order to contrast the Holy Spirit from an impersonal force or energy that vaguely *exists*. As Chen Zemin of the China Christian Council notes, "If you only regard the Holy Spirit as a kind of force (or energy or strength or power), that is a misunderstanding of the Holy Spirit."[42]

Free and Sovereign

There is, instead, a dynamic interaction between the Spirit and all that She has made (more on this in chapter 5, below). She is lively, on the move, responsive, proactive, and purposeful. In her work, her passion is visible, enacting the fulfillment of all God's purposes in the realm of God. This distinguishes her from an impersonal force or power, like electricity. She is not a vague "divine energy," lacking in will and purpose.

The Spirit is free and sovereign, just as the Trinity as a whole is free and sovereign. There is no external compulsion or greater power that causes the Spirit to act in a particular way, as if there were a principle "behind" the Spirit that has more authority. The biblical image of *wind* reinforces this throughout the First and Second Testaments, especially in John 3:8. Here Jesus tells Nicodemus, "The wind [*pneuma*, also meaning Spirit] blows where it chooses, and you hear the sound of it, but you do not know where it comes from or where it goes." The freedom of the wind is an analogy

38. Ambrose, *Holy Spirit* 2.10.

39. Basil, *On the Holy Spirit* 9.22.

40. Basil, *On the Holy Spirit* 23.54.

41. Ramsey, *Holy Spirit*, 16.

42. Chen, "Spirit, Please Come Upon Us," 250.

of the freedom of the Spirit. The wind and the Spirit are "incalculable and unpredictable," according to John Dow of The United Church of Canada: "It comes and goes unaccountably, and no [one] claims it as an abiding possession."[43] The freedom and sovereignty of the Spirit mean that human beings relate to her in an attitude of reliance, not rule-over, and with an awareness of contingency, not control.

It is also good to make room for the wildness and playfulness of the Holy Spirit:

> We sing of God the Spirit,
> faithful and untameable,
> who is creatively and redemptively active in the world.
> The Spirit challenges us to celebrate the holy
> not only in what is familiar,
> but also in that which seems foreign.[44]

The Spirit is always seeking new irruptions of life, always rumbling in the green and growing places. As Calvin writes,

> It is the Spirit who, everywhere diffused, sustains all things, causes them to grow, and quickens them in heaven and in earth. . . . He is circumscribed by no limits . . . in transfusing into all things his energy, and breathing into the essence, life, and movement, he is indeed plainly divine.[45]

The surprising movements of the Holy Spirit might take us off guard or make us laugh. After all, the Holy Spirit is Someone who comes to us not from a place of precise definition or from a static, unchanging corner of the universe, but from a place of mystery, wonder, activity, and joy. "God's Spirit cannot be manipulated or coerced," writes Simon LeSieur of The United Church of Canada.[46] The Spirit who is like the wind that blows where it wills is unlikely to follow a script, let alone a script of human expectations. The uncontrollability of the Spirit is an essential attribute that humbles human aims. The Spirit might laugh at the prayer imagined by Raniero Cantalamessa: "Come, Holy Spirit, come . . . but not right now and especially no strangeness."[47] The Spirit's wild, unconstrained freedom draws the human creature into wonder and joyful obedience, not into attempts to assert power over God. As Patricia Wells of The United Church of Canada reflects,

43. Dow, *This Is Our Faith*, 55, 56.

44. United Church of Canada, "Song of Faith."

45. Calvin, *Institutes* 1.13.14.

46. LeSieur, *Come, Holy Spirit*, 126.

47. Cantalamessa, *Mystery of Pentecost*, 61.

regarding this freedom, "In his resurrection and ascension [Jesus's] life-giving Spirit was released into the world and made available to all people of all time."[48]

A New Proposal

To conclude this chapter, I would like to introduce a nuance about how theology might speak of the three Persons of the Trinity, and to propose an alternative. For centuries, and still today, Christianity has routinely referred to the "threeness" of the Trinity by way of the term "person" and "persons." It is commonplace to speak of the Father as the First Person, the Son (Jesus Christ) as the Second Person, and the Holy Spirit as the Third Person. This way of speaking of the triune God is linked to a term for a physical device that was employed on the stage in ancient Greece: a special kind of mask. This mask was the *prōsōpon*. The physical mask worn by the actor enabled the audience to see the character that was being portrayed as well as their emotional state (such as joy, anger, or surprise). The mask might also have had a role in amplifying the actor's voice. It was from this aspect of dramatic arts that early theologians borrowed the Latin version of the term (*persona*) and applied it to the three "Persons" of the Trinity.

Karl Barth preferred to call the Spirit a "mode of being" of the one God, rather than a Person.[49] This can be confused with the heresy of *modalism*. Moreover, there might be some advantages in retaining the notion of Person. Not least among those advantages is to understand that the Holy Spirit has purpose, direction, and "personality" (so to speak), and is not merely a power, a principle, a force, or a function. That Person, the Spirit, has volition and intention, and thus is not *impersonal*.

At the same time—and this is critical—to say that the Spirit is a divine Person is not to claim that there are three "centers of consciousness"[50] in the way that a human "person" is an individual. The three divine Persons do not operate independently, not even in tandem, in harmony, nor in concert. That would lean too far toward tritheism or imagining that there are three Selves within the Trinity. "Person" also creates some confusion, because modern psychology often makes us fascinated with an individual's "personality." Looking back, we can note that Augustine suggested that *persons* is a term of convenience, anyway: "[It] has been agreed to say it like that, simply

48. Wells, *Welcome*, 4.

49. Barth, *Church Dogmatics*, 1/1, cited in Rogers, *After the Spirit*, 22.

50. Rogers, *After the Spirit*, 22.

in order to be able to say something when asked, 'Three what?'"[51] Later, he writes that nowhere does the Bible refer to three persons as a way to speak of God.

The limits of "personality," tritheism, modalism, and the distance from the original meaning of *persona* leave us with a quandary. To resolve this, I propose speaking of the threeness of the triune God as *Identities*. This word is less confusing and less suggestive of tritheism. A human analogue is easy enough to imagine, although (like all analogies for the Trinity) it is imperfect and in a way creates new difficulties. What does it mean for a single someone to have three identities? A human being called Ashley might be a shop owner, a sister, and a friend. In all those relationships, that individual is still Ashley. She relates to the customers in her shop in terms of buying and selling; to her siblings as their sister with whom they share a unique bond; and to her friends as the one with whom they have developed a history and another unique set of links. Through it all, she is still Ashley, fully herself in every relation. Her three identities do not turn her into three individuals, three persons, or three selves. If this is so, then we could helpfully construe the triunity of God in terms of Identities. It helps us to conceive of God in relational and not functional terms. An *identity* is accordingly to be encountered and discovered. The relationship cannot be forced, devised, imposed, or extracted.

No human language will fully capture the fullness of the mystery of the triune God. But to enrich and refresh the conversation, from this point on, I will use *Identity* in place of the traditional *Person*.

FOR REFLECTION OR DISCUSSION

1. This chapter speaks of three common errors that someone might make when talking about the Trinity: thinking of the Trinity as three separate gods; thinking about each of the three Persons of the Trinity as one-third of God; and placing the three Persons in a hierarchy. Often when we talk about the Trinity, we use analogies (such as the three leaves of a clover; the three phases of ice, water, and steam). What analogies have you heard used for the Trinity? Do any of these analogies fall into one of the errors listed in this chapter?
2. How would God as "Trinity" be changed if we took the Holy Spirit out of the relationship?

51. Augustine, *Trinity* 7.3.7.

3. The end of this chapter introduces new language for the three Persons of the Trinity, naming them as three *Identities*. Do you find this language helpful? Why or why not?

Chapter 3

How to Discern the Spirit

The Holy Spirit is the Spirit of God and is one with God. . . .
The Spirit is the living, creative, personal,
and immediate presence and power
of the transcendent God that extends into the world
and is at work in it and in us.
—Uniting Presbyterian Church in Southern Africa, The Manual of Faith and Order

If God is One, and three, and eternally One (and never anything except One in Three), what sense does it make to speak of any one of the Identities of the Trinity apart from the others? This is a perplexing question. To affirm the Oneness of God is also always to affirm the unity of God's will, purposes, and mind. To say "God is One" cannot allow for three independent agents or a pantheon of gods who are out and about doing their own thing. There is an old story in Homer's *Iliad* about Zeus being unavailable to respond to human prayers because he is away from Olympus, attending a feast in Ethiopia. This image of divine "separability" is a significant distance from the unity of the godhead to which Christianity attests. The conundrum of the Christian belief in divine threeness-in-oneness is intensified when encountering the theological principle of *communicatio idiomatum*, or the communication of attributes. According to this principle, everything that one member of the Trinity experiences or expresses is experienced and expressed by the other two. After all, God is One, not a trio. "All" of God experiences everything that God experiences. The fullness of the Trinity is present when we speak of any one Identity of the Trinity being present. Yet there is also threeness in the oneness, for God is triune.

The principal way to address this quandary in Christian theology is to employ the *doctrine of appropriation*. To a given Identity within the Trinity, we "appropriate" or associate a particular action. It is usually actions, rather than God's characteristics or dispositions that are treated in this way. For example, when Paul proclaims that God was in Christ reconciling the world to God (2 Cor 5:19), the conviction emerges that Jesus Christ is the Reconciler and Redeemer: Jesus is the Identity of the Trinity who reconciles and redeems. Or again, when the prophet Micah tells of the Spirit's influence on his work, the empowering of the prophets is "appropriated" or attributed to the Holy Spirit.[1] This does not take away from the core conviction that the whole Trinity acts as One, for there is no division in the purpose and mind of God. As Augustine testifies, "I will say however with absolute confidence that Father and Son and Holy Spirit, God the creator, of one and the same substance, the almighty three, act inseparably."[2] Appropriation also enables theology to guard against giving "essence to the Father and deny personality to the others [Son and Spirit], and make them only powers of God."[3] In other words, the Son and Spirit are One with the Father, but are more than "aspects," agents, or instruments of the Father.

Instead, appropriation tries (imperfectly) to remain consistent with the testimony of the Bible and the creeds. Drawing on the Bible, Calvin teaches, "To the Father is *attributed* the beginning of activity, and the fountain and wellspring of all things; to the Son, wisdom, counsel, and the ordered disposition of all things; but to the Spirit is *assigned* the power and efficacy of that activity."[4] This convention—attributing certain activities to certain Identities of the Trinity—is long-standing. Care must be taken, however, lest this division in human language veer into modalism, which imagines erroneously that God's three Identities act separately within separate spheres. God is always One in being, purpose, and action.

Ephrem uses poetry to describe the united-yet-distinctive character of the triune God:

> Three names are visible within the fire,
> Yet each one stands on its [own] authority,
> And each appears [distinctly, or simply] in its action,

1. "But as for me, I am filled with power, with the spirit of the Lord, and with justice and might, to declare to Jacob his transgression and to Israel his sin" (Mic 3:8).

2. Augustine, *Trinity* 4.5.30.

3. Gregory Nazianzen, *Fifth Theological Oration* §32.

4. Calvin, *Institutes* 1.18.18 (emphasis added).

> Unique strengths mingled together.
> Fire marvellously, heat distinctly,
> And light gloriously dwell together with one accord.[5]

Here Ephrem communicates subtly but effectively that each of the Three-Who-Are-One has a distinct identity, but never acts or operates as if they (singly) had an independent will or purpose. At the same time, Christian thought often attributes certain actions to one Identity more than to the other two. The Father is most often thought of as the Creator, for example, even though truly all of God-in-Triunity creates. The Son is said to die and thereby to redeem humankind, even though it is God-in-God's-fullness who enacts salvation.

The Shy Friend

The Holy Spirit, characteristically, is less frequently evoked in this theological habit of appropriation. The Spirit might be seen as the one who sanctifies, inspires, or guides, which are "invisible" actions, in a sense. Thomas O'Laughlin helpfully notes that Augustine "links the hidden work of God with the work of the Spirit."[6] This hidden aspect of the Spirit keeps the Spirit from taking center stage. Perhaps this is intentional. There is a tendency within Christian thought to regard the Holy Spirit as deferential, silent, or even shy. The farewell discourse of Jesus in John 16:13–14 gestures in this direction:

> When the Spirit of truth comes, he will guide you into all the truth, for he will not speak on his own but will speak whatever he hears, and he will declare to you the things that are to come. He will glorify me because he will take what is mine and declare it to you.

Jesus here points to a Spirit whose role is to glorify the Son, not herself. The gifts given by the Spirit are understood as deriving from Jesus as the source of the gifts. This deferential characteristic might underlie the remark in Eph 4:30 that the Holy Spirit can be "grieved." Vulnerability [Latin: *vulnere*; to wound] is suggested here, rather than an overpowering dominance. The Spirit is "wound-able." Or again, the language of "grieving of the Spirit" might be a way to express the Spirit's own discouragement when war, chaos, harm, sin, and suffering continue in the human family.[7] She gives gifts, but

5. Ephrem, *Hymns* 40.8.
6. O'Laughlin, "St Augustine's View," 89.
7. I suspect this is in mind when Paul writes, "Do not quench the Spirit. . . . Abstain

does not overpower human will. Human opposition to the divine purposes is a source of grief for God.

The Spirit is also described in selfless terms in John 14:25, pointing to Jesus, not herself ("The Holy Spirit . . . will teach you everything and remind you of all that I have said to you"). This can be a problematic interpretation, if it is taken to suggest that women or others with less power ought *only* to be selfless servants. That is certainly not a reading I would endorse. In another interpretation, it can suggest to persons with an overdeveloped sense of self-importance that the role of servant is appropriate for them. Either way, we should note that it is the Spirit's nature to display humility, but not a humility that requires subservience.

The Holy Spirit is also shy with respect to her appearance in Christian theological reflection. Despite the Spirit's popularity among Christians, sustained doctrinal reflection on pneumatology often takes second, third, or last place in systematic theological work, especially in the West. This is not to suggest that there is no doctrinal work available. There are many substantial contributions.[8] But the overall attention given to pneumatology is far less than that given to areas such as Christology, the Trinity, and ecclesiology, for example. One theologian well-known among readers in English, Douglas John Hall of The United Church of Canada, despite his prolific publishing, wrote little on the Holy Spirit. Tellingly, his sweeping major trilogy (*Thinking the Faith*, *Professing the Faith*, and *Confessing the Faith*), has no distinct chapter on the Spirit, despite its fifteen-hundred-page length. Here and there, the Spirit makes an appearance in Hall's work, but pneumatology is always a lesser consideration.

Much of the rest of this book seeks, in contrast, to notice this "shy friend" with appreciation, and to shed light on the identity and action of the Spirit by emphasizing what can be said on the basis of the doctrine of appropriation. Without it, one would be compelled to remain silent about the Holy Spirit, or to couch all pneumatology within a kind of general unitarianism. But for the sake of clarity, I want to ask the "shy friend" to step forward and to be seen.

The Holy Spirit and Gender

Is the Holy Spirit male or female? Or neither? Or both? Eugene Rogers notes, "It is well known that Christian God-language works in such a way

from every form of evil" (1 Thess 5:19, 21).

8. Recent excellent titles include Peterson, *Holy Spirit*; Kärkkäinen, *Pneumatology*; Kim, *Holy Spirit*; Crisp and Sanders, *Third Person*; and Boff, *Come Holy Spirit*.

as to transcend gender, and necessarily so."[9] Among the writers of the ancient Christian period, there are many examples of feminine imagery and pronouns for God. In the writing of Syriac Christian authors, we see that "in Syriac the word for Spirit is grammatically feminine."[10] Ephrem's poetry showcases the Holy Spirit in feminine terms:

> Because the Holy Spirit did not receive a body,
> She is exalted above voices and above the words
> Spoken about the divinity
> Of our Lord, and his humanity.[11]

Isaac of Nineveh (c. 613–700) similarly lifts up "the fact that the Holy Spirit acts tenderly and in a motherly fashion. Isaac states that one who is born of God and nurtured by the Holy Spirit may suck life-giving nourishment from the breasts of the Spirit and enjoy the smell of her ardour."[12] Rogers also reminds us that in Augustine, as well as in the Eleventh Council of Toledo (675), ancient Christian Syriac poetry, and in Cistercian theology of the Middle Ages, there are references to both the Father and the Son having a "womb." Thomas Aquinas (c. 1225–74) speaks of God the Father "giving birth" to the Son.[13]

These are strikingly feminine images. We do well also to recall the language of Gen 1:27—"So God created humankind in his image, in the image of God he created them; male and female he created them." To say that the "image of God" is both male and female is evocative, and puts to the test the notion of God as exclusively male. Jürgen Moltmann provides a thorough overview of understandings of the Holy Spirit as "mother" and "motherly," especially in the ancient Syriac and Egyptian churches, and among the Moravian Brethren in the eighteenth century.[14] Many Indigenous cultures also warmly embrace *Mother* as a divine image.[15]

In this book and in my teaching, I most often refer to the Holy Spirit with feminine pronouns (She/her). This is intentional and intentionally provocative. It reflects a similar move in some of the United and Uniting Churches, and in some other contemporary and historic Christian movements and denominations. But it is also meant to provide an alternative

9. Rogers, *After the Spirit*, 111.
10. Rogers, *After the Spirit*, 138n8.
11. Ephrem, *Hymns* 59.8.
12. Seppälä, "Holy Spirit in Isaac of Nineveh," 140.
13. Thomas, *Summa Theologiae* 3.35.5.
14. Moltmann, *Spirit of Life*, 157–60. See also Congar, "Motherhood in God."
15. Jacobs, "Holy Spirit," 168.

to the male-centric and male-only language that has overwhelmingly predominated in Christian discourse for two thousand years. The long history of Christian speech about the Holy Spirit using only masculine "he" pronouns might reflect mere convention, or it might point to a male-oriented bias among Christian writers. The critique of male-centric language for God is well articulated in authors such as Rosemary Radford Ruether, Delores Williams, and Mary Daly.[16] Sallie McFague has also made an important contribution by diversifying the terms that could be used for God, including feminine images.[17] I recognize that there is no consensus on the use of feminine terms for the Holy Spirit. Many will object for a variety of reasons. Some feminist theologians suggest that "feminizing" the Holy Spirit might make perceptions of God's "maleness" even worse. I acknowledge that there is no perfect solution to this dilemma. But this effort has more advantages than liabilities.

As we have seen, feminine imagery and pronouns for God are not without precedent in the Christian tradition. Again, Rogers is helpful in noting that not all languages require male terms for the Spirit, which "takes masculine pronouns in Latin, neuter in Greek, and feminine in early Syriac. I follow Jerome's remark," says Rogers, "that God is beyond gender."[18] Yes, *beyond gender* might be a helpful concept. *Inclusive of all genders* is another. There are certainly cultures and linguistic systems in which there are more than two genders in binary pairs. Some Indigenous cultures reflect this,[19] as do the Jewish Talmud and the Mishna.[20] However one sorts out the linguistic challenge, there is merit in subverting, broadening, and nuancing the male-centric norms of Christian theology.

FOR REFLECTION OR DISCUSSION

1. The doctrine of appropriation associates different actions with different Identities of the Trinity, without dividing the Trinity into thirds. This chapter names the Spirit as "the one who sanctifies, inspires, or guides." Are there other actions that you associate with the Holy Spirit?
2. This chapter refers to the "hiddenness" of the Holy Spirit, the "shy friend." Is this in keeping with your understanding of the Holy Spirit,

16. See Ruether, *Sexism and God-talk;* Williams, *Sisters in the Wilderness*; Daly, *Beyond God the Father.*

17. See McFague, *Models of God.*

18. Rogers, *After the Spirit*, 21n9.

19. See Sterritt, "Indigenous Languages."

20. Kukla, "Terms for Gender Diversity."

either in your own experiences of God, or in how you speak about God?

3. Why do you think that the Holy Spirit doesn't feature more prominently in Christian theological reflection?

Chapter 4

Language, Names, and Terms for the Holy Spirit

WHO IS THE HOLY Spirit? In the simplest terms, the Holy Spirit is God. To speak of "the Holy Spirit" is at the same time to speak of God. The Spirit is the non-material reality who both transcends and inhabits the material order of creation, and is the Source of life, power, grace, and love. The Holy Spirit is not "part" of God, but is *one with* God, the Trinity. The Holy Spirit's divinity was settled at the Council of Constantinople (381) and the resulting revision of the creed consolidated Christian consensus. In Christian theology and practice, there has been no serious effort since that time to separate the Holy Spirit from God: that which is *God* is also the Holy Spirit. The Spirit is "none other than God . . . reaching into the souls [God] has made," writes John Dow of The United Church of Canada.[1] In the same way, there is no Christian theologian in more than one thousand years who has supposed that the Holy Spirit of the First Testament is not the same as the Holy Spirit of the Second Testament. The only exceptions are those whose thinking is considered heretical by the church as a whole.

Good theology will also help us see that the Holy Spirit is not simply a theory, a principle, nor a undifferentiated force generically at work in the universe or in human beings. The Holy Spirit is a *Someone*, an Identity of the triune God who is present and at work within creation and human creatures in specific ways. Although one with the triune God who is Creator of all, the Holy Spirit is also the way that human beings experience God's "immediacy . . . and intimacy."[2] The Holy Spirit "with the Father and the Son . . . *is God*,"

1. Dow, *This Is Our Faith*, 62.

2. Shinn, *Confessing Our Faith*, 77.

as the Heidelberg Catechism (1563) teaches.[3] The gospel according to Matthew tells of Jesus commissioning his followers to go and "make disciples of all nations, baptizing them in the name of the Father and of the Son and of the Holy Spirit" (Matt 28:19). Elsewhere, Jesus says more directly, "God is Spirit" (John 4:24). The ancient Christian bishop and theologian, Basil of Caesarea, clarifies that the Holy Spirit is not a created "something" that God has made separately. The Spirit "is rightfully and properly called 'Holy Spirit,' which is above all the name of everything incorporeal, purely immaterial, and indivisible."[4] In biblical terms, then, and in the overwhelming majority of Christian teaching, *the Holy Spirit is God*, not a separate entity; nor a created reality apart from God; nor a power, instrument, or tool of God; nor "part" of God. "To call the Spirit 'Holy' is to speak of the life of God," attests the United Reformed Church (UK). "God is holy—distinct, perfect, not dependent on us, yet shaping our world with goodness."[5]

The Divine Spirit

It is worth clarifying that the word "spirit" in English and in many other languages can refer to human spirits, the divine Spirit, or other spirits. It is a flexible word and does not have a fixed, single reference. In English, we can speak of the "spirit of the age," "God's Spirit," or the "human spirit," using the same term but meaning different things. In brief, the term usually means something non-material, eternal, and invisible, but still real.

When a word in any language is used for the Spirit, it is always a reference. This is a basic feature of all language. Words can only *refer* to something (or someone), because a word is never the thing (or the person) itself. The words we use can only refer to the reality we intend to suggest. This becomes especially relevant when the words used for the Holy Spirit are metaphors and images. To say the Spirit is "fire" or "breath," for example, is always to say that She is *something like* fire and breath. Metaphors are an approximation, but they reveal something of the reality to which they refer without entirely capturing and containing the fullness or essence of it. Psalm 91:4 describes the protection offered under God's "pinions" and "wings," yet God is not a bird. Still, the analogy and the metaphor of a bird protecting her young in the nest is evocative and helpful in understanding

3. The United Church of Christ (USA) claims the Heidelberg Catechism as authoritative. See Thayer and Jacobsen, *Christ, Creeds and Life*, 92; "Heidelberg Catechism [1563]," 53.

4. Basil, *On the Holy Spirit* 9.22.

5. United Reformed Church [UK], *What Do We Believe About*, 4.

God's divine care. So theology does use words, metaphors, and analogies for the Spirit, even if they are imperfect.

There is a wide range of terms for the Holy Spirit in the Bible. Some are names; some are metaphors; some are images; and some are attributes. Each of these offers a partial understanding of the complex wonder of God the Spirit. We can never capture, contain, nor fully express the mystery of God the Spirit, but they are helpful. Some biblical terms allude to the relational nature of the Spirit within the Trinity and toward human beings:

Spirit of God (Job 33:4; 1 Cor 2:11)
Spirit of Christ (1 Pet 1:11)
Spirit of the Father (Matt 10:20)
Spirit of [God's] Son (Gal 4:6)
Spirit of adoption (Rom 8:15)

Many references to the Holy Spirit offer adjectives that convey a sense of what God is like, using attributes to describe the Spirit:

Spirit of grace (Heb 10:29)
Spirit of holiness (Rom 1:4)
Holy Spirit (Isa 63:10–11)
Spirit of life (Rom 8:2)
Spirit of the living God (2 Cor 3:3)
Spirit of truth (John 16:13)
Spirit of wisdom, understanding, counsel, might, knowledge (Isa 11:2)
Spirit of wisdom and revelation (Eph 1:17)
Spirit of glory (1 Pet 4:14)
Eternal Spirit (Heb 10:29)

The choice of "eternal" as a descriptor of the Holy Spirit within the statement of faith of the United Church of Christ (USA]) is deliberate: "We believe in you, O God, Eternal Spirit."[6] The phrase suggests "a reality not of our own creation, a reality prior to ourselves. . . . We do not fabricate and manipulate or confer deity upon God. God is not a human projection but the power who has given life and imagination to human beings."[7] This confession of faith looks beyond human powers to see that the One who made all things and infuses all things with love and life is the Holy Spirit, eternal, God forever. This one God was present as the Spirit at the beginning of all things, creating life (Gen 1:2). The powerful Spirit of God "breaks the cedars of Lebanon" (Ps 29:5) and, in Jesus, quiets the tumult of a storm at sea

6. United Church of Christ [USA], "Statement of Faith (1981)."

7. Shinn, *Confessing Our Faith*, 37.

(Mark 4:35–41). At the same time, the Spirit of God can come as the "sound of sheer silence" (1 Kgs 19:12). The World Council of Churches reminds us of the importance of the subtlety with which the Spirit can act: "The Spirit often speaks to us in silence in the quiet of our ordinary life. Signs and wonders are not necessarily the norm."[8]

Hebrew and Greek Terms

The First Testament gives us a term that recurs again and again in a huge range of contexts, from Genesis and elsewhere in the Torah to the Psalms and the prophets. The word is *ruach*. It is a gendered noun, like most nouns in Hebrew and some other languages like Greek, Latin, French, and German. Modern English has few gendered nouns, and they are exceptions (such as "fireman" and "actress.") But *ruach* is gendered, and specifically, it is a feminine noun. That is one of the reasons that the pronoun "she" is appropriate when speaking of the Spirit. *Ruach* suggests something like *wind*, *breath*, or *spirit* of God. We see it first in Gen 1:2, where the *ruach* (Spirit-breath-wind) "swept over the face of the waters" of creation. Another way to think of *ruach* is as life-force or life-principle, but not in a generic or non-personal way. It is specifically the life of *God* that flows through all that lives. Cognate words in other languages carry the same meanings (wind-Spirit-breath) and the feminine gender:

Hebrew: *ruach*
Syriac: *rûḥâ*
Arabic: *rūḥ*

Ruach (breath-wind-Spirit of God) appears not only at the first moment of the creation, but frequently throughout the First Testament (Gen 8:1; Exod 15:8–10; Num 11:31; Ps 143:10; Is 32:15, Ezek 37:1). It is by *ruach*-Spirit "that the world and [hu]mankind are created and nature is continually sustained."[9] Another Hebrew word for the Spirit with a meaning close to *ruach* is *neshamah/nephesh*. The term is first seen when God breathes life into the *adam*, the first human creature: "Then the Lord God formed man from the dust of the ground and breathed into his nostrils the breath [*neshamah*] of life, and the man became a living being" (Gen 2:7). *Neshamah/*

8. World Council of Churches, *Come, Holy Spirit*, 19. The World Council of Churches will be cited frequently in this book, as it is the ecumenical body in which nearly all United and Uniting Churches participate. It has shared authority for these denominations.

9. Ramsey, *Holy Spirit*, 11.

nephesh suggests something like "life-breath." Again, this is not "life in general," but specifically the life that comes from God.

Other terms for the Spirit of God in Hebrew include *ḥokhma* and *shekinah*; *ḥokhma*, the wisdom of God, is "the divine agent in creating and sustaining the world and illuminating the human race"[10] (see Prov 8). From a Christian theological point of view, God as a whole (the fullness of the Trinity) is Wisdom, not only the Spirit; but it is to the Spirit that theology most often assigns the Wisdom of God.[11] We also want to distinguish between divine Wisdom and the wisdom that God creates. Human wisdom is something God makes and develops in the human creature. For shorthand, we could call this the human capacity for sound judgment. But when we speak of God *as* Wisdom, or the Holy Spirit *as* Wisdom, we are not talking about a capacity that God has. In God, Wisdom is not a what but a *Who*. We can say that God the Spirit *is* Wisdom, but not that God *has wisdom*. Thus, any use of *ḥokhma* (or its Greek version, *sophia*) is more like a name for God the Spirit, rather than a property of God. For any attribute of God—such as wisdom, love, or justice—theology doesn't begin with an idea of the attribute and then apply it to God. Rather, God defines these realities by *being* them. God *is* Love, *is* Justice, *is* Wisdom.

The beautiful and evocative word *shekinah* and its root, *shakan*, point toward the dwelling of the divine presence among the people (Exod 24:16; Num 10:12). That word is used, for example, in relation to the divine presence with or within the ark of the covenant (Exod 25:8). The term suggests that God is among the people. The Spirit chooses to be in the midst of the people, not controlled or contained by them, but freely choosing to be and freely flowing in the midst of the people of God.[12]

The Second Testament has another array of evocative terms for the Holy Spirit. The Greek word most often used for the Holy Spirit (*pneuma*) parallels closely the Hebrew word *ruach*. Like *ruach*, *pneuma* suggests wind, breath, and spirit. It is the root word for *pneumatic* in English, having to do with air pressure or the lungs. *Pneuma* is the word Jesus uses in John 3:7–8 for the Spirit who gives (spiritual) birth and who "blows where it chooses." There is a strong theological relationship between the breath-wind of God (*ruach*) that was at work at creation (Gen 1), and the breath (*pneuma*) breathed by the risen Jesus in the upper room when he commissioned his followers (John 20:22), as well as the powerful wind sent at Pentecost to

10. Ramsey, *Holy Spirit*, 17.

11. See Augustine, *The Trinity* 15.5.29.

12. The precise form of the term as *shekhinah* appears in the Talmud, but not in the First Testament.

bring the church to birth (Acts 2:2). The Holy Spirit (Greek: *hagia pneuma*) is the one who baptizes believers with the Spirit (Acts 11:16).

Other words for the Holy Spirit are *Lord* (*kyrios* in 2 Cor 3:17–18, and in the Niceno-Constantinopolitan Creed) and *paraclete* (*paraklētos* in John 14:16, 15:26). The use of *kyrios*, Lord, is a direct equivalent for readers of Greek to the Hebrew term YHWH or *Yahweh*, meaning the Lord God. *Kyrios* is also used repeatedly in the Second Testament in reference to Jesus Christ, with whom the Spirit is united in the Trinity. If the Spirit is Lord, there is nothing subordinate about the Spirit within the Trinity. The fullness of God is the Lord, and the Spirit shares in that fullness—indeed, the Spirit is *one with* that fullness. However, in this case, lordship does not mean domination or "lording over." It does not mean unjust or oppressive power. The form of lordship that God exercises (as seen in both Jesus and the Spirit) is an authority that lovingly serves the good of others, blesses creation and its renewal, and brings about the joyful fulfillment of the realm of God. In relation to this, it is worth noticing that the Old English word that is the root of "Lord" in modern English is *hlafwaerd*. A *hlafwaerd* is the person in the household who ensures that everyone has enough bread. The lordship of the Spirit is a lordship of service, ensuring all receive what they need.

In contrast, there is no single word in English that captures the dense set of meanings packed into *paraclete*. Translations range from "comforter" or "advocate," to "counsellor" or "encourager." "When the Advocate [*paraklētos*] comes," says Jesus, "whom I will send to you from the Father, the Spirit of truth who comes from the Father, he will testify on my behalf" (John 15:26). In John's account, the *paraclete*-Spirit has a particular set of roles, such as witnessing to Christ, convicting the world of sin, reminding the followers of Jesus about his ministry, and comforting them. This latter role is sometimes overlooked. Jesus promises that through the *paraclete*-Spirit, or Advocate, peace will be his personal gift to his followers: "Peace I leave with you; my peace I give to you. I do not give to you as the world gives." As a result of that gift, which will arrive through the Spirit, Jesus can offer this assurance: "Do not let your hearts be troubled, and do not let them be afraid" (John 14:27). In a world of many stresses, strains, and troubles, this is a profound promise.

The Character of the Spirit of God

Multiple characteristics of the Holy Spirit are scattered throughout the Biblical accounts and later Christian writings. One of the most distinctive aspects of the Holy Spirit is *freedom*—to act or not to act, to will or not to will, to give or to withhold gifts, and so on. The richest expression of this is in John 3:8, where Jesus says, "The wind [*or breath or Spirit*] blows where it chooses, and you hear the sound of it, but you do not know where it comes from or where it goes." This indicates both autonomy and unpredictability. As Roger Shinn of the United Church of Christ (USA) notes, "Nobody could set a timetable for the arrival of the Spirit."[13] Even the usual expectation that baptism will coincide with the arrival of the Spirit cannot be guaranteed. In Acts 8:16, some converts who had been baptized did not immediately receive the Spirit (see Acts 19:1–7 for a similar story). Although Christians pray earnestly for the Holy Spirit to come—in sacramental celebrations or in private prayers—no one can guarantee that the Spirit will show up. If it were otherwise, and we could say certain words that would *cause* the Spirit to arrive, we would be talking about magic, not the free relationship between a free Holy Spirit and the free creation. "God's presence is disturbing," writes Shinn,

> because it is out of our control . . . [and has] a capacity to break through conventional boundaries of law and authority. . . . Pentecost . . . makes clear that the Spirit is not a possession of the church.[14]

If the Spirit is free, then the Spirit is correspondingly the source of freedom: "Now the Lord is the Spirit, and where the Spirit of the Lord is, there is freedom" (2 Cor 3:17). Writing to the Roman emperor, Gratian, Ambrose of Milan pointedly takes up this theme: "The Holy Spirit is not subject to a foreign power or law, but is arbiter of His own freedom, dividing all things according to the authority of His own will."[15] This is an important caution to any earthly power that tries to co-opt or claim the power of God. The Spirit is not interested in being a prop in our political agendas.

This Spirit is called *Holy*, in contrast to other spirits (1 Cor 2:7–13; Gal 4:9). The adjective *holy* indicates that this Spirit is one with the triune God. Holiness is not a kind of gift from God to the Spirit. The Spirit *is* Holy. As Basil suggests, "For the Spirit, holiness is an essential part of his nature, so that he is not made holy but makes holy . . . and has goodness as his substance."[16] The Holy Spirit is the *Giver of Life*, as the Niceno-Constantinopolitan Creed states, echoing John 6:63 and 2 Cor 3:3. The Holy Spirit is *filled with grace* (Zech 12:10). The ways God acts as the Spirit, how the

13. Shinn, *Confessing Our Faith*, 76.

14. Shinn, *Confessing Our Faith*, 78–79.

15. Ambrose, *Holy Spirit* 1.18. Ambrose directed his treatise to Gratian, at the Emperor's request.

16. Basil, *On the Holy Spirit* 19.48.

Spirit moves, and the effects of the Spirit's work, can all be described as grace-filled. There is nothing about the Spirit that suggests the opposite, such as hateful, spiteful, death-dealing, or cruel. In the Spirit, we see only the goodness of God, even when the Spirit's work seems contrary to what we desire or will for ourselves. The purposes of God always lead to the greater good. The Holy Spirit is also known for *power*, as Ambrose writes: "Where, then, there is the manifestation of the Spirit, there is the power of God."[17]

Non-Personal Language for the Spirit

Among the language options for the Holy Spirit are a number of non-personal terms. A broad range of metaphors for the Holy Spirit is used throughout the Bible and Christian writings. The Holy Spirit appears as a *dove* at the baptism of Jesus in all four Gospels. Another term, *arrabon*, suggests something like what English would call a foretaste, pledge, or deposit.[18] The Spirit in this sense is "a down payment of the coming glory . . . or the first installment of the believer's inheritance in the kingdom of God."[19] As a "foretaste," the Holy Spirit's presence and action in human life and creation is a sign, a foreshadowing, of the fullness of all that God intends in the new creation. In a related way, Paul speaks of the *first fruits* of the Spirit (Rom 8:23). The *fire* of the Spirit is seen on the day of Pentecost (Acts 2:2–3). Fire is a symbol of transformation and purification. As we shall see in Part Two, transformation is a principal purpose of the Spirit. Other metaphors used for the Spirit include *incense*, *river* (John 7:38–39), *seal* (Eph 4:30), *sword* (Eph 6:17), *teacher* (Luke 12:11–12), and *water* (Isa 44:3; John 4:10; 1 Cor 12:13). As noted in chapter 2, Augustine speaks relationally of the Holy Spirit as the "bond of communion" between the Father and the Son.

One of the influential Western philosophers who spent a great deal of time thinking about the Spirit is Georg Wilhelm Friedrich Hegel (1770–1831). For Hegel, the favored term is *Geist*. This suggests "Spirit." Linguistically, it is related to the English term *Ghost*, which also can refer to the Holy Spirit. *Geist* is as close to a word like "God" as Hegel was likely to use. *Geist* is a principle, an energy, or even a kind of mind. Hegel's distinctive use of the term points toward something like *the world-becoming-process principle*. Geist has purpose and direction, and is unfolding continuously in time, history, and material reality. But it is not exactly a *Someone* in the way that the Bible, ancient Christianity, and most other expressions of Christianity have

17. Ambrose, *Holy Spirit* 2.12.

18. See 2 Cor 1:22 and 5:5; Eph 1:14.

19. Kärkkäinen, *Holy Spirit*, 7.

identified the Spirit: "Radically deviating from Christian tradition, Hegel taught that God is a Spirit permeating everything rather than the transcendent Creator of the world."[20] Those who, like Hegel, are more philosophically inclined rather than biblically inclined with respect to theology, might find this conceptualization attractive and helpful.

What remains difficult to reconcile is how a world-unfolding spirit (as implied by *Geist*) is different from just "what is." That is to say, could we simply look at the world or history and say, "here is the world" or "here is history," without pointing to anything like *Geist*, and yet mean essentially the same thing? And if that is possible, why have a separate word and concept for it? If *Geist* is simply the world unfolding through a series of processes, then it has no identity apart from material reality and its history. From a non-theological perspective, we would have to allow that this might be so. However, Christian theology that is rooted in the Bible will have endless quarrels with that perspective, as they are finally mutually exclusive. The triune God who acts within (and beyond) material reality, who has an existence that is not strictly dependent on materiality (even while choosing to interact with matter, with creation), and who is incarnate in Jesus Christ to save and transform, cannot be squared with Hegel's *Geist*. Most urgently, *Geist* can be conceived and described with no reference at all to Jesus Christ. Indeed, that is characteristic of Hegel—but a problem for trinitarian Christianity.

In this sense, it is impossible to locate *Geist* as one with the Trinity, as Christian thought invariably does with the Holy Spirit. The Holy Spirit apart from the Trinity and apart from Jesus Christ is not a Christian account of reality. The Spirit to which the Bible testifies should not be confused with something "masquerading as a generic term for human religiosity or world process," as Amy Plantinga Pauw says critically of *Geist*.[21] While Hegel certainly has his advocates (past and present), his conception of the Holy Spirit as *Geist* falls short in theological terms.

However, Hegel's teaching on *Geist* continues to echo down to the present. In the vernacular of our current era, there is a concept of the Spirit that is not attached to the Trinity at all. In such uses of the term ("spirit"), there is again a gap or separation from trinitarian reference and from the key relationship between the Holy Spirit and Jesus Christ. Process theology, which has other strengths, has an unfortunate tendency to speak of the Spirit as a something like the *process of the universe becoming itself*. One can see here the connection to Hegel. Others will speak of *spirit* without

20. Kärkäinnen, *Pneumatology*, 90.

21. Pauw, "Holy Spirit and Scripture," 31.

the designators of "the" or "Holy" in front of it—just simply "spirit." Here, the word seems to refer to a kind of undifferentiated force or energy that is somehow present in the universe. But it is difficult to distinguish it. It is unclear what this force or energy is all about. Where is it anchored? What are its goals and purposes? Is it benevolent or malign, and how can we know?

Or again, in the twenty-first-century West, everyday use of the term "spirit" is "relegated to the realms of the psychological and the paranormal. Cultural understandings of 'spirit' is linked with pixies, fairies and demons in the fantasy world of wizards and witches, remembered in fairy tales."[22] Annexed to this dilemma is the fact that

> in modernity, the language and reality of the Holy Spirit . . . has often been regarded as nothing more than "metaphysical speculation" and "largely irrelevant." So the [Holy] Spirit was assigned to the realm of values, or to the human mind, or religious experience, and the link to divinity was obscured.[23]

These imprecise treatments are unsatisfying. But I think it is clear, even if it is unacknowledged or people are unaware of it, that this vague way of thinking about "spirit/Spirit" owes a certain debt to Hegel. His approach means that history, people, Geist, and nature are unified and "unfolding" as a whole, but there is little clarity about the destination or purpose of that unfolding. In contrast, the clarity given to Holy Spirit language by the Bible, liturgy, and trinitarian theologians is far preferable. This specific *Holy* Spirit has personhood, character, and distinctive purposes and actions, and is undoubtedly one with God. Undifferentiated "spirit/Spirit" could mean anything—helpful or unhelpful, sinful or righteous, of God or anti-God.

The Human Spirit

In Hebrew, the language of the First Testament of the Bible, the common word *ruach* is used in several contexts. Very often, it refers to God; but it can also refer to other senses of "spirit." *Ruach* can speak of more than one kind of spirit, as well as to physical phenomena such as the literal, material "wind" and "breath." This sense of *ruach*-spirit is something found in nature, both human and non-human: "Who knows whether the human spirit [*ruach*] goes upward and the spirit [*ruach*] of animals goes downward to the earth?" (Eccl 3:21). Here, the term conveys something like a "life-force,"

22. Kim, *Holy Spirit in the World*, 1.
23. Kim, *Holy Spirit in the World*, 2.

the animating element that makes a creature live and thrive. Without it, the creature dies, as in the great flood:

> And all flesh died that moved on the earth, birds, domestic animals, wild animals, all swarming creatures that swarm on the earth, and all human beings; everything on dry land in whose nostrils was the breath of life [*neshamah-ruach*] died.[24]

A similar use of *ruach* as life-force appears when the hero Samson, exhausted from battle, needs to recover and regain his strength: "God split open the hollow place that is at Lehi, and water came from it. When he [Samson] drank, his spirit [*ruach*] returned, and he revived" (Judg 15:19). There are moments in which animal and human spirits interact or intersect with the divine Spirit (God). This occurs when specifically the Spirit *of God* gives life and breath to creatures. As Elihu testifies to Job, "The spirit [*ruach*] of God has made me, and the breath of the Almighty gives me life" (Job 33:4). The same relationship is signalled in the Second Testament, as in Paul's remark, "For what human knows what is truly human except the human spirit [*pneuma*] that is within? So also no one comprehends what is truly God's except the Spirit [*pneuma*] of God" (1 Cor 2:11). *Ruach* and *pneuma*, on their own, do not tell us if the "spirit" to which they refer is divine or creaturely, but the intentionally close correspondence between the *Spirit of God* and the *spirit of creatures* in the biblical languages is clear. A deep relationship is implied in the very words.

Other Spirits and Their Dangers

There are still other "spirits and powers" that are not of God. These are abundantly attested in the Bible and in many cultures. North Atlantic cultures, under the influence of the Enlightenment, are often resistant to acknowledging these powers, attributing talk about them to superstition. United and Uniting Churches in the global North, typically, are also reluctant to speak of these other spirits or to account for them theologically. This is a shortsighted mistake. As Kirsteen Kim notes, "A theology of the Spirit for today must take into account the other spirits encountered in an increasingly plural world."[25] Many societies that have not been overpowered by the anti-superstitious presuppositions of the Western Enlightenment have a robust sense of living in a world filled with spirits of all kinds. Yet rationalistic explanatory models are prone to "finding social and psychological

24. Gen 7:21–22.

25. Kim, *Holy Spirit in the World*, 3.

explanations for believing in the spirits."[26] For example, the living spirits who are recognized in many traditional African societies have often been dismissed by Western intellectuals as subconscious human forces and latent emotions. Again, there is an unwarranted theological and cultural superiority embedded in that dismissal.

In contrast, the Bible testifies frequently to other spirits that are present and at work beyond the divine Holy Spirit that shares life with the human and non-human creatures of creation. Some of these spirits are God's messengers and assistants, called *angels* (Num 22:31; Heb 1:13–14). Some have names, such as Michael and Gabriel, or are grouped into categories such as cherubim, seraphim, "thrones or dominions" (Col 1:16).

Still other spirits have evil intentions. The one that might come most easily to mind is Satan or the devil. Both the First and Second Testaments refer to this non-material spirit (Job 1:6–12; Mark 3:23–27). This spirit is considered an adversary of God ("the enemy" as Jesus calls him in Luke 10:18–19). There are further malign spirits, often called *demons* (Deut 32:17; Luke 10:17). Some have names, such as Azazel and Beelzebub. One Second Testament author speaks of "the rulers . . . the authorities . . . the cosmic powers of this present darkness . . . [and] the spiritual forces of evil in the heavenly places" (Eph 6:12). The United Church in Jamaica and the Cayman Islands upholds the importance of the Holy Spirit's gift of discernment in light of these other spirits' potential influence:

> This gift is the ability to recognize the difference between expressions of spiritual life that are divine, human or demonic in origin. It enables one to help others to learn whether their gift is of the Holy Spirit or from some other source.[27]

Unlike the majority of United and Uniting Churches, many charismatic-Pentecostal Christian traditions and many Christians in non-Western contexts recognize and acknowledge spirits that are not the Holy Spirit, and often consider these to be spirits in conflict with the one God.

In a measured tone, the World Council of Churches speaks of non-divine spirits that are adversaries to God's purposes. These are forces that

> oppose God's will for justice and peace on earth. They find expression in social and economic systems that divide humankind and perpetuate the deep divisions based on race, religion,

26. Kim, *Holy Spirit in the World*, 152.

27. United Church in Jamaica and the Cayman Islands, *Our Church*, 86.

> colour, and sex . . . in the arms race and in the violations of the rights of people.[28]

These other spirits threaten and attempt, as Pauw says, "to usurp the place of the Holy Spirit and to demand idolatrous service and loyalty from Scripture" and indeed from human beings.[29] Speaking in this way of "other spirits" in non-personal terms allows us to identify other abstract societal forces such as militarism, consumerism, inhumane ideologies, racism, sexism, classism, and homophobia as anti-God spirits.

All "other spirits," who are false claimants to human allegiance, must be rejected in favor of the Holy Spirit whose perfect will and goodness alone command our obedience. Obedience here does not mean docile submission to an overpowering will. Obedience in terms of our relation to the Spirit means that our wills *desire to cooperate with God's will* to achieve God's purposes. Desiring what God desires is the result of the process of sanctification. I will say more about this in chapter 13.

Distractions and forces that draw human beings away from serving God are not new to our era. In ancient times, Micaiah prophesied against the false prophets advising King Ahab:

> A certain spirit came forward and stood before the Lord, saying,
> "I will entice [Ahab]."
> "How?" the Lord asked him.
> He replied, "I will go out and be a lying spirit in the mouth of all his prophets."[30]

In the Second Testament, Paul scolds the ancient Christians in Rome about their lack of discernment about non-divine spirits: "For if someone comes and proclaims another Jesus than the one we proclaimed, or if you receive a different spirit from the one you received, or a different gospel from the one you accepted, you put up with it readily enough" (2 Cor 11:4). All gifts given by the Holy Spirit, in contrast, are aligned with and serve the purposes of God's mission in the world. Nothing that runs counter to that can come from the Holy Spirit. The task of discerning spirits, then, falls to all Christians, according to the writer of 1 John: "Beloved, do not believe every spirit, but test the spirits to see whether they are from God, for many false prophets have gone out into the world" (1 John 4:1). All such malign spirits, however they are conceived, are forces and agents that run counter to God's purposes. Paul (in Gal 5:19–21) outlines several of the evil outcomes of such

28. World Council of Churches, *Come, Holy Spirit*, 9–10.

29. Pauw, "Holy Spirit and Scripture," 26.

30. 1 Kgs 22:1–28.

spirits' work. Then he contrasts them with the fruit of the Holy Spirit—"love, joy, peace, patience, kindness, generosity, faithfulness, gentleness, and self-control" (Gal 5:22–23).

It is essential to distinguish the false powers from the Holy Spirit, for they will lead us away from the purposes of God. For this reason alone, retaining the adjective "Holy" when referring to the Spirit of God is a crucial move. The Holy Spirit designates a *specific* Spirit, the one divine Spirit, and not any other. When they are open to the Holy Spirit's guidance, the community of the faithful can discern the true Spirit of God, and the false spirits can be rejected. The United Church of Canada cites favorably a "Litany from Canberra," a prayer resource from the Seventh Assembly of the World Council of Churches (Canberra, Australia, 1991):

> O Spirit of truth . . . consume, as a mighty fire,
> the powers of evil that bind your people
> and set us free to walk in your light.[31]

False powers and spirits take many forms, including the neglect of the Holy Spirit's power and presence. There are moments when the dynamic and intricate realities of the human spirit—and human spirits as they combine in societies, cultures, and civilizations—can obscure the capacity to perceive and receive the Holy Spirit. We humans are notoriously egocentric and routinely overestimate our own significance. Liberal theology in the nineteenth and early twentieth centuries had a tendency to reduce the Holy Spirit to mental or ethical activity, as if anything non-material about the make up of human beings was the same as the Holy Spirit, without distinction. This simultaneously demoted and desacralized the Spirit of God while elevating the importance of human creatures (but without elevating other creatures). From time to time in the last century, the legacy of this conflation has reared its ugly head and the differences between human creatures and the divine triune Creator have nearly been erased. This was part of Karl Barth's reaction to classical theological liberalism, when he reemphasized the radical distinction between humans and God. The United Church of Canada echoes this distinction by referring to God as "wholly other."[32] The Holy Spirit must not be confused with other spirits, nor conflated with human beings' best intentions.

Because we can and must name these false powers, we can and must oppose them and give our allegiance to God alone. This is modelled by Jesus, when he names and casts out demons who oppose God's will (Luke

31. Cited in United Church of Canada, *Mending the World*, 1.

32. United Church of Canada, "Song of Faith."

4:33–36). Indeed, Jesus indicates that those who follow him will also cast out demons (Mark 16:17). As the Uniting Presbyterian Church in Southern Africa attests, "The Spirit is thus fully God in basic contrast to every other existing or supposed spirit, whether ancestral or supernatural."[33] God's charge to the people at Mount Sinai comes to mind: "You shall have no other gods before me" (Exod 20:3).

~

There is considerable breadth of meaning to this one small word, "spirit." In contemporary English, in the languages of the Bible, and in other Christian writings, we can find everything from "force" to "principle" to the life-energy that inhabits human or non-human creatures, and from collective impersonal powers to angels and demons. But above all is the sense indicated by the "Holy" Spirit, who is one with the Trinity, the eternal and everlasting God, "the Lord and Giver of life." Stanley J. Samartha of the Church of South India has suggested that sharply distinguishing between phrases like "breath of God," "the Holy Spirit," and "the Spirit of Christ" may be futile, when trying to express the reality of the Spirit. It is "like trying to slice a flowing river with a razor blade."[34] There is truth to this. We can dance endlessly on the head of the proverbial pin and we will never resolve the divine mystery. It has always been thus, and it is incumbent on good theology to admit its limitations. As Robert Jensen notes, "The Spirit cannot be confined by our language."[35] The best we can do is to access the metaphors and images, the attributes and characteristics of the Holy Spirit that our spiritual ancestors have discerned, and to continue the conversation, in continuity with the past, seeking prophetic insight and faithfulness.

FOR REFLECTION OR DISCUSSION

1. Both *ruach* (Hebrew) and *pneuma* (Greek) have multi-layered meanings of *spirit*, *breath*, and *wind*. How would you describe the connection between spirit, breath, and wind, which are three different words in English?
2. Metaphors can help us speak about God, because the holiness of God is impossible to capture with human language. Metaphors always convey

33. Uniting Presbyterian Church in Southern Africa, *Manual*, 25.
34. Samartha, "Holy Spirit and People of Various Faiths," 21.
35. Jensen, "Introduction," xiii.

a meaning of "like" and "not like." An example used in this chapter is a bird protecting her young. God is *like* the bird in offering care; God is *not like* a bird, since God does not have literal wings and a beak. What metaphors have you heard used to describe the Holy Spirit? How is the Holy Spirit like and unlike these images or analogies?

Chapter 5

Who Is the Holy Spirit for Creation and Humankind?

THE HOLY SPIRIT'S IDENTITY is rightly lodged first of all within the Trinity, as we have seen in earlier chapters. The Spirit is not separate from God, nor one more created entity, and not a rival demigod. The Holy Spirit is not just God's tool or instrument, and not merely an agent or impersonal power. The Spirit is always already *one with* the triune God. The Holy Spirit has many names and images associated with her, and many distinctive actions of the one God are habitually associated with (appropriated to) the Spirit. We can now continue the investigation into the question "Who is the Holy Spirit?" with these things in mind.

We can reflect on the triune God in terms of God's *immanent* nature (God "inwardly," so to speak; God's relations within the Trinity), as we have done above, in chapter 2. But this reflection needs also to follow the lines of what is called the *economic* Trinity. To say "economic" in this case has nothing to do with trade or money. It has to do with how God relates and acts toward the created order. Within this frame—the *economic* Trinity—there are many important things to say about the Holy Spirit.

Above all, theology that is grounded in the Bible and Christian tradition asserts that the Spirit is not a mere phantasm, nor a principle, nor distant from creation. She is present to and with creation, without being the same as creation. The biblical narratives are especially good at helping us see how the Holy Spirit is active within and toward creation. As David Jensen points out, "A disembodied Spirit does not exist in Biblical narratives, only a Spirit who descends on bodies in creation."[1] Consider the physicality emphasized in the *Catechism* of the China Christian Council: "The Holy

1. Jensen, "Discerning the Spirit," 1.

Spirit dwells within us, our body becomes the temple of the Holy Spirit, the place where God, through the Holy Spirit, may reside."[2] Matter *matters* to the Holy Spirit.

Embodiment is a key theme in Indigenous Christian understandings of the Holy Spirit too. Adrian Jacobs worked for many years with The United Church of Canada, and is Haudenosaunee, of the Handsome Lake Longhouse religion of the Cayuga nation, and a Christian. Jacobs notes that in the Haudenosaunee community, the Spirit's life is profoundly embodied, through community gathering, dancing, singing, smudging, dropping tobacco, feasting, storytelling, and teaching. In Western thinking, says Jacobs, the Holy Spirit is too often "extracted from the body . . . and is no longer a practically animating force in the here and now." This is problematic, given that Christian faith is meant to be "embodied in action."[3] One of the many detrimental consequences of this disembodiment—which is antithetical to authentic Christianity, as Jacobs describes—were the atrocities and abuse perpetrated by European settlers/invaders in Canada and elsewhere.[4]

Alive and at Work

From a biblical perspective, then, what can be said about the Spirit must always attend to how She is vibrantly at work *within and through* creation, rather than apart from or beside it. This perspective, which I adopt here and which is easily found in United and Uniting Church perspectives, is called panentheism. Note the *en* in the middle of that word. It should be distinguished from panthesism (without the "*en*"), which is the belief that God and nature are the same, without distinction. In pantheism, all that exists is the same as God; and all that is God is identical with the material world. Pan*en*theism, in contrast, respects the divine reality that exists outside of or at least beyond the created order, since God is the Creator prior to the existence of creation. Yet God also values and celebrates the divine presence "in" creation. The foremost theologian of panentheism was Jürgen Moltmann (1926–2024), who worked to discover God "in all the beings he has created and to find his life-giving Spirit in the community of creation

2. China Christian Council, "Introduction to Doctrines: Important Q&A."

3. Jacobs, "Holy Spirit," 158.

4. Many Euro-descended Canadians and others currently speak of being "settlers." But there is also important truth in admitting candidly that we are also invaders, coming to places like Canada with military force and often waging war to assert territorial dominance. See Budden, *Following Jesus in Invaded Space.*

that they share."[5] Elsewhere Moltmann writes, "Through his Spirit God is also present in the very structures of matter."[6]

Although Christians customarily look first to the divine presence of the Spirit in Second Testament accounts such as the baptism of Jesus or the day of Pentecost, there are multiple accounts of the Holy Spirit in the First Testament. The Spirit sweeps with life-giving power over the waters of creation (Gen 1:1–2). The Spirit gives life to the human creature (Gen 2:7; Job 33:4). The Spirit empowers and gives gifts to prophets and judges. The Spirit teaches and leads the people. In the midst of the people in their exodus from Egypt, the Spirit is in pillars of cloud and fire, in the camp, on the holy mountain, and later in the ark of the covenant. God's freedom-loving Spirit is everywhere the psalmist can think to look:

> Where can I go from your Spirit?
> Or where can I flee from your presence?
> If I ascend to heaven, you are there;
> if I make my bed in Sheol, you are there.
> If I take the wings of the morning
> and settle at the farthest limits of the sea,
> even there your hand shall lead me,
> and your right hand shall hold me fast.[7]

The prophet Haggai overhears God assuring the people in a time of despair: "Take courage . . . I am with you . . . my Spirit abides among you; do not fear" (Hag 2:4–5). In these and other ways, we can think of the Holy Spirit as the outward movement of God toward creation and human beings. While conventional religiosity (ancient or contemporary) might suppose that the material and the spiritual are radically separate, that assumption does not bind and limit God, nor does it need to bind the theological reflections of pneumatology. God is not limited by Western Enlightenment binaries that radically separate physical and spiritual reality.

The Holy Spirit and the Material Order

One expression of this truth—that spiritual and physical realities are not radical binaries—is found in Jesus Christ, in whom God took up a human

5. Moltmann, *God in Creation*, xi.

6. Moltmann, *God in Creation*, 212. For a dynamic and inspiring treatment of the related Jewish concept of *zimzum*, see his chapter 6 of *God in Creation* ("The Space of Creation"). See also his chapter, "The Origin and Completion of Time," in *Science and Wisdom*.

7. Ps 139:7–10.

identity. This conviction is profoundly ancient and central to Christianity. In the incarnation of the Second Identity (the Word, the Son) in human form, we see the uniting of the spiritual and material realms in an astonishing way. But long before the moment of Jesus's incarnation in Mary's womb, the acts of creation described in Genesis reveal that the Holy Spirit was already well acquainted with and active within the material order. She sweeps or hovers (depending on the translation) over creation as *ruach*—the breath-wind-Spirit of God. As Sergius Bulgakov notes, the physical world of materiality "is not closed off from or alien to the Spirit. Created out of nothing, the world receives its reality, matter, and elements from the Holy Spirit."[8]

At the baptism of Jesus, the Spirit is physically manifested as a dove. After his resurrection, in the physical forms of wind, ecstatic speech, and flames of fire, the Holy Spirit is made manifest among the thousands gathered in Jerusalem on the day of Pentecost (Acts 2). Many people today report physical manifestations of the Spirit's presence such as warmth, tingling, and light.[9] These physical expressions are especially significant to and most frequently reported by persons affiliated with charismatic and Pentecostal forms of Christianity, but is not limited to these groups. I, too, can testify to physical sensations that I associate clearly with the presence of the Holy Spirit.

In ancient times, Basil asked, "What sort of nature should [the Spirit] be thought to have, who exists everywhere and co-exists with God?"[10] Such a nature is coeternal with the triune God, to begin with, as we described in chapter 2. The same God who is omnipresent, wise, gracious, loving, and powerful is already one with the Holy Spirit—there is no distinction in essence or substance. While the First Identity of the Trinity (the Father) is often considered the Creator, the whole Trinity is involved in the making and sustaining of the created order. There are good reasons to seek non-gendered words for the First Identity, and United and Uniting Churches will sometimes substitute *Mother* for *Father*, or introduce the hyphenated *Mother-Father*. But a straight substitution of *Creator* for *Father* distorts the teaching that the whole Trinity shares in the work of creation. The Holy Spirit's creating role is clear, again, in passages such as Gen 1:1–2 and 2:7, Job 33:4, and more. The Holy Spirit as the creative presence of God is alluded to in Prov 8:22–31, where She is called the Wisdom (*ḥokhma*) of God, and Ps 33:6, where the *ruach* of God's mouth makes the inhabitants of heaven. The Wisdom-Spirit who is God is present from before the beginning of all things,

8. Bulgakov, *Bride of the Lamb*, 401.

9. See Inbody, "Sensing God."

10. Basil, *On the Holy Spirit* 23.54.

and remains active in the ongoing creative and sustaining work of the triune God in relation to the created order—all things "visible and invisible" as the Niceno-Constantinopolitan Creed attests. Dhirendra Sahu of the Church of North India concurs: "The Holy Spirit is the pouring out of [God's] love in endless fresh creativity."[11] The ongoing presence of the Spirit in creation has an immediacy to it, giving a sense of God's freshness, dynamism, "nearness and interiority" within creation and creatures.[12] Every good thing that exists is the work of the Spirit. As Basil indicates, "No gift at all comes to creation without the Holy Spirit."[13] Diversity, freshness, and fruitfulness within creation are also hallmarks of the Holy Spirit's work. Consider the "command to the heavens, lands, and seas to bring forth multiple kinds and 'every living creature that moves' and 'everything that God has made.'"[14] Indeed, diversity is "an expression of the Spirit's creativity expressed in the infinite variety of creation, of culture and of the natural world."[15]

Keeping it Together

In reflecting on the life of the Holy Spirit in relation to creation and humankind, an important theological principle applies: *opera Trinitatis ad extra indivisa sunt*—the works of the Trinity toward that which is outside the Trinity are indivisible. In other words, the way that the three triune Identities act toward and within creation cannot be strictly separated from each other. When the Father acts, the Son and Spirit are also acting. Rogers provides two illustrations: "Not only is the Father the Creator, but so is the Spirit; not only is the Son the Redeemer, but the Spirit [is] also."[16] Thus, all of God creates, so to speak. The fullness of the Trinity sustains life. Through the doctrine of appropriation, it might still be useful to associate the First Identity, God the Father, with creating. But it would also be useful to associate the redemption of creation with the Second Identity, Jesus who is the Christ. Similarly, it is the Holy Spirit who is known as the Identity of God that sustains the life of creation, reinvigorates life, and brings healing, growth, greenness, freshness, and renewal. Those conventional appropriations can be useful in understanding that the whole of the Trinity is always at work toward and within creation. This is a deeply held and deeply felt

11. Sahu, *Church of North India*, 294.
12. Leahy, "'Hiding Behind the Works,'" 18.
13. Basil, *On the Holy Spirit* 24.55.
14. Rogers, *After the Spirit*, 65.
15. Macleod, "On Not Losing the Way," 103.
16. Rogers, *After the Spirit*, 11.

conviction for those in the United and Uniting Churches. Shinn writes, "The Holy Spirit represents the immediacy of God in human experience. . . . The Holy Spirit is God experienced in intimacy, God's liberating presence in persons and communities."[17]

This experiential dimension of the Holy Spirit is often the most compelling aspect of pneumatology. It goes beyond doctrinal wranglings to get at the heart of God's presence among the people—just as the Spirit was present among the peoples of ancient Israel and the earliest church. The Spirit is still alive and well and at work within creation.

FOR REFLECTION OR DISCUSSION

1. Panentheism, or an understanding of the divine presence in creation, is one way to understand how the Holy Spirit relates to creation and humankind. Does this understanding resonate with you, or are you challenged by it? Why?
2. Have you ever experienced physical manifestations of the Holy Spirit's presence? What were the circumstances? What did it feel like?
3. This chapter speaks of the Holy Spirit being the heart of God's presence with the people. How do you experience the presence of the Holy Spirit in the people around you?

17. Shinn, *Confessing Our Faith*, 77.

Chapter 6

Christological Pneumatology or Pneumatological Christology?

THERE IS A CRUCIAL element in pneumatology that I have only touched upon so far: the close relationship between Christology and pneumatology. We could even ask, "Is pneumatology Christological? Or is Christology pneumatological?" Christian theology continually affirms that when we are speaking of the Holy Spirit, we are speaking of the "Spirit of Christ." There is no coherent Christian theological speech about the Holy Spirit that does not have close reference to Jesus Christ. They are not independent entities or sub-deities. At the same time, the affirmation of the Trinity means that, as Calvin teaches, "Father and Son and Spirit are one God, yet the Son is not the Father, nor the Spirit the Son."[1]

The intimate relationship between Jesus Christ and the Holy Spirit is attested again and again in Scripture and throughout the history of Christian writing. Paul speaks of God sending "the Spirit of his Son" (Gal 4:6). The traditional expression found in the revised Western version of the Niceno–Constantinopolitan Creed indicates that the Holy Spirit "proceeds" from the Father *and* the Son.[2] Yet the relationship between Son and Spirit is a co-unity, and not a cooperative partnership between separate entities. "The Spirit of Jesus Christ" is the phrase favored in Phil 1:19. Acts 16:7 uses "the Spirit of Jesus." While in John 14:16, Jesus speaks of the Father sending

1. Calvin, *Institutes* 1.13.5.

2. It is crucial to note that the Eastern Christian communities have never accepted this phrasing, preferring instead the original Niceno–Constantinopolitan Creed of 381, which attests that the Spirit proceeds only from the Father, not from both Father and Son.

the Spirit (John 14:16), later he refers to himself as sending the Spirit (John 16:7). The unity of the three Identities is reinforced in these passages.

Long before, the prophet Isaiah spoke of the coming of the messiah. Isaiah relates that "the Spirit [*ruach*] of the Lord shall rest upon him, the spirit [*ruach*] of wisdom and understanding, the spirit [*ruach*] of counsel and might" (Isa 11:2). Isaiah's messianic-prophetic voice is heard again in the phrases of Isa 61:1–2:

> The spirit of the Lord God is upon me
> because the Lord has anointed me;
> he has sent me to bring good news to the oppressed,
> to bind up the broken-hearted,
> to proclaim liberty to the captives
> and release to the prisoners,
> to proclaim the year of the Lord's favor.

When Jesus reads these words from the scroll in the synagogue in Nazareth, he applies them to himself, as the one upon whom the Spirit of God has come: "Today this scripture has been fulfilled in your hearing."[3] As the Evangelical Church in Germany testifies, "The speech of God the Son as the Reconciler and the speech of God the Holy Spirit as the Savior are mutually dependent."[4]

The Spirit Enfleshed

Many other testimonies to the closeness and indeed unity between the Spirit and the Son can be named. It is important to note the Spirit's role in the incarnation, for example. Mary's body—her womb—becomes the location of the Spirit's divine activity: "She was found to be pregnant by the Holy Spirit" (Matt 1:18–20). As Ephrem poetically put it, "Fire entered the womb."[5] From Mary's body, the divine-human child, Jesus, is born. The two "co-present" divine Identities of Spirit and Son are active within Mary, whose faithfulness enables the coming of the Messiah into the world to serve and to save. The Uniting Presbyterian Church in Southern Africa professes that "the eternal Word . . . by the Holy Spirit took on our humanity in the Virgin Mary's

3. Luke 4:16–22. See also Matt 12:18.
4. Beintker and Philipps, eds., "Handeln Gotte," 55.
5. Ephrem, *Hymns* 4.2.

womb."[6] As Brendan Leahy writes, "Through the incarnate Son the Spirit is becoming present in history in a new way."[7]

The baptism of Jesus is another example of the co-presence of the Spirit and the Son. The cousin of Jesus, Baptizing John, sees the Spirit "descending like a dove and alighting" on Jesus when he is baptized (Matt 3:16).[8] Attested in all four Gospels, his baptism reveals the presence of the Holy Spirit to empower and indwell Jesus Christ in his earthly ministry. These dramatic scenes reveal the dynamic interplay and cooperation between the Spirit and the Christ. The stories are strategically placed near the start of each Gospel, so that there is little doubt that all that follows in the life and work of Jesus is already invested with the Holy Spirit's presence and power. As one who comes into this world in the flesh, Jesus himself is the One who baptizes with the Holy Spirit and with fire.[9] This work of narratively stitching together the Holy Spirit and Jesus Christ in the Gospel accounts testifies once again the singleness of the will, purpose, and power of the triune God. There is no presence or action of the Holy Spirit that is not also saturated with the Christ-Identity, for they are One. The work of the Spirit always has the aroma of Christ.

There is a common misperception that Jesus "became" the Christ at his baptism, or "became" the Son of God at that moment. This is contrary to the teaching of the Bible, and especially the Second Testament, in which the pre-existence of the Word (also called the Son and the Christ) is disclosed in places such the first chapter of the gospel according to John. That is, the eternal Word of God (the Son of God, the Christ) was made incarnate—took on human flesh—but Jesus did not "become" the Word, the Christ. As Augustine exclaims, "It would be the height of absurdity to believe that he only received the Holy Spirit when he was already thirty years old . . . [when] he was baptized by John."[10] I raise this misperception to highlight the Christian teaching that the oneness and coeternality of the Trinity always precedes any earthly or historical action. Father, Son, and Holy Spirit are always already One, from eternity and for eternity. Thus when we reflect on the Spirit, we are always already reflecting on the Father and the Son. There are many biblical instances in which the Son and the Spirit are mentioned together, mutually indwelling or mutually interacting. As Basil says

6. Uniting Presbyterian Church in Southern Africa, *Manual*, 23.

7. Leahy, "'Hiding Behind the Works,'" 21.

8. The same testimony is offered in Mark 1:10; Luke 3:22; and John 1:32–33.

9. Matt 3:11; Luke 3:16.

10. Augustine, *Trinity* 15.6.46.

of Jesus, "His every act was performed in the presence of the Spirit. . . . The Spirit was inseparably present to him."[11]

After his baptism, the Spirit remains the accompanying presence and power of Jesus's earthly ministry. She leads him into the wilderness (Luke 4:1) and fills him after his testing there: "Then Jesus, in the power of the Spirit, returned to Galilee" (Luke 4:14). Among the four Gospel writers, Luke is especially interested to "present Jesus as one whose life is perpetually guided by the Spirit, one who is full of the Spirit."[12] The narrator of the gospel according to John relates that Jesus "speaks the words of God, for he gives the Spirit without measure" (John 3:34). The climactic scene after his resurrection sees Jesus breathing on his followers and saying, "Receive the Holy Spirit"—confirming that it is his to give (John 20:22). Not long after, on the day of Pentecost, when the gathered crowd receives the gift of the Spirit, Peter tells them that it is Jesus who has poured out the Spirit (Acts 2:33). In short, the Gospel writers see in Jesus and the Holy Spirit the closest of connections. It is in and through the Spirit that Jesus drives out demons, heals bodies, raises people from the dead, and is himself raised from the dead. It is the Spirit who teaches believers to know the Son.

Two United Identities

Further theological reflection on the unity of the Spirit and the Son unfolds in the Second Testament and the early centuries of the church. Paul tells the Christians in Corinth that their sanctification and justification are accomplished "in the name of the Lord Jesus Christ and in the Spirit of our God" (1 Cor 6:11). The first letter attributed to John relates that "we know that we abide in him [Christ] and he in us, because he has given us of his Spirit" (1 John 4:13). Ambrose writes that "where the Spirit is, there, too, is Christ . . . [and] where Christ is, there also is the Holy Spirit."[13] This affirmation of co-presence underscores the deep conviction of a trinitarian view of the Holy Spirit. Much later, writers within the United Church of Christ (USA) will echo the same notion: "Jesus remains deeply and intimately connected with us and our world and, through the work of the Holy Spirit, he comforts and empowers us."[14] At this level, it would be incoherent to try to pry apart the presence and work of the Son and Spirit. They are one in action, presence, and purpose. It is common enough to attribute an action to one or the

11. Basil, *On the Holy Spirit* 16.39.

12. Ramsey, *Holy Spirit*, 20.

13. Ambrose, *Holy Spirit* 3.9.

14. Thayer and Jacobsen, *Christ, Creeds and Life*, 87.

other, but there is a seamlessness in Spirit and Son because ultimately they are One.

When considering the Holy Spirit, then, how closely do we need to consider Christology, the doctrine about Jesus Christ? There is little doubt that the two need to be considered in tandem. Zizioulas goes so far as to say, "Christ exists *only* pneumatologically."[15] There is a great deal of Christian teaching, narrative, and testimony that makes it clear that Jesus is a *Someone* whose life is inextricably intertwined with the Spirit, both in earthly and eternal terms. Kärkkäinen, drawing on the thought of Wolfhart Pannenberg, contends that "everywhere the work of the Spirit is closely related to that of the Son, from creation to salvation to the consummation of creation in the eschaton [the final completion of God's purposes]."[16] Many believe that it is through the Holy Spirit that Jesus continues to be at work in the world today. For example, the Augsburg Confession, which is claimed as authoritative by the United Church of Christ (USA), notes that it is "through the Holy Spirit" that Jesus is active to "sanctify, purify, strengthen, and comfort."[17] It is by virtue of the Holy Spirit's work that we can come to know Jesus Christ and his significance.[18]

Still, there is merit in discerning and discussing the Holy Spirit in a focused way—which is of course the purpose of this book. But given what we have seen in this first section ("Who Is the Holy Spirit?"), it is hard to avoid thinking and talking in terms of a "Christological pneumatology" or a "pneumatological Christology." After all, the Trinity is One, not three gods. The close Christ-Spirit connection, indeed their unity, will always frame the way we consider pneumatology.

This can present a certain liability. As Ennis Macleod of the Uniting Church in Australia argues, in relation to that denomination's *Basis of Union*, "An underdeveloped pneumatology results in the Holy Spirit having no agency of her own, and the Church being unevenly responsive to the inspiration and guidance of the Holy Spirit. The Spirit becomes, not a Person to be known, but a conduit for the Person of Christ."[19] There is deep value, then, in preserving the principle of appropriation, which enables us

15. Zizioulas, *Being as Communion*, 111.

16. Kärkäinnen, *Pneumatology*, 124.

17. "Augsburg Confession," §III, cited in Thayer and Jacobsen, *Christ, Creeds and Life*, 92.

18. "So without the Spirit there is no seeing the Word of God . . . knowledge of the Son is through the Holy Spirit." Irenaeus, *Proof of the Apostolic Preaching* §7. So also Calvin: "Christ cannot be known apart from the sanctification of his Spirit." *Institutes* 3.2.8.

19. Macleod, "On Not Losing the Way," 102.

to perceive the Spirit's distinctive work. At the same time, the Holy Spirit's life, identity, and work is always thoroughly conformed to the life, identity, and work of Jesus Christ, for God is One, not three gods. What we see in Jesus is the embodied will of the Holy Spirit. What we see in the Holy Spirit is the freely flowing will of Jesus throughout creation. When the church is led by the Spirit, it is toward the truth of Christ.[20]

SUMMARY OF PART 1

So far, we've seen that a study of the Holy Spirit—or any theological subject—benefits from remembering to keep silent before launching into too much language. Whatever we say will always be partial and inadequate. Nevertheless, we work toward clarity and appropriate nuance in theological speech, so that our faith can be better understood and more deeply held. We've examined the eternal unity among the three Identities of the Trinity, and reflected on the importance of de-emphasizing a hierarchical relationship among them. The freedom, divinity, and sovereignty of the Spirit—always One with the Trinity—are crucial to bear in mind. Appropriation, or associating certain actions to the Holy Spirit, helps clarify our perception of God's work in the world. The value of feminine language for the Holy Spirit—and the richness of many other terms, names, and images—have been lifted up. The reality of other spirits and the human spirit reinforces the importance of using the key adjective "Holy." The Holy Spirit's deep attachment to the created order and human beings has been established. Finally, we've considered the intertwined nature of Christology and pneumatology. All this has helped answer the vital question, "Who is the Holy Spirit?"

Ahead of us is another vital question: "What does the Holy Spirit do?" Part 2 address this in dynamic and energetic ways. We will see how the transformative goals of the Spirit result in constant, purposeful action. The Holy Spirit is alive and at work within creation as a whole, and working within each person to inspire, guide, and give gifts. The Spirit sanctifies and renews. For the sake of all, both in the church and throughout all creation, the Spirit empowers and enables Scripture, the sacraments, Christian service, and more, en route to the fulfillment of the realm (kingdom) of God.

20. Ramsey, *Holy Spirit*, 108.

FOR REFLECTION OR DISCUSSION

1. This chapter deals with the close relationship between pneumatology (the doctrine of the Holy Spirit) and Christology (the doctrine of Jesus Christ). Does linking them together but still keeping them distinct make sense to you?
2. There are at least two moments in the Bible where the Spirit and the Son are in a close, obvious relationship: at the incarnation and at Jesus's baptism. Are there other places in the Bible where you see a similar relationship?
3. What distinctions can you see between the work of the Holy Spirit and the work of Christ?

PART TWO

What Does the Holy Spirit Do?

Chapter 7

Interlude: Transformation

So far, we have considered the *identity* of the Holy Spirit, working to answer the question, *Who is the Holy Spirit?* We've seen that her life within the Trinity and creation is a crucial consideration. The doctrine of appropriation is important to remember. Names, terms, and images shape how one thinks of the Spirit. Her life in relation to creation orients the question of identity, and the ways pneumatology and Christology intersect and influence each other are essential to examine. Now, in Part 2, we turn our attention toward another vital question: *What does the Holy Spirit do?*

In Part 2, I want to draw attention to a central motif: *transformation*. Above all else, the Holy Spirit's work is to transform. This is not purposeless, vague, nor indiscriminate change. Nor is it change for the sake of change. The transformation the Holy Spirit brings is oriented always toward the good purposes and will of God for creation and humankind. *Transformation* summarizes and expresses in the briefest way what She is interested in accomplishing. The transformation of creation, including human creatures, in a Godward and Christ-image-bearing way, is the heart of the Spirit's work. This is a strong theme throughout the Bible.

Paul expresses this in a way that helpfully links transformation with the Spirit's work: "All of us, with unveiled faces, seeing the glory of the Lord as though reflected in a mirror, are being *transformed* into the same image from one degree of glory to another, *for this comes from the Lord, the Spirit*" (2 Cor 3:18; emphasis added). Basil of Caesarea was also captivated by the Spirit's power to transform: An individual who "clearly fixes his eyes on the Spirit is somehow *transformed* by the Spirit's glory into something brighter as his heart is illuminated by the truth of the Spirit, as if by a light."[1] The

1. Basil, *On the Holy Spirit* 21.52 (emphasis added).

transformation of creation, communities, and the human creature takes time, and the Spirit is patient with this.[2] Instantaneous transformation is neither the norm nor the expectation. (Paul's sudden conversion on the road to Damascus in Acts 9 is a noteworthy exception.) Moreover, the Spirit's patient transformation over time takes place in the context of community. It is "inseparable from concrete times and spaces."[3] Human transformation, then, is not just a hope, a notion, or an aesthetic affectation. It is truly the will and purpose of God.

God is so intent on human transformation that the Spirit makes it her particular business to enact it and influence it through a myriad of means. The Spirit, whom the Niceno-Constantinopolitan Creed calls "the Lord and Giver of life," is deeply invested in the quality and nature of life. Life is more than mere existence. The Spirit heals, brings peace, provokes repentance, and endows persons and communities with gifts that enable them to advance the mission of God in the world. These endowments are universal: "Then afterward I will pour out my spirit on *all* flesh; your sons and your daughters shall prophesy, your old men shall dream dreams" (Joel 2:28; emphasis added). Drawing "all flesh" into the joyful, hopeful, love-filled work of the triune God, the Spirit transforms with power and intent. Every aspect of this work is deeply relational, meant for whole communities, nations, and the planet—and indeed for the whole creation, "all things visible and invisible" as the Niceno-Constantinopolitan Creed phrases it—and not only for the private enjoyment of individuals. The transformation the Holy Spirit brings for the sake of each one is also for the sake of all; and the transformation of all blesses each one.

To help us to see the character of the transformation the Spirit intends and shapes, we'll focus again on language and terms, this time with respect to verbs and actions. How does language reveal the activity of the Holy Spirit? Next, we'll consider how the Spirit is transformative within creation as a whole, en route to God's purposes and plans. Third, we'll look at how the Spirit operates "for the sake of each one," acting in, through, and toward individuals. Finally, we shall see how She is active "for the sake of all," inspiring collective action and acting through communities as a whole, both within and beyond the church.

2. Rogers, *After the Spirit*, 183.

3. Rogers, *After the Spirit*, 188.

FOR REFLECTION OR DISCUSSION

1. The key action of the Holy Spirit to transform humankind. What examples of transformation have you seen in your life or others' lives?

Chapter 8

The Language of Action

WHAT DOES THE HOLY Spirit *do*? To begin to describe and understand what the Holy Spirit does, it is helpful to focus on the actions and verbs that are associated with her in the Bible and in various Christian writings. These words and phrases make more obvious the ways in which people of faith express their sense of the Holy Spirit as One who *acts*. (In relation to the Trinity, the way theology speaks of the Spirit's actions is closely linked to the idea of *appropriation*, as discussed above in chapter 2.) Part of the weakness of pneumatology in Western Christianity is the unhelpful vagueness that sometimes replaces clear speech about the Spirit. It is not uncommon to believe or to say that the Holy Spirit does "something," without being more specific about what that means. Western pneumatology is similarly impoverished when it suggests that the Holy Spirit does "everything," with no distinction from the other trinitarian Identities or from other forces and powers (including human beings). Indeed, it is a grave error to fail to clarify that the Spirit does *not* in fact do everything. She does only that which is in alignment with her character and purpose. For example, it would be wrong to state that the Spirit harms, destroys, disunites, hates, or kills. "The Lord and Giver of life," on the contrary, is all about healing, unifying, loving, transforming, and bringing life. So we will step back from these inadequate conceptions (*something* and *everything*) and start by specifying what the Holy Spirit does in terms of the actions and verbs that are properly associated with her.

In summary, the Holy Spirit acts in a purposeful and personal way:

1. within creation as a whole;
2. within individual human creatures (for the sake of each one); and

3. within humankind as a collective (for the sake of all), both within the church and beyond it.

It is in these *actions* that we are best able to see what the Spirit does. As Rogers remarks, Christians know "this character [the Holy Spirit, as narrated in the Bible] in her actions, rather than by conceptual analysis."[1] The openness to observe and describe these actions will give us a better foundation for understanding what the Spirit does than would complex reasoning that corresponds only to a theoretical framework. It is often the *effects* of the Holy Spirit's work—what happens when She acts—that we can best speak about, feel, or observe. Orthodox theologian Florensky notes that "what is usually known is not the Holy Spirit but His grace-giving energies, His powers, His acts and activities" toward creation and human creatures.[2]

In the biblical testimony and a wide range of Christian writing, several key verbs arise repeatedly in reference to the Holy Spirit as One who *acts*. Some of these include *inspire*, *accompany*, *anoint*, and *consecrate*. The Spirit *appoints* the elders in Ephesus, according to Paul: "Keep watch over yourselves and over all the flock, of which the Holy Spirit has made you overseers, to shepherd the church of God" (Acts 20:28) The Spirit *breathes* and *commands* (Acts 13:2). According to Jesus, the Spirit "*proves* the world wrong" about certain truths, such as sin and righteousness (John 16:7–8; emphasis added). One with the triune God, the Holy Spirit *creates*, as Job attests: "The spirit of God has made me" (Job 33:4); and as Augustine confirms: "We cannot deny the Holy Spirit the right to be called origin either, because we do not exclude him from the title of creator."[3]

As One who *descends* (John 1:32–33), the Spirit *speaks to*, *directs*, *renews*, *empowers*, and *leads* the people of God. She *enlightens* and *illuminates*, especially by *revealing* the significance of Jesus Christ (1 Cor 2:10) and continuing the work and truth of Jesus in the present era. She *bears witness* to Jesus and *testifies* in the sense of *vouching for* him (John 15:26; 1 John 5:6). The One Spirit *redeems*, *regenerates*, *sustains*, *sanctifies*, *strengthens*, and *sends* (Acts 13:2–4). To individuals, the Spirit *gives gifts*; and within the church, it is distinctively the work of the Spirit to *unite*. More on these themes later.

All the actions listed above are oriented toward transforming human creatures, societies, nations, the church, and all creation. *Transformation* is the central motif of the Spirit's work, the promised goal of her will and desires. Guided not by human standards and norms but by divine purposes,

1. Rogers, *After the Spirit*, 208.

2. Florensky, *Pillar*, 90.

3. Augustine, *Trinity* 5.3.14.

the Holy Spirit works in and though human beings, the created order, and even the processes of history to transform that which *is* toward that which *will be*. The United Free Church of Scotland affirms, "We believe that God has revealed Himself in nature, conscience, and history."[4] The United Church of Canada uses nearly identical terms: "We believe that God has revealed Himself in nature, in history, and in the heart of [people]."[5]

A word of caution about history is warranted here: the United Reformed Church [UK] notes that "It is not clear whether all historical developments are to be regarded as the work of the Holy Spirit, or only some."[6] Discernment is needed. Does an historical development display the fruit of the Spirit, the mind of Christ, and the wisdom of God? Since God's wisdom envisions the fullness of the Kingdom (Realm) of God, with all the graces of justice, joy, peace, and bread for all, God the Spirit does not rest content with the way things are, but is restlessly active to bring about change in the direction of that Realm. Toward these ends, the Spirit "works through historical events and historical figures in unforeseeable ways" and yet "may work to accomplish its own ends which are not intended or are even contrary to those sought by the individual or social group."[7] The sovereign freedom and purposes of the Holy Spirit should be acknowledged in any assessment of history.

"One characteristic of the Holy Spirit," writes Shinn, "is a capacity to break through conventional boundaries of law and authority."[8] To this we could add the Spirit's power and desire to break through the powers of sin and death to redeem and restore God's people. This *breaking through* is seen again and again in the Biblical record and among God's people throughout time. It is sometimes expressed theologically as the *vivifying* work of the Spirit. To vivify is to *give life*, as the Niceno–Constantinopolitan Creed professes (Latin *vivificantem*, life-giver). The dry bones in Ezekiel's vision (Ezek 37) lie disconnected and dry in the valley, but at the word of the Lord, the Holy Spirit stitches them together:

> Suddenly there was a noise, a rattling, and the bones came together, bone to its bone. I looked, and there were sinews on them, and flesh had come upon them, and skin had covered them.

4. United Free Church of Scotland, "Statement of Faith," §8.
5. United Church of Canada, "Basis of Union," art. 2.
6. United Reformed Church (UK), "[Response]," 104.
7. Schweitzer and Kwon, *Hope Peace Unrest*, 31, 30.
8. Shinn, *Confessing*, 78.

But still there was no life in them. So the Spirit moves again:

> I prophesied as [the Lord God] commanded me, and the breath [wind, Spirit] came into them, and they lived and stood on their feet, a vast multitude.[9]

Ezekiel's vision points toward an actual, visually apparent work of the Holy Spirit, who self-discloses through the flourishing of life. But there is also the hidden work of the Spirit, no less vivifying. For example, the whimpering infant Jesus does not immediately reveal the fullness of the incarnation, and yet the Spirit is fully present in and with him. So also, we could say that in times of human languishing, despair, or trouble, the Holy Spirit is still at work to comfort, sustain, and vivify. There is inwardness and invisibility to such movements of the Spirit. The language of the Niceno-Constantinopolitan Creed—"all things visible and invisible"—is so evocative in this respect. The Spirit is often at work in ways we don't perceive, imagine, or understand. Yet in it all, "It is the office of the Holy Spirit to make alive."[10]

Ezekiel's vision of the Spirit's transformative power, and the silent role of vivification, are embodied most powerfully in the resurrection of Jesus. The Spirit's work on that third day, to transform the shell of Jesus's dead body into the living One whose eternal life is shared with all, has defined and empowered the Christian way all through the ages.

FOR REFLECTION OR DISCUSSION

1. The Holy Spirit doesn't do everything; her role is specific. What connections do you see between this chapter and chapter 4 that talks about preciseness in naming the Holy Spirit?
2. Many different verbs or actions in the Bible describe the work of the Holy Spirit. Which of these action verbs are easy to see or comprehend? Which (if any) of these action verbs are more challenging to you?

9. Ezek 37:1–10. See also Rom 8:11–13.
10. Luther, *Lectures on Genesis 1–5*, 9.

Chapter 9

The Spirit Within Creation as a Whole

Come Holy Spirit
Heal our wounds
Renew the whole creation!
—World Council of Churches, "A Prayer"

ANOTHER WAY TO FOCUS attention on what the Spirit *does* is to notice how She acts within creation as whole. This action arises in relation to the nature of God as Spirit. God-who-is-Spirit acts within the material and spiritual realms of creation—but without being *the same as* creation. She is spiritual but not material. God the Holy Spirit works *as Spirit* in spiritual terms within the created order, but is not herself the physical, created order. Accordingly, it is a core teaching in Christianity that God is both transcendent and immanent. That is, God the Spirit is both fully beyond the created, material order (transcendent) but also chooses to be present and participate within it (immanent). "The reciprocal indwelling of Spirit and earth is neither an absorption of the one into the other nor a confusion of the two," writes Mark Wallace. "Insofar as the Spirit abides in and with all living things, Spirit and earth are inseparable and yet at the same time distinguishable."[1]

Taken exclusively, a God who was only *transcendent*, as seen in Deism, would in no way participate in creation, but would only fabricate the world and then watch it from afar. In this way of thinking, the notion of a divine incarnation in human flesh, or in fact any sense of God's presence in the world, would be a delusion or an error. On the other hand, a God who

1. Wallace, "Green Face of God," 319.

is exclusively *immanent*, fully and only present in creation, would be ultimately indistinguishable from the material, natural world, or from matter in general. This perspective is characteristic of pantheism: the world/universe is God, and God is the world/universe. There is no way to distinguish one from the other.

Neither of these extremes is taught by Christianity. Deism and pantheism may be the sincerely held beliefs of some persons, but they are not Christian beliefs. In contrast, Christian theology teaches that God is both transcendent and immanent. God is not the same as creation, but neither is God radically cut off from it.

One with the triune God, the Holy Spirit's transcendence was emphasized in chapter 2, in our discussion on the Trinity. Now, we can focus on her actions toward and within creation as a whole in an immanent frame. Toward and within creation as a whole, the Holy Spirit acts in a purposeful and personal way. She is "the life principle and bond of unity between God and creation, as well as among the creatures."[2] She is not *the same as* creation or materiality. But She does not disdain creation nor reject materiality. Nor does She hold herself apart from it in divine, celestial aloofness. She freely chooses to be involved with the universe, and to be a mutual participant in the life of the created order. As Calvin teaches, "The beauty of the universe . . . owes its strength and preservation to the power of the Spirit . . . it is the Spirit who, everywhere diffused, sustains all things, causes them to grow, and quickens them in heaven and in earth."[3]

Not Just Us People

The work and life of the Holy Spirit within and through creation is not limited to human creatures. Neither is She a generic power, or some kind of undifferentiated energy that is vaguely present within the created order. Rather, She is a creative and purposeful actor. Indeed, One with the Trinity, She *is* the Creator. "The world is neither self-originating nor self-sustaining," says Kärkkäinen.[4] In Wang's terms, "The fundamental origin or source [of everything] is the Holy Spirit that nurtures or produces life."[5] The world is always deriving its life from the Spirit. As Job tells his conversation partners in the First Testament,

2. Kärkäinnen, *Spirit and Salvation*, 45.

3. Calvin, *Institutes* 1.13.14.

4. Kärkäinnen, *Spirit and Salvation*, 62.

5. Wang, "Holy Spirit Gives and Nurtures Life."

But ask the animals, and they will teach you,
the birds of the air, and they will tell you;
ask the plants of the earth, and they will teach you,
and the fish of the sea will declare to you.
Who among all these does not know
that the hand of the Lord has done this?
In his hand is the life of every living thing
and the breath [*ruach*] of every human being.[6]

Here, in Job's voice, the life-giving action of the Holy Spirit is again noticed and celebrated. We see her impact and effect on and in the world. "The Spirit speaks through all of creation," writes Jacobs. "The energy of the Holy Spirit has always been present in all of creation and is not limited by abstract theologizing or human imagining." Jacobs refers to eagles, wind, and stars as some of the ways that the Spirit communicates through the natural order, alongside elders' teaching and human intuition.[7]

The Spirit's work and life is present everywhere then, throughout creation and all creatures. Nothing that lives does so apart from her life-giving power. It is not only that materiality simply exists; it is brought to life through the Spirit's action. The Spirit is Life with an uppercase "L." All that is living, then, shares in that Life. This is true of the local and the cosmic. Microscopic and subatomic particles live because She-who-is-Life causes them to have life. The whole range of the universe (and perhaps multiverse, if it exists) is living, pulsing, and flowing by the work of She-who-is-Life. Even without today's scientific knowledge, the ancient psalmist could write,

By the word of the Lord the heavens were made
and all their host by the breath [*ruach*] of his mouth.[8]

When Ps 139:7 asks, "Where can I go from your spirit? Or where can I flee from your presence?," we learn that the answer is "nowhere." There is nowhere to go where God is not present. God the Spirit is omnipresent: present in all places, working with care and for good. The term "life-giver" for the Spirit in the Niceno–Constantinopolitan Creed "refers to creation not just at the beginning of time but continuously: the Spirit is the unceasing, dynamic flow of divine power that sustains the universe, bringing forth

6. Job 12:7–10.

7. Jacobs, "Holy Spirit," 166.

8. Ps 33:6.

life."[9] The pouring out of the Holy Spirit is intended for "the renewal of all life."[10]

Fruitful and Green

From ancient Christian teachers such as Basil, we learn that through the Spirit, "the Gospel bears fruit in every creature under heaven."[11] That fruitfulness, or fruiting-forth, is a characteristic action of the Spirit. She flows through and embraces creation with love, and works throughout its forms and creatures to accomplish God's purposes. Health, wellbeing, restoration, balance, thriving life—these are all signs of the Spirit at work. The result of the pouring out of the Spirit [*ruach*] upon a wasteland is described in the First Testament. In that place, "the wilderness becomes a fruitful field." There, "justice will dwell . . . and righteousness abide," alongside peace, quiet, trust, and security (Isa 32:16–17).

Mystical writer Hildegard of Bingen (1098–1179) refers to the Holy Spirit in terms of the Latin word *viriditas*—"greening." Hildegard used gardening, watering, and "greening" images to describe the Spirit's activity. In one of her visions, a mystical figure says,

> I am likewise the fiery life of the substance of divinity.
> I flame over the beauty of the fields and sparkle in the waters,
> and I burn in sun, moon, and stars.
> And with an airy wind that sustains all things with invisible life,
> I raise them up vitally.
> For air lives in greenness and flowers, waters flow as if alive,
> the sun, too, lives in his light, and when the moon comes to her decline
> she is kindled by his light, as it were to live again. . . .
> Thus I, the fiery force, am hidden in [the winds],
> and they take fire from me,
> just as breath continually moves a man,
> and as a windy flame exists in fire.
> All of these live in their essence and are not found in death,
> because I am life.[12]

9. Johnson, *Women, Earth, and Creator Spirit*, 42. See also Johnson's very significant contribution toward pneumatology in *She Who Is*.

10. World Council of Churches, *Come, Holy Spirit*, 7.

11. Basil, *On the Holy Spirit* 28.69.

12. Cited in Jones, "Theological Interpretation of 'Viriditas.'"

In Hildegard's poetic vision, we see multiple ways and forms through which God is at work in creation. Many of these recall the biblical images of the Spirit: fire, life, flame, water, light, wind. Some are visible and some are hidden, or visible only through their effects.

The Spirit's work in creation, therefore, is diverse and takes many forms. It is both evident to human perception and also invisible to our senses and intuitions. In ways that we cannot fully grasp, it is properly the Holy Spirit's work to sustain all creation: all that is human and non-human; all that is animal, mineral, or vegetable; all that is of Earth and all that is beyond it, extending to the whole universe; all that is "seen and unseen." The psalmist praises God, the sustainer-Spirit, for this ongoing work:

> You make springs gush forth in the valleys;
> they flow between the hills,
> giving drink to every wild animal;
> the wild asses quench their thirst.
> By the streams the birds of the air have their habitation;
> they sing among the branches.
> From your lofty abode you water the mountains;
> the earth is satisfied with the fruit of your work.
> The trees of the field are watered abundantly,
> the cedars of Lebanon that he planted.
> In them the birds build their nests;
> the stork has its home in the fir trees.
> The high mountains are for the wild goats;
> the rocks are a refuge for the coneys.
> These all look to you
> to give them their food in due season;
> when you give to them, they gather it up;
> when you open your hand, they are filled with good things.
> When you hide your face, they are dismayed;
> when you take away their breath, they die
> and return to their dust.
> When you send forth your spirit, they are created,
> and you renew the face of the ground.[13]

Such affection and care for the created order is surely in mind for Rogers when he suggests that "the Spirit befriends matter."[14] This idea of the Holy Spirit as a friend to Earth, to creation, and all creation's creatures is beautiful and transformative. It provides a gentler notion of God, who can sometimes be seen in the popular imagination only in terms of wrath, vengeance, or

13. Ps 104:10–13, 16–18, 27–30.

14. Rogers, *After the Spirit*, 55.

judgment. Yet on the contrary, God the Spirit reveals a tender, nurturing Creator whose affection for creation wraps all that exists with a caring, sustaining, healing embrace.

Science and Faith

The full scope of the Holy Spirit's work of cosmic transformation undoubtedly exceeds human observation and analysis, let alone full understanding. In the modern and late modern eras, many are attached to a scientific-materialist way of thinking, in which all phenomena can be studied, examined, mapped, measured, and manipulated. But the eye of Christian faith sees more. This is not a rejection of science, but an openness to supplementing what science on its own can reveal.

Sometimes the transformation brought by the Spirit within creation is clear and obvious to people of faith, and our perception of it is indeed aided by contemporary scientific methods and instruments. In this category, we could consider the transformation of the egg to the caterpillar, then to the chrysalis and the beautiful spreading wings of the butterfly. The distant transformation of a star into a red giant cannot be detected in real time by humans, but its latent effects leave a trail that astronomers and physicists can piece together to describe its development. Some Christians look to the processes of genetic evolution and see in them evidence of the Holy Spirit at work.

In other respects, however, this theological claim (that the Holy Spirit is at work to transform all of creation) completely confounds scientific-materialist modes of thinking. Is it coherent, within the disciplinary boundaries of physics and biology, to say that the Spirit is at work in a spark, or a slug, or sedimentary rock? Probably not. Is there measurable, material evidence, as contemporary science would seek, to justify a faith claim that the Holy Spirit works within natural processes to develop a caterpillar into a butterfly, or a human embryo into a baby within the womb?

No. These can be observed in scientific terms, but it is specifically a theological or faith claim to say that they reveal the Holy Spirit at work.

The good work of the Spirit is present, clear, or hidden, in all these beloved aspects of creation, which are precious to the Lord. As Jesus teaches, "Look at the birds of the air: they neither sow nor reap nor gather into barns, and yet your heavenly Father feeds them. . . . Consider the lilies of the field, how they grow; they neither toil nor spin, yet I tell you, even Solomon in all his glory was not clothed like one of these."[15] God the Holy Spirit is at work

15. Matt 6:26, 28–29.

through and within creation to sustain and transform all that God has made with love and care. This ministry of sustaining creation is a distinctive work of the Spirit.

Mystery and Beauty

To say that the Holy Spirit acts in purposeful and personal ways toward and within creation as a whole runs aground again, in strictly logical terms, when we admit that we cannot truly conceive of what "all creation" even means. Human beings cannot conceive fully and adequately what the Holy Spirit is doing in the transforming, let alone why. Even so, Christian faith and theology claim it is true that the Spirit is at work. That claim in turn is empowered by the gift of faith that the Spirit grants to Christian hearts and minds. Through the Spirit, God "is made known to the world."[16] We could add, "and is made known *through* the world."

Popular spirituality often speaks of how human beings can intuit God in and through nature. Many people *feel* God in the natural world, often in ways that can't be expressed in words. This is especially true via scenes of beauty and wonder, such as a sunrise, beholding a birth, or marvelling at the stars or the sublimity of patterns and symmetry. Alice Finnamore of The United Church of Canada sings of this intuition in hymn lyrics:

> Holy, holy, holy, Wild Sacred Presence
> Early in the morning, I come outside to see
> What the Wild will show me,
> What the birds will tell me,
> of Sacred Presence
> In the world today.[17]

The destructive chaos of natural disasters, or one animal fatally attacking another, are less likely candidates for this sense of awe and grandeur. Although Calvin argues that the Bible is needed for accurate human comprehension of God, even he makes room for the reality that "God . . . sets forth to all without exception his presence portrayed in his creatures." Remembering Ps 19:1 ("The heavens are telling the glory of God"), Calvin confirms that God "calls all peoples to himself by the contemplation of heaven and earth." Even so, as Calvin has it, "another and better help is needed"—namely the "spectacles" of Scripture to help us to see and

16. Sahu, *United and Uniting*, 82.

17. Finnamore, "Holy, Holy, Holy."

understand aright the world and especially God's saving work within it.[18] Thus to discern the presence of the Holy Spirit in creation is not automatic.

It stands to reason then, that while Christianity affirms the transforming activity of the Holy Spirit within creation, humans cannot fully grasp the scope and significance of this activity. In chapter 5 we noted the conviction that the fullness of the Trinity is involved in all of God's work: *opera Trinitatis ad extra indivisa sunt*—meaning that the works of the Trinity toward that which is outside the Trinity are indivisible. It is not a mistake, then, to see the work of the Spirit in God's creating and redeeming actions. God the creating-redeeming Holy Spirit sustains and comes to the aid of "the whole creation [that] has been groaning together as it suffers" (Rom 8:22). The liberator-Spirit is at work to free creation from its bondage. This is another way to think of panentheism—God in ("*en*") creation. God is not the same as creation, but is at work within it, by the Holy Spirit.

Learning to Love Creation

Jürgen Moltmann had an expansive view of the Spirit's work and presence throughout the created order. Indeed, the sanctifying work of the Spirit is not limited only to human creatures. Earlier Christian theology often restricted its reflection on the Holy Spirit to how the Spirit can assist human brings. Yet Moltmann affirms the value of seeing the Spirit

> in nature, in plants, in animals, and in the ecosystems of the earth. The experience the fellowship of the Spirit inevitably carries Christianity beyond itself into the greater fellowship of all God's creatures. For the community of creation . . . is also the fellowship of the Holy Spirit.[19]

One way to participate and to be in alignment with the life-affirming and life-transforming passion of the Spirit is to grow in love for creation. "Discovery of the cosmic breath of God's Spirit," teaches Moltmann, "leads [us] to respect for the dignity of all created things."[20]

Millions, maybe billions, of persons can tell a story of how they have experienced a divine Presence in the natural world, whether in beholding a sunset or the brilliance of the stars, in the beauty of a flower or a raging river's power. For those attuned to the Spirit in this way, there are often special feelings in these moments, such as closeness, intimacy, fullness, vulnerability,

18. Calvin, *Institutes* 1.6.1, 1.6.4.
19. Moltmann, *Spirit of Life*, 10.
20. Moltmann, *Spirit of Life*, 10.

awe, unity, wholeness, love, and longing. I, too, have felt this—many times. It is cause for deep gratitude and celebration. Some persons even weep with joy and wonder at the beauty of creation. Deep within the human creature there seems to be an intuition, as The United Church of Canada expresses it, that God "works still, through the Spirit, to bend the broken creation back into the unity and wholeness for which it was made."[21]

These intuitions and feelings are pervasive in the human family, and have propelled the writings and prayers of mystics for generations, both Christian and otherwise. English poet William Wordsworth (1770–1850) felt deeply connected to a kind of divine reality through his experiences in nature. In one poem, he writes of feeling

> a presence that disturbs me with the joy
> of elevated thoughts; a sense sublime
> of something far more deeply interfused,
> whose dwelling is the light of setting suns,
> and round ocean and the living air,
> and blue sky and in the mind of man.

Wordsworth continues, saying he is

> well pleased to recognise
> in nature and in the language of the sense,
> the anchor of my purest thoughts, the nurse,
> the guide, the guardian of my heart, and soul
> of all my moral being.[22]

Nature, in Wordsworth's evocative poetry, is saturated with something, or Someone, who is transcendent (beyond creation) and yet also immanent (within and around creation). I would say, even if Wordsworth doesn't quite say it, that this is the Holy Spirit. In more theologically precise language, Clark Pinnock confirms that the Spirit is ever-present, "directing the universe toward its goal, bringing to completion first the creational and then the redemptive purposes of God. Spirit is involved in implementing both creation and new creation."[23]

21. United Church of Canada, *Mending the World*, 10.

22. Wordsworth, "Lines Written a Few Miles Above Tintern Abbey."

23. Pinnock, *Flame of Love*, 9.

Destructive Dominion, or Stewardship?

Yet centuries of exploiting creation and its resources have now brought us to the point of ecological catastrophe. That exploitation has been justified by a misreading of the Genesis creation story. When Gen 1:26–28 is translated as "having dominion," countless generations have taken this to mean that the Bible grants permission to us humans to "lord it over" creation, to "dominate" it and "use" it in whatever way we wish. This turn of phrase, "having dominion," relies on the Latin Vulgate translation of the Bible. "Dominion" (Latin: *dominum*, lordship) has notoriously been taken to mean that humans are themselves like the *Dominus*—the Lord God—or even to mean that we have authority to act in God's stead, as God. In this interpretation, creation is ours to rule in a monarchical way, or worse.

But what if *dominion* could mean something else? Could we reshape our sense of dominion after the pattern of the Holy Spirit, the Lord, who loves in vulnerability rather than controlling power? Could we choose stewardship, care, and love instead of consumption and waste? If we embrace courage and conviction, and open ourselves to the Spirit's guidance, dominion could mean not exploitation, but servanthood and even sacrifice for the Other—in this case, for Earth itself. Jesus's model of being the Lord (*Dominus*) embodies care and service, after all.

If dominion could mean care and love, the Holy Spirit can assist us to "participate in Christ's undoing of the fall by befriending nature instead of seeking like Adam to rise above it."[24] If dominion could mean stewardship and service, we would be allies and partners in seeking the planet's health and wellbeing, united with creation in seeking the planet's health and wellbeing. Each in our small or large ways, and all of us together, would then be agreed and aligned with the passion of the Holy Spirit to transform all of creation, "all that is seen and unseen."[25] This accords with the vision of the Wisdom of Solomon:

> Although she [Wisdom, the Spirit] is but one, she can do all things,
> and while remaining in herself, she renews all things;
> in every generation she passes into holy souls
> and makes them friends of God and prophets,
> for God loves nothing so much as the person who lives with wisdom.[26]

24. Rogers, *After the Spirit*, 41.

25. This phrase comes from the Niceno-Constantinopolitan Creed.

26. Wis 7:27.

We can trust the Spirit "who can do all things" to do all that we cannot, and all that is well beyond us. In the meantime, we can become friends and partners with this vulnerable, suffering planet and love it much better than we have. We could join the psalmist in singing, "When you send forth your Spirit [*ruach*, breath] . . . you renew the face of the ground" (Ps 104:30). For humans to embrace Earth in friendship, rather than in domination and exploitation, is to embrace the Holy Spirit as She draws us into the work of loving creation. As we embrace the Spirit, She in turn "collapses the distance so that the distance between Creator and creation is contained within the trinitarian embrace."[27] Kärkkäinen calls this affectionate embrace among humans, the Spirit, and creation a "Green Pneumatology."[28] Developing an orientation toward loving creation—in the way that the sustainer-Spirit loves it—will radically change our encounter with our one and only terrestrial home. Leslie Boseto, the first indigenous moderator of the assembly of the United Church of Papua New Guinea and the Solomon Islands, wisely remarks,

> No human community . . . can survive unless our Mother earth is sustainable. Our communal society in the Pacific has no problem in understanding that life is integrated with creation through and in the Spirit, and therefore our whole being must struggle and "groan" with God's Spirit which is in us and in the world.[29]

To seek the wellbeingof the earth is to be in alignment with the purposes of the Holy Spirit of God, who has created and passionately loves all that exists.

No Need to Wait

There can be a temptation to despair when the promises of the Spirit seem far off and "when the current crisis has not only filled our lives with fear, but revealed the cruelty of the systemic injustices that have left hundreds of millions in this emergency without sufficient health care, work, food and basic services," writes Andy Lang of the United Church of Christ (USA). "The struggles we face can crush our hope."[30] Can we wait for the Spirit to deliver on her promises? The vision of a renewed creation in which a new creation

27. Shaw, *Creating Space*, 10.
28. Kärkäinnen, *Spirit and Salvation*, 58.
29. Boseto, "Mission and Unity," 287.
30. Lang, "Come, Holy Spirit."

will emerge (someday), with an end to all pain and suffering, is captivating (see Rev 21:1–4), even if it is still unfulfilled.

Yet we need not wait as passive bystanders for some future cataclysm, nor despair that the fullness of God's realm has not yet materialized. The renewal of creation might well start today, with the renewal of the human heart and mind, so that human actions will express care and stewardship of the earth and all its creatures, rather than domination and exploitation. Ezekiel perhaps foresaw this: "A new heart I will give you [says the Lord], and a new spirit I will put within you . . . I will put my spirit within you" (Ezek 36:26–27). As Wang Weifen of the China Christian Council says, "The renewal of God's sons and daughters in the Holy Spirit is part of his renewal of the whole universe."[31]

The many physical representations of the Holy Spirit in theological and biblical writings gesture toward immanence. These symbols point toward her continuing involvement in the created order: dove, fire, wind, light, water, breath, and so on. Each of these images evokes a sensibility and conveys a link to the materiality that human beings experience every day. They bring the abstraction of a spiritual "something" into much closer view through their physicality. The Holy Spirit, through these images and metaphors, does not remain distantly transcendent or inert.

At the same time, human language always has limitations. The philosophical tradition might prefer abstractions such as principle, force, *Geist*, or mind when referring to the Spirit. But the biblical habit of using physical elements to symbolize the Spirit reveals a faithful intuition about the link between the transcendent and immanent God-who-is-Spirit, both beyond and among us.

This deep intuition and faith claim—that the Holy Spirit is present and working within creation as a whole—leads to certain theological convictions about other aspects of life. For example, one could look upon the final meal that Jesus shared with his disciples as simply a sad farewell feast. Yet because Christians believe that the Holy Spirit does not simply watch the created order from far, far away in some celestial easy chair but chooses instead to be involved in human lives and the created order, a theologian like Rogers can state, "At the Last Supper the Spirit transforms the blood of murder into the blood of redemption for the whole world."[32] Obviously, this is Christian speech and theological interpretation about what might appear to be a simple meal, followed by an arrest and an (unjust) state execution. The faith awakened by the Holy Spirit, however, prompts Rogers and others

31. Wang, "Holy Spirit Gives and Nurtures Life," 210.

32. Rogers, *After the Spirit*, 145.

to see that Jesus's death on the cross, on the day after the Last Supper, represents and enacts God's work of worldwide redemption. The life, death, and resurrection of Jesus are Spirit-infused actions *within the created order* that prompt, prod, and finally transform that which is into that which God desires, through the gift of saving grace.

FOR REFLECTION OR DISCUSSION

1. This chapter gives several examples of ways we can observe the Holy Spirit working in and transforming non-human members of the community of creation, such as an egg becoming a caterpillar, then a chrysalis, then a butterfly. What examples come to mind when you think of the Holy Spirit transforming creation?
2. Have you ever experienced awe and wonder when you have perceived God's presence in the natural world? What were the circumstances?
3. If the Holy Spirit is a friend to all creation, how does that affect your thinking about things in creation that appear harmful, such as cancer cells or a deadly virus?

Chapter 10

For the Sake of Each One

Just as the Holy Spirit acts in a purposeful and personal way within creation as a whole, She also acts within individual human creatures, for the sake of each one. As the United Church of Christ in the Philippines succinctly states, "In the Holy Spirit, God is present in the world, empowering and guiding believers to understand and live out their faith in Jesus Christ."[1]

There are multiple accounts of the Spirit's work in and through individuals in the Bible and Christian writings. There are many descriptions of the Spirit as the one who inspires, guides, gives gifts, transforms, sanctifies, and more. The ancient origin story told in Genesis sees God tenderly raising up a human creature from the earth: "Then the Lord God formed man [human creature, *ha-adam*] from the dust of the ground [*ha-adamah*] and breathed into his nostrils the breath [*nishmat*] of life, and the man [*ha-adam*] became a living being" (Gen. 2:7). James Weldon Johnson's poem, "The Creation," beautifully retells this moment:

> Up from the bed of the river
> God scooped the clay;
> And by the bank of the river
> He kneeled him down;
> And there the great God Almighty
> Who lit the sun and fixed it in the sky,
> Who flung the stars to the most far corner of the night,
> Who rounded the earth in the middle of his hand;
> This great God,
> Like a mammy bending over her baby,
> Kneeled down in the dust

1. United Church of Christ in the Philippines, "Statement of Faith."

Toiling over a lump of clay
Till he shaped it in is his own image;
Then into it he blew the breath of life,
And man became a living soul.
Amen. Amen.[2]

Upon this same creating Spirit all human lives depend. Job's companion Elihu warns: "If [God] should take back his spirit [*ruach*] to himself and gather to himself his breath [*nishmat*], all flesh would perish together, and all mortals [*wa-adam*] return to dust" (Job 34:14–15).[3] Human dependence upon God's creating and sustaining Spirit continues for the whole duration of each person's life. Awareness of God's supportive presence in life arises from the work of the Spirit.[4]

The Holy Spirit and Mary

Mary, the mother of Jesus, provides an exemplar of the way that the Holy Spirit is at work in human creatures. Mary is first of all a real human being, a woman from Nazareth who lived in the first centuries BCE and CE.[5] Her real humanity is the site of human–divine interaction. In her human response to the annunciation by the angel Gabriel, she is an emblem or sign of the possibility of individual encounter with the Holy Spirit.[6] It is by virtue of the Spirit's work and Mary's cooperation that Mary conceives the messiah, Jesus Christ, in her womb (according to the gospels of Matthew and Luke, as well as the creeds). The United and Uniting Churches are largely silent on the matter of the virgin birth and the exclusion of a male partner in the conception of the embryo that became Jesus's body. So also, they are largely silent on the significance of Mary, quite unlike the profound veneration and affection for Mary in the Roman Catholic and Eastern traditions. This silence ought not to be seen as dismissal, however.

Although the place and veneration of Mary is different between Roman Catholic and Protestant traditions, Mary is still highly regarded by Protestants. Her willingness to collaborate with God the Spirit in bringing

2. Johnson, "Creation," 20.

3. See also Ps 104:29: "When you hide your face, they are dismayed; when you take away their breath, they die and return to their dust."

4. Beintker and Philipps, eds., "Handeln Gotte," 26.

5. If Jesus was born in the "year zero" or a few years before (as is now often thought), then Mary his mother must have lived before and after that year, in two centuries, so to speak.

6. See Luke 1:29, 34, 38, 46–55.

the Christ into the world is admired and embraced. Her affirmation of her place in God's purposes is a model for all human beings, displaying a faithful response to the Spirit's initiative.

More could and indeed should be said (and has been said by others) about Mary as a faithful example of a person who in her own life and body says "Yes!" to the Holy Spirit, who desires to work (literally and bodily) in and through her.[7] The Spirit–Mary connection is a beautiful and illuminating partnership.

No Passive Pigeons, Please

The personal nature of the Spirit's interaction with each individual is manifested in the distribution of a range of gifts. Not all human creatures receive every spiritual gift. They are broadly distributed (see 1 Cor 12:14–31). Further, the Spirit herself can "indwell [a person], not abstractly, but for a purpose: to catch the whole world up into their common life with the Father."[8] This common purpose is embedded in the theological vision of the China Christian Council: "The Spirit bestows wisdom and ability and every grace, in order to together build up the Body of Christ."[9]

Frequently, the Bible and the early Christian tradition speak of this interaction between the Spirit and individuals in the language of descending, alighting, or resting upon a person or persons. But this should not be conceived of as a passive roosting, like a pigeon on a pole. Rather, the dove of the Spirit alights and rests upon a person in order to work in and through them. *Descending* and *resting* are metaphors for the transmission of the Holy Spirit's purpose and power to make something happen in and through a human creature. She comes, as the World Council of Churches testifies, to "lead [people] to the full accomplishment of their vocation."[10] Each individual person, in the sight of the Lord who is the Spirit, has a role to play in the Realm of God. For this reason, all the faithful are chosen. The resting, alighting Spirit comes upon them to energize their lives and service by living in and through them.

In a parallel way, the Holy Spirit is invoked and, as Christians hope and pray, She descends upon the bread and wine at communion and transforms

7. As Rogers notes, in Mary's pregnancy we see that "God desires and loves and befriends human bodies. God the Spirit does not have disgust at the physical . . . she loves and befriends it." Rogers, *After the Spirit*, 103–4.

8. Rogers, *After the Spirit*, 59.

9. Joint National Conference, "Church Order," 3.

10. World Council of Churches, *Nature and Purpose*, 9.

them into the body and blood of Christ (or, depending on the eucharistic theology that is embraced, confers upon it the power to remind us of Christ's sacrifice). Once the bread and wine are thus inhabited by the Spirit, the communion elements embody the capacity to do what they are meant to do for individuals and the church as a whole. They draw the Christian closer to Christ, bringing Christ literally or symbolically into a person, and in this way transform them in a Godward direction. Through these Spirit-filled material elements, God works to change individuals and ultimately the whole world. Perhaps this is what Calvin intended when he wrote of "the secret energy of the Spirit, by which we come to enjoy Christ and all his benefits."[11]

Spirit, Fill Us!

Christians often pray that the Holy Spirit would "fill" a person or a place, again with the desire that She would make something happen by working in and through that person or place. Such prayers share the faith of Basil that "the Spirit is present to each one who is fit to receive him, as if he were present to him alone, and still [the Spirit] sends out grace that is complete and sufficient for all."[12] The prayer to be filled by the Holy Spirit is another expression of the collaborative willingness that Mary and other ancestors in the faith have demonstrated.

The work of the Holy Spirit in and through individuals is pervasive and takes multiple forms. The Spirit is "the one who overshadows Mary, descends over the Jordan, drives into the wilderness, waits to be sent, participates in the resurrection, alights on the disciples."[13] Throughout the story of God's people, the Spirit comes again and again to work through persons for their good as well as the goodness of God's purposes. The psalmist rejoices that God the Spirit brings forth from the earth "bread to strengthen the human heart" (Ps 104:15). In the midst of his call to serve as a prophet, Ezekiel writes, "the spirit of the Lord fell upon me" (Ezek 11:5). As Samson grew up, "the spirit of the Lord began to stir him" (Judg 13:25). Isaiah foretold the Spirit's anointing of the Messiah:

> The spirit of the Lord shall rest on him,
> the spirit of wisdom and understanding,
> the spirit of counsel and might,

11. Calvin, *Institutes* 3.1.1.
12. Basil, *On the Holy Spirit* 9.22.
13. Rogers, *After the Spirit*, 53.

the spirit of knowledge and the fear of the Lord.[14]

The anointing was fulfilled in the person of Jesus when Baptizing John "saw the heavens torn apart and the Spirit descending like a dove upon him [Jesus]" (Mark 1:10). A little later in his ministry, Jesus, "full of the Holy Spirit," claims for himself the ancient prophecy:

The Spirit of the Lord is upon me,
because he has anointed me
to bring good news to the poor.
He has sent me to proclaim release to the captives
and recovery of sight to the blind,
to set free those who are oppressed,
to proclaim the year of the Lord's favour.[15]

The history of the Christian movement after the biblical era is filled with stories of continuous individual interactions with the Spirit.

A Caution

As much as an individual might long for, pray for, and delight in the Holy Spirit's work within and through them, She cannot be taken for granted. A request for such a blessing is not a conjuring trick. One with the Trinity, the Spirit remains sovereign over the giving of her gifts. Some persons will receive gifts as hoped, and other gifts will come unbidden. Some persons might receive no gifts, or none that are evident. Once given, the Spirit aids us in developing and expressing them. After all, the gifts themselves are meant to bring joy, as well as the awareness that we have received a blessing and are participating in God's good purposes. In living out our gifts and delighting in them, we share in the joy of God.

Yet the gifts given cannot be assumed to be permanent, as if they became the possessions of the recipients. The gifts of the Spirit remain hers—to give or to withdraw. Ancient King Saul squandered his responsibilities to

14. Isa 11:2. There might be an echo of this in the book of Revelation, which speaks of the "seven spirits of God" (3:1; see 1:4). The figure of the Lamb in Rev 5:6 has "seven horns and seven eyes, which are the seven spirits of God." John, the writer of Revelation, doesn't provide enough information to be certain about his reference. Traditionally, the "seven spirits" in Revelation are considered to be attributes of the *one* Holy Spirit, and perhaps correlate to the "seven gifts of the Spirit" named in Isa 11:2–3. That passage (Isa 11) is similarly linked in Christian interpretation with the Messiah (the Lamb, the Christ). Taken together (Revelation and Isaiah), these passages once again link the Son and the Spirit in their common single mission.

15. Luke 4:1, 18–19.

the nation and to God. As a result, "the spirit of the Lord [*wa-ruach Yahweh*] departed from Saul" (1 Sam 16:14). Basil cautions that "those who grieve the Holy Spirit by their evil lives or those who do not further cultivate what they have been given will be deprived of what they have received, and the grace will be given to others. . . . This cutting off is understood to be complete alienation from the Spirit."[16] Basil is uncompromising, and this teaching is hard to bear.

In the United and Uniting Churches, the language is never as harsh as that of Basil. Indeed, the teaching that the Spirit might be withdrawn is not addressed by them. The perception of the Spirit as generous and gracious is pervasive, and rightly so. This graciousness makes it all the more difficult to absorb the idea that the Spirit's gifts might be withdrawn. "The Spirit's absence is difficult to contemplate," writes Kirsteen Kim, "but only if there is acceptance of the possibility that there may be places or occasions that God's Holy Spirit does not inhabit or endorse, is there a possibility of critical engagement with the world."[17] In other words, how can God stand in judgment against that which is false, or inhabited by a false spirit, if all things, moments, places, movements, and persons are fully saturated with the Holy Spirit? That which is not *of God*, or stands against God, must be critically named and prophetically denounced. We can only do so if there is a possibility, as Kim says, that "there may be places or occasions that God's Holy Spirit does not inhabit or endorse." In an example of this, The United Church of Canada testifies:

> The Spirit judges us critically when we abuse scripture
> by interpreting it narrow-mindedly,
> using it as a tool of oppression, exclusion, or hatred.[18]

We return, then, to the teaching that the free and sovereign Spirit is always sovereign over her gifts and their deployment. Holy Spirit, gifts, and human creatures are never *fused* into one thing, and human beings never *own* the Spirit's endowment. There is always an important distinction, and the nature of the gifting is never uniquely the decision of the recipient. No gift that one might receive is ever a possession. In every case, it is something for which a person can only be a steward, a trustee. All the Spirit's gifts, writes Paul, "are activated by one and the same Spirit, who allots to each one individually just as the Spirit chooses" (1 Cor 12:11).

16. Basil, *On the Holy Spirit* 16.40.
17. Kim, *Holy Spirit in the World*, 150.
18. United Church of Canada, "Song of Faith."

FOR REFLECTION OR DISCUSSION

1. One image that this chapter explores is that of the Holy Spirit "descending like a dove" to rest on a person. Do you find the image of the Holy Spirit like a bird to be helpful or unhelpful in understanding her work?
2. Mary is an example of someone collaborating with the Holy Spirit to fulfill God's work in the world. What other examples of this sort of collaboration can you see, either in the Bible, the church, or the wider world?
3. What do you think of the idea that the Holy Spirit can be withdrawn?

Chapter 11

Inspire and Guide

The Spirit equips us with an abundance of gifts and talents to build up the Body of Christ
and empowers us to serve and witness to Christ in the world. . . .
Through the Spirit God guides us in our daily lives.
—Uniting Presbyterian Church in Southern Africa, The Manual of Faith and Order

THROUGHOUT JEWISH AND CHRISTIAN traditions, including the First and Second Testaments, there is ample testimony to the presence and activity of the Holy Spirit in the lives of individuals. Chief among those actions is the Spirit's work to inspire and guide. The Holy Spirit is alive in the conscience, to teach right and wrong. Chen Zemin of the China Christian Council proclaims, "The Holy Spirit is like a double edged sword. It opens up our soul and bones and sinews. Without this sword, we cannot distinguish beauty from ugliness, good from evil. Without this sword, we cannot see ourselves clearly."[1] In prayer, the Spirit guides and shapes human character and action, drawing each person closer to the heart of God. As the United Church of Christ in the Philippines states, "We can recognize the Holy Spirit through experience guiding us and giving us power to do what God wants us to do."[2] The Spirit moves us toward praise and love of God, and is at work to assist the human will to become aligned with the Word and will of God. As Basil writes, "All that live virtuously desire [the Spirit], as they are watered by his

1. Chen, "Spirit, Please Come Upon Us," 251–52.
2. United Church of Christ in the Philippines, *Confirmation Manual*, 21.

inspiration and assisted toward their proper and natural end."[3] Inwardly, then, the Spirit works upon human creatures to align them with God's purposes and desires. John Wesley raises the temperature on this claim: "We are convinced that . . . [it is] impossible for us even to think a good thought without the supernatural assistance of [the] Spirit."[4]

Outwardly, the Spirit works to influence human behavior toward peace, justice, and reconciliation, for the fullness of God's realm is a reality characterized by justice, joy, peace, and bread. Unlike some Christian communities, United and Uniting Church perspectives do not hold that God's realm of *shalom* is the result of a divine, catastrophic intervention that shatters the world. Rather, the realm of God, the consummation of all divine purposes, arises through the mutual cooperation of God and humankind. To that end, the Holy Spirit shapes and empowers through the giving of gifts to help human beings to will what God wills. As Jessica Heatherington of The United Church of Canada puts it, "The hope of the Holy Spirit is within communities, both human and other-than-human, who are crying out for justice, crying out for healing, crying out for revolution and transformation."[5] *The Pastor's Manual* of the Armenian Evangelical Church includes a prayer that by the Holy Spirit

> we may be guided in times of temptation, in times of making difficult decisions, and in times of witnessing before others. May this light shine through our lives into the hearts of those around us.

The prayer continues, asking that the Spirit's work would serve

> to guide us into all truth, to deter us from sin, to enrich us with your gifts, to refresh us with your peace, and to rule in our hearts.[6]

Moral formation of this kind is the particular work of the Spirit. The guidance of the Holy Spirit was at work in the council at Jerusalem noted in Acts 15. Of this meeting, K. H. Ting of the China Christian Council notes, "The Holy Spirit personally took part in this meeting, personally led and moved some people's hearts, opening their ears to God's own way of acting."[7] Ting remarks on the apostles and the Spirit *collaborating*—in this case, in the task

3. Basil, *On the Holy Spirit* 9.22.
4. Wesley, "Circumcision of the Heart," 403–4.
5. Heatherington, "Looking for the Light."
6. Tootikian, *Pastor's Manual*, 20, 17.
7. Ting, "What the Spirit Is Saying," 391.

of advising gentile believers: "It has seemed good to the Holy Spirit and us" (Acts 15:28).

Personal Awareness of the Holy Spirit

This activity of influence, inspiration, and guidance is revealed through personal awareness of the Spirit. It is also possible for the Spirit to be at work before an individual can sense it. But awareness dawns, in time. In the thought of Isaac of Nineveh, "the operation of the Holy Spirit is usually sensed during prayer, when [a person] is fully concentrated on God."[8] This corresponds in a way to Friedrich Schleiermacher's "feeling of absolute dependence" that has been so influential in the modern era. He writes, "The feeling of absolute dependence, accordingly, is not to be explained as an awareness of the world's existence, but only as an awareness of the existence of God, as the absolute undivided unity."[9] Many individuals report "feeling" the Spirit, either in physical sensations such as coolness, heat, tingling, goosebumps, and so on; or in an inward emotional state of being aware of the divine presence, calm, accompaniment, or peace. Inward "movement" of some kind is often attributed to the Spirit's presence when She inspires poets and other artists. "Kinship with God comes through the Spirit," says Basil.[10] Knowledge of the Spirit's presence and activity might also defy description: a person might simply say, "I just *know* the Spirit is here." For many Christians, this divine Presence is a vital aspect of their faith and spirituality. As the United Church of Christ (USA) professes, "God promises to all who trust in his gospel . . . [the] presence of the Holy Spirit in trial and rejoicing."[11]

How God the Holy Spirit might move and enter the awareness of an individual is "not according to our own will," according to John Wesley. We can't demand it, orchestrate it, nor expect that it will flow in a predictable way. Rather, "the means into which different [persons] are led, and in which they find the blessing of God, are varied, transposed, and combined together [by the Spirit] a thousand different ways."[12] It is God's initiative to stir within the human creature and to self-reveal in a way that accords with God's logic and purposes. "Have a care therefore," advises Wesley, "of

8. Seppälä, "Holy Spirit in Isaac of Nineveh," 139.

9. Schleiermacher, *Christian Faith*, 132.

10. Basil, *On the Holy Spirit* 19.48.

11. United Church of Christ [USA], "Statement of Faith [Moss Adaptation]."

12. Wesley, "Means of Grace," 395.

limiting the Almighty. He doth whatsoever and whensoever it pleaseth him. . . . He is always ready, always able, always willing to save."[13]

In the gospel according to Luke, awareness of the presence of the Holy Spirit energizes a response of passionate praise in Elizabeth (Luke 1:39–45), in Zechariah (Luke 1:67–79), and in Simeon (Luke 2:25–32). The presence of the Spirit provokes praise and gratitude, to be sure, but also empowers various gifts of service. In serving, the appropriate disposition is not pride but modest obedience. As Ephrem puts it,

> Who has seen chaff presume to examine
> The wind's force with questions?[14]

In nature, the chaff of the grain blows where the wind drives it. So also, the presence of the Spirit ought to draw the human creature into humble, joyful participation in the work of God, not vain self-assertion. In Ephrem, his choice of words for "wind" (*rûḥâ*) is ambiguous in Syriac, meaning either "wind" or "spirit"—or both.[15] Ultimately, in a mature faith, to serve with the gifts of the Spirit is a joy, for we understand ourselves to be participating in God's work of healing and redeeming the world.

Scripture and Interpretation

Among the Holy Spirit's many gifts, perhaps foremost are the gifts connected with the Bible. I say "foremost" because of the unique and essential revelatory role of Scripture. The First and Second Testaments provide the most significant collection and source of wisdom for Christian theology and Christian life. Other ways of knowing God are vital—from personal experience to church tradition to all that creation reveals. But the Bible holds a unique place of importance and authority. The United and Uniting Churches are agreed in this conviction, as are most Christians: "The same Spirit who spoke through the prophets and Jesus and the apostles inspired the writing of the Scriptures. . . . The Spirit guided the community of faith to recognize these writings as the unique and faithful record of the Word of God."[16] As Augustine notes, it was "the Spirit who gave authority to Mark

13. Wesley, "Means of Grace," 395–96.

14. Ephrem, *Hymns* 29.5.

15. See the note from Jeffrey T. Wickes in Ephrem, *Hymns* 29.5n6.

16. Uniting Presbyterian Church in Southern Africa, *Manual*, 26–27. Among dozens of others, the Armenian Evangelical Church affirms the same in its statement of faith (Tootikian, *Pastor's Manual*, 162).

and Luke to preach and to compose their Gospels in writing."[17] Calvin says that the Holy Spirit is "the Author of the Scriptures."[18]

The gift of inspiration given by the Holy Spirit to the biblical writers and editors enabled them to listen to the world, their community, their experiences, and the inward voice of God to compose their best and most faithful work. Indeed, "God's Spirit has worked in and through the whole process in the formation of the Bible," writes the United Church of Christ in the Philippines. "The storytellers, writers, compilers, editors, those who canonized, translators, and even interpreters of the Bible are all instruments of the Divine Spirit in making the truth of God's self-revelation alive then and now."[19] The Waldensian Evangelical Church (the Union of Methodist and Waldensian Churches) claims the confession of the Reformed Churches of Piedmont (also known as the Waldensian Confession of Faith of 1655). In this document, we hear the same trust and regard for the work of the Holy Spirit in the composition of the Bible:

> We acknowledge the divinity of these sacred books, not only from the testimony of the church, but more especially because of the eternal and indubitable truth of the doctrine therein contained, and of that most divine excellency, sublimity, and majesty which appears therein; and because of the operation of the Holy Spirit . . . who opens our eyes to discover the beams of that celestial light which shines in the Scripture.[20]

This active work and presence of the Holy Spirit in its composition does not make the Bible perfect and flawless. It remains an entirely human set of documents, liable to err. Nor does it mean that the Bible is the result of God dictating each word to each writer. Each writer was always and only human. But ultimately, all biblical writers were graced by the Spirit's gift of inspiration. "The Holy Spirit wields her transcendent influence on biblical writers," teaches Meng Yanling of the China Council of Churches, "such that their writing has a sacred nature."[21] Despite what modern biblical scholarship would later point out as flaws or inconsistencies in the Bible, Augustine holds to the notion that "the Spirit [was] working secretly in the texts'

17. Paraphrased in O'Laughlin, "St. Augustine's View," 91.

18. Calvin, *Institutes* 1.9.2.

19. Dingayan, *Catechetical Guide*, 6.

20. "Confession of the Reformed Churches of Piedmont (Waldensian Confession of Faith)," §IV.

21. Meng Yanling, "Approach to Biblical Exegesis," 188.

composition."[22] That "secret work" was instrumental in the development of the many writings that finally came together as the Bible.

It is rare to find a person in the modern or postmodern era who supposes that the Bible holds magical powers. It is always fully a set of human documents. This is certainly the commonly held view among the United and Uniting Churches. The Bible is thus a fully human document, liable to errors and mistakes. Consequently, critical and thoughtful interpretation is essential. Still, we recognize that the biblical authors and editors were assisted by the Spirit in bringing Scripture into being. This is indeed the sense of the word *inspire* when we speak of the Bible as "inspired." The Spirit (Latin: *spiritus*) is "in" the word: *in-spire*. The Second Testament gestures toward this: "All scripture is inspired [*theopneustos*] by God" (2 Tim 3:16). The United Church of Canada refers to biblical writers are those "who spoke as they were moved by the Holy Spirit."[23] This does not require a view that the Spirit literally spoke each syllable and the biblical scribes merely wrote it down—although some Christians do believe this. The United and Uniting Churches make use of the tools of modern scholarship in their interpretive work, and do not teach a theory of divine "dictation."

Despite its imperfections, the Spirit takes up the Bible as uses it, like an instrument or tool, to bless, guide, teach, inspire, correct, and encourage its readers and hearers. Calvin writes that without the Spirit, we are "bereft of the whole light of truth."[24] The Bible is a central means of God's self-revelation. For this reason, the "word" of God can be heard through the Bible. The words on the page are not "God's words." But the self-communicating God uses these human words to reach out to every generation. No other book compares in value. For this reason, the United and Uniting Churches are strongly committed to Scripture, but are not literalists or inerrantists. They look to the Holy Spirit to guide their understanding, helping them to interpret wisely and faithfully.

Trust and Nurture

In the thousands of years since those ancient documents were composed, the transmission and interpretation of the Bible has also been guided by the grace of the Holy Spirit. Augustine's view is that Christians accept the authority of the Scriptures "in spite of all the difficulties they present to us

22. O'Laughlin, "St. Augustine's View," 92.

23. United Church of Canada. "Basis of Union," art. 2.

24. Calvin, *Institutes* 1.9.3.

in understanding them, because the Spirit dwells within us."[25] If that is so, then a reader's approach to the Bible can adopt an attitude of trust, seeking goodness and blessing in the encounter with the ancient writings: "God calls us to engage the Bible trusting God's Spirit to enliven our understanding and to empower our acting."[26]

This does not mean that critical faculties and tools should be set aside. But it does mean that the Spirit's desire to bless readers and hearers of the Bible is trustworthy: "The dead letter of Scripture becomes God's own living and active Word to us, when Christ speaks through it in the power of the Spirit. . . . In and through the words of Scripture God in person speaks to us."[27] Yes, God the Spirit speaks to us *through* the Bible. One of the key reasons Christianity values the Bible is its power to unveil the life, death, and resurrection of Jesus, and their significance. Remarking on John, the fourth gospel, Ephrem notes that the author (or authors) made use of words, as the Spirit directed, to help us understand what Jesus was like:

> The pattern that the Spirit sketched for us through John
> Is impressed upon our heart, mind, and thought.[28]

That initial openness to what Scripture will disclose is the first step in interpretation, a process that is likewise guided by the Spirit. The right hearing of that which the Bible offers is only possible if we "are caused by the Spirit of God to do so."[29] What will be found within the pages of the Bible might surprise and challenge, because reading and understanding is not exclusively a human project. We are not in full control of it. As the Church of North India says, "The church must always be ready to correct and reform itself in accordance with the teaching of [the] Scriptures as the Holy Spirit shall reveal it."[30] The Spirit might well reveal something unexpected in our encounters with the Bible.

Thus human readers and hearers rely upon the Holy Spirit to make the wisdom of the Bible accessible. As Douglas John Hall of The United Church of Canada writes, "There is no special quality of the book as such which would guarantee its effectiveness as the unique medium of God's Word. . . . [The] words of this book must be transformed. . . . The Spirit must make

25. O'Laughlin, "St. Augustine's View," 92.

26. United Church of Canada, *Authority and Interpretation of Scripture*, v.

27. Uniting Presbyterian Church in Southern Africa, *Manual*, 28.

28. Ephrem, *Hymns* 33.2.

29. Hall, *Thinking*, 120.

30. Church of North India, *Constitution*, clause 2.

these words live."[31] Calvin, an important forerunner of many United and Uniting Churches, similarly claims that "the testimony of the Spirit is superior to reason. For as God alone can properly bear witness to his own words, so these words will not obtain full credit in the hearts of [people], until they are sealed by the inward testimony of the Spirit . . . [who] must penetrate our hearts."[32]

Since the Bible is inspired by God, it is God the Spirit who will reveal its meanings to those who read under her influence. Calvin teaches that the Holy Spirit works within those who read the Bible, reaching "into our hearts to persuade us that they [the biblical authors] faithfully proclaimed what had been divinely commanded." It is "the secret testimony" of the Spirit that opens the truth of Scripture to God's people.[33] Two centuries later, Methodist cofounder Charles Wesley (1707–88) penned a hymn in which he sang,

> Come, Holy Ghost, for moved by thee,
> thy prophets wrote and spoke;
> unlock the truth, thyself the key,
> unseal the sacred book.[34]

That single verse nicely sums up the understanding of the Holy Spirit (Holy Ghost) as the one who both inspired the composition of the Bible and enables its interpretation. A more recent witness echoes the theme: "The Spirit who breathed life-giving air into the nostrils of humanity has also breathed life-giving power into both the writing and the engaging of Scripture."[35]

The reading and interpretation of the Bible under the guidance of the Holy Spirit enables the faithful to become aligned with God's purposes, to be formed into the image of Christ, and to be preserved as the Body of Christ, the church, both inhabiting and housing the gifts of the Spirit in their midst. "The Spirit makes the Word of God come alive," says the Uniting Church in Sweden.[36] When the Holy Spirit guides the reading of the Bible, the reader encounters the faith and the failures of those who have gone before.

31. Hall, *Thinking*, 443. In this, Martin Luther concurs: "No one can correctly understand God or His Word unless he has received such understanding immediately from the Holy Spirit." Outside of the "school of the Spirit," says Luther, "nothing is learned but empty words and prattle." Luther, *Sermon on the Mount and the Magnificat*, 299.

32. Calvin, *Institutes* 1.13.14.

33. Calvin, *Institutes* 1.7.4.

34. Wesley, "Come, Holy Ghost."

35. United Church of Canada, *Authority and Interpretation of Scripture*, 34. See also, "The Spirit breathes revelatory power into scripture" (note the present tense) in United Church of Canada, "Song of Faith"

36. Uniting Church in Sweden, "Theological Foundation," 4.

Through their witness, we can draw nearer to God. It is no accident that Bible reading and study are considered *spiritual exercises*, for the "muscle" of the human spirit is conditioned and strengthened by the activity of the Holy Spirit within our encounter with the Bible. The Spirit-enabled acts of reading and interpreting transform Christians toward greater faithfulness. Calvin went so far as to say that "without the illumination of the Holy Spirit, the Word can do nothing."[37] While neither the Bible nor the reading of it should be regarded as infallible, Amy Plantinga Pauw argues that the Spirit's accompaniment of the reader ensures that "these writings are sufficient to nurture and shape our love to God and neighbour."[38] Through instruction, inspiration, correction, and above all the testimony of God's great love for all, the Holy Spirit uses the Bible to nurture God's people.

FOR REFLECTION OR DISCUSSION

1. If bringing about the realm of God results from collaboration between the Holy Spirit and humankind, how can we make sure that we are collaborating with her, rather than going at it alone to make the world better?
2. Many churches include a prayer for illumination during worship services, usually before the Bible readings or the sermon. How does the prayer that you pray or hear in your worship context relate to what this chapter has to say about the Holy Spirit's role in interpreting Scripture?
3. What are the practical implications of this chapter to your walk of faith as you read, share, and discuss the Bible?

37. Calvin, *Institutes* 3.2.33.
38. Pauw, "Holy Spirit and Scripture," 30.

Chapter 12

The Gift Giver

Because the Holy Spirit herself is free, it is her purpose *to make free*—to liberate—all those who are in Christ, and indeed, all of creation. Inspiration and guidance are key parts of that story, as we saw in the last chapter. But the Spirit has more in mind, for She is ambitious for the fulfillment of the realm of God. To build and grow that realm, the Holy Spirit distinctively gives a vast range of gifts to humankind, empowering us to serve the greater good alongside the triune God of all. A gift from the Spirit is also called a *charism*, following the Greek term found in the Second Testament.

These gifts come in great diversity and are given for the sake of blessing the world. Individuals and communities who receive the Spirit's gifts are inwardly renewed and outwardly commissioned to share in God's mission. As the Uniting Church in Sweden notes, "The Holy Spirit gives the congregation a multitude of gifts so that the whole abundance of the Gospel may be expressed."[1] Many such gifts are easy to see and recognize. Wang, of the China Christian Council, enumerates "human intelligence, talent, knowledge, learning, conception, design, wisdom, strategies, thinking, inspiration—they all come from the Holy Spirit."[2] But no one person receives all the gifts. The whole community of the church (and creation) is therefore drawn together for mutual blessing as the gifts are shared.

Some gifts are practical, as seen in the Torah:

> The Lord spoke to Moses, "See, I have called by name Bezalel son of Uri son of Hur, of the tribe of Judah, and I have filled him with a divine spirit [*ruach elohim*], with ability, intelligence, and knowledge, and every kind of skill, to devise artistic designs, to

1. Uniting Church in Sweden, "Theological Foundation," 7.
2. Wang, "Holy Spirit Gives and Nurtures Life," 205.

> work in gold, silver, and bronze, in cutting stones for setting, and in carving wood, to work in every kind of craft."[3]

Bezalel's gifts from the Spirit enabled him to serve the community and to serve God. This dual pattern recurs throughout the biblical accounts. One of the most well-known and important passages in this respect is from Paul's first letter to the church in Corinth:

> Now there are varieties of gifts but the same Spirit, and there are varieties of services but the same Lord, and there are varieties of activities, but it is the same God who activates all of them in everyone. To each is given the manifestation of the Spirit for the common good. To one is given through the Spirit the utterance of wisdom and to another the utterance of knowledge according to the same Spirit, to another faith by the same Spirit, to another gifts of healing by the one Spirit, to another the working of powerful deeds, to another prophecy, to another the discernment of spirits, to another various kinds of tongues, to another the interpretation of tongues. All these are activated by one and the same Spirit, who allots to each one individually just as the Spirit chooses.[4]

Note here the range and diversity of the gifts! Note also the emphasis on the community's wellbeing: "To each is given the manifestation of the Spirit *for the common good*" (emphasis added). The gifts the Spirit gives are never for the aggrandizement of the individual, nor to make them feel extra special, holy, or righteous. It is always for the common good. As the China Christian Council teaches, "If we use the gifts of the Spirit in order to show off, or as a device for gaining a reputation, this is to misuse the gifts of the Spirit, and is of no benefit either to one's self or to others. . . . If one is concerned simply to edify one's self and not the Church, this too is undesirable."[5]

The Source of All That Is Good

As the Giver of gifts, the Holy Spirit is one with the Trinity. The three Identities do not work at cross-purposes or independently. As Cyril of Jerusalem (c. 315–86) teaches, "The gifts of the Father are none other than those of the Son, and those of the Holy Ghost; for there is one Salvation, one Power, one

3. Exod 31:1–5.
4. 1 Cor 12:4–11.
5. China Christian Council, "Introduction to Doctrines: Important Q&A."

Faith."[6] In speaking of the Holy Spirit as One who gives gifts, the starting place is surely the gift of the Spirit herself. That is, the Spirit's *self*-giving is the paradigm of all other gift-giving. It may be paralleled with the self-giving of Jesus Christ on the cross, in that the self-giving of the Spirit is intended to bring life, health, and transformation.

The Spirit's gift-giving is purposeful and intentional. Dhirendra Sahu of the Church of North India remarks that the Spirit's self-giving is foundational, for example, for the work of ecumenism and church union: "It is the living Spirit which can and does give its own life to bodies which lack in some measure the fullness of Christ's true teaching and order."[7] In other respects, the Spirit's offering of herself animates the Christian life as a whole, providing all things necessary for faithful living. This self-giving reflects the deeply relational nature of the Spirit, who does not remain aloof from creation and human creatures, but is profoundly concerned for and involved with the life of creation. As Moltmann beautifully writes, "Where the Holy Spirit is present . . . [human beings] experience whole, full, healed, and redeemed life." To call upon the Holy Spirit and receive her gift of self reveals that "the Spirit is more than just one of God's gifts among others; the Holy Spirit is the unrestricted presence of God in which our life wakes up, becomes wholly and entirely living, and is endowed with the energies of life."[8] Just as parents (human and non-human) give themselves wholeheartedly to the wellbeing of their offspring, the Spirit is attentive and ready to give all that is needed from her own resources to nourish and to bless. Consider just a few biblical witnesses to the Holy Spirit's generous self-giving:

> Even before his birth he [Baptizing John] will be filled with the Holy Spirit.
>
> If you, then, who are evil, know how to give good gifts to your children, how much more will the heavenly Father give the Holy Spirit to those who ask him!
>
> He [Jesus] breathed on them and said to them, "Receive the Holy Spirit."
>
> God anointed Jesus of Nazareth with the Holy Spirit and with power . . . he went about doing good and healing all who were oppressed by the devil, for God was with him.[9]

6. Cyril, *Catechetical Lectures* 16.24.
7. Sahu, *Church of North India*, 152.
8. Moltmann, *Source of Life*, 10–11.
9. Luke 1:15; 11:13; John 20:22; Acts 10:38.

An enormous range of other gifts of the Spirit appears throughout the Bible and is attested in a variety of places in Christian history. Without being exhaustive, the next section groups together several of these pneumatic (Spirit-filled) gifts under six themes: relational gifts; gifts of service; gifts of knowledge and ability; gifts of faith; gifts of character; and gifts of human thriving. (Missing from this account is a word about "ecstatic" or "charismatic" gifts. I will return to these in chapter 19.)

RELATIONAL GIFTS

The Gift of the Fruit of the Spirit

Given that the relational triune life of God is itself a model for all of creation, the relational nature of God the Spirit as gift giver is expressed over and over. Paul's celebration of the fruit of the Spirit—the outward expressions of the inward working of the Spirit—is characterized by this relational dimension. "The fruit of the Spirit," Paul writes, "is love, joy, peace, patience, kindness, generosity, faithfulness, gentleness, and self-control" (Gal 5:22–23). Each of these nine fruit, or attributes, is found in interpersonal relating. The work of the Holy Spirit in each person is meant to transform the relational dynamic among human beings in a Godward direction. The fruit of the Spirit are "those graces that make for the upbuilding and enriching of community life," remarks John Dow of The United Church of Canada.[10] Love receives special attention, both here (as the first fruit named) and also in Rom 5:5—"God's love has been poured into our hearts through the Holy Spirit that has been given to us." The Holy Spirit, who is Love, awakens love in us. Augustine advises, "It is God the Holy Spirit proceeding from God who fires [humankind] to the love of God and neighbour." We love because God the Spirit has made it possible for us to love.[11] In Rom 14:17, Paul further develops the importance of this theme (the Spirit's fruit) by naming the kingdom (realm) of God itself as "not food and drink but righteousness and peace and joy in the Holy Spirit." The peace and joy given by the Spirit remain, writes John Wesley, and "overflow [even] in the depth of affliction"; and the gift of love makes it possible for us to love others "with a love not

10. Dow, *This Is Our Faith*, 71.

11. Augustine, *Trinity* 15.5.31; see also 1 John 4:19—"We love [God], because [God] first loved us."

only ever burning in your hearts, but flaming out in all your actions and conversations."[12]

The Gifts of Accompaniment and Adoption

Psalm 139:7 and following rejoices in God's steadfast presence in and as the Holy Spirit: "Where can I go from your spirit? Or where can I flee from your presence?" No matter where one goes, the psalmist knows that "your right hand shall hold me fast." Such confidence in the Spirit's presence is received as comfort and reassurance. More profoundly, by the work of the Holy Spirit, human beings become the children of God. As Paul writes, "For you did not receive a spirit of slavery to fall back into fear, but you received a spirit [*pneuma*] of adoption. When we cry, 'Abba! Father!' it is that very Spirit bearing witness with our spirit that we are children of God" (Rom 8:15–16). Through the Spirit, the human–divine connection becomes a family relationship, free from domination. Paul's word choice, *abba*, is a term of tender embrace. The Maker of all things does not seek to control and manipulate, but to be in loving relationship. Through the Spirit, we are drawn into communion with the fullness of the Trinity. To receive this gift from the Spirit is to encounter and interact with the very self of God, who confers on the believer the status of family.

The Gift of Reconciliation

In a world constantly riven by war and conflicts of all kind, the gift of reconciliation is deeply desired. As an apostle of Jesus following the resurrection, Peter relates that in Joppa (today, part of modern Tel Aviv), he was given a vision that no foods should be treated as unclean. In other words, the hard divisions between Jew and gentile should be set aside. According to the book of Acts, Peter goes on to say,

> At that very moment three men, sent to me from Caesarea, arrived at the house where we were. The Spirit told me to go with them and not to make a distinction between them and us. These six brothers also accompanied me, and we entered the man's house. . . . As I began to speak, the Holy Spirit fell upon them just as it had upon us at the beginning. . . . If then God gave them

12. Wesley, "Marks of the New Birth," 425–28.

> the same gift that he gave us when we believed in the Lord Jesus Christ, who was I that I could hinder God?[13]

If indeed it is God's will that all persons should be reconciled in Christ, through the power of the Holy Spirit, who are we to defy God's purposes? Better still, it is a blessing to acknowledge and delight in the grace that the gift of reconciliation is given for the sake of peace and harmony among the peoples.

GIFTS OF SERVICE

The Gifts of Leadership, Administration, and Teaching

The theme of relational giving is again expressed in how the Holy Spirit empowers some to serve in particular ways. Through the service human beings offer, the desire of God to provide for human beings and all creation can be seen. When I am in need of something I cannot do on my own, I must look to others to serve me, just as I in my turn will serve them. This reciprocity seems to be constitutive of God's purposes and design. In the book of Numbers, God instructs Moses to gather seventy elders to serve as leaders of the people. When they have come together, the Lord says,

> I will come down and speak with you there, and I will take some of the spirit [*ruach*] that is on you [Moses] and put it on them, and they shall bear the burden of the people along with you so that you will not bear it all by yourself.[14]

Jesus's commissioning of the seventy-two in Luke 10:1–12 echoes this distribution of the work of leadership. Through leaders, God the Spirit is at work to provide for certain human needs, providing such things as care, coordination, and oversight. Through Spirit-led leaders, God might even "rescue communities from distress and . . . create a flourishing society out hopeless, dis-spirited people."[15]

A specific gift of leadership, administration (*kubernēsis*), is identified by Paul as one of the distinctive gifts of the Spirit (1 Cor 12:28). This is not the practice of bureaucratic busy-work. *Kubernēsis* is derived from a Greek word related to steering a ship. Without that leadership gift, a ship

13. Acts 11:11–17.

14. Num 11:16–17.

15. Schweitzer and Kwon, *Hope Peace Unrest*, 49.

(or a church) is in danger of foundering on rocks or navigating in the wrong direction. Similarly, those with the gift of teaching advance the purposes of God by communicating truth and wisdom to guide the community, by the Spirit's power.[16]

The Gifts of Power and Strength

Power in every human context is an ambiguous reality. It can harm and it can heal. The ways the Holy Spirit gives power are consistent with the divine purposes to bring life and redemption to the world. When Samuel anoints David for his future kingship, "the spirit of the Lord came mightily upon David from that day forward" (1 Sam 16:13) in order to make him a better ruler, not just to make him powerful. The legendary physical strength of Samson was attributed by Ambrose to "the Spirit of the Lord [who] directed him" in service to the nation.[17] Samson's bloody killing of thousands of Philistines at various points in his life and at the moment of his death (Judg 16:23–30) is regarded by the biblical authors as praiseworthy. The bloodthirstiness of these accounts illustrates the ambiguity of the use of power, however. It is hard to reconcile that vengefulness with the loving purposes of God. Such stories should be assessed alongside the gifts of the Spirit to reconcile and unify.

The Gift of Prophecy

Prophecy is rarely represented in Scripture as predicting the future. Rather, it is the gift of describing the present with clarity and faithfulness, to point out the errors of sin, and to indicate the future paths that accord with God's will. In this sense, prophecy is entirely a gift of service to others. As Michael Ramsey notes, "It is by *ruach* that the prophets prophesy."[18] The stories of the biblical prophets are often accompanied by a commission from the Holy Spirit. This was true, for instance, in the cases of Ezekiel and Micah:

> He said to me: "O mortal, stand up on your feet, and I will speak with you." And when he spoke to me, a spirit [*ruach*] entered into me and set me on my feet, and I heard him speaking to me. He said to me, "Mortal, I am sending you to the people."[19]

16. See Rom 12:6; Eph 4:11–12.
17. Ambrose, *Holy Spirit* 1.2.
18. Ramsey, *Holy Spirit*, 11.
19. Ezek 2:1–3.

> But as for me, I am filled with power, with the spirit [*ruach*] of the Lord, and with justice and might, to declare to Jacob his transgression and to Israel his sin.[20]

Others, such as Zechariah and Simeon, are filled with the Spirit in order to prophesy in a special circumstance (Luke 1:67ff.; 2:25ff.). More generally, the Spirit's gift of prophecy is promised to "all" in Joel: "I will pour out my spirit on all flesh; your sons and your daughters shall prophesy" (Joel 2:28). Joel's theme is taken up much later among the thousands who gathered in Jerusalem on the day of Pentecost. Peter publicly identifies the phenomenal appearance of the fire and wind of the Holy Spirit with the words of the prophet: "This is what was spoken through the prophet Joel" (Acts 2:16).

Despite the association between the Holy Spirit and the gift of prophecy, the prophets are not always willing partners. They do not immediately provide the resounding "Yes!" that Mary the mother of Jesus is reported to have said. As Rogers notes, "It is typical of prophets to resist their call . . . Moses, Jonah, Isaiah, Paul characteristically require coercion into working for justice; the Spirit drives them."[21] The biblical accounts of prophetic empowerment are not stories of the prophets needing only gentle nudges to get up and do what they felt like doing anyway. The Spirit works in and through them, sometimes *despite* them. When the message, circumstances, or urgency of their calling contradicts the dominant voices and trends around them, the prophets may be understandably reluctant. The world might not be eager to hear their message—or indeed, the world might violently reject it. And yet, "the essential character of Hebrew prophecy was resistance to dominant powers as empowered by the Spirit."[22] It is precisely into those challenging and God-resisting contexts that the Spirit send the prophets.

As a result, the Spirit must often be insistent and persistent in calling forth the gift of prophecy. From Augustine's perspective, "it was the Holy Spirit who directly raised their [the prophets'] minds to see divine reality in the same way that the angels see it. . . . When prophets prophesy, they do so through what they have learned through the action of the Holy Spirit."[23] Like Scripture itself, the prophets are *theopneustos*—that is, "God-inspirited," or God-inspired (see 2 Tim 3:16). The work of Jesus and his cousin John in the Second Testament is in continuity with the work of the ancient prophets. "John the Baptist was filled with the Holy Spirit even when he

20. Mic 3:8.

21. Rogers, *After the Spirit*, 105.

22. Wells, "Resistance to Domination," 173.

23. See Augustine, *De consensu evangelistarum* 1.24.37, referenced in O'Laughlin, "St. Augustine's View," 89–90.

was in his mother's womb," testifies Wang Weifen. "He was not afraid of the powerful, and he bravely pointed out the social evils of the society."[24] All of these persons in the prophetic tradition are empowered by the same Spirit.

The ongoing gift of prophecy is little emphasized among the United and Uniting Churches. A test for the presence of this gift would be its fidelity to the biblical purposes of prophecy: describing the present faithfully, pointing out sin, and indicating the ways that align with God's purposes. The United Church in Jamaica and the Cayman Islands helpfully notes that "the gift of prophecy is the means by which the mind and will of God are communicated to God's people [and] it is for the purposes of edification, exhortation, and comfort."[25] It is presumptuous to think that God the Spirit no longer calls prophets to prophesy. Attentive awareness of the voices of protest and critique in our societies today might reveal something else altogether.

GIFTS OF KNOWLEDGE AND ABILITY

The Gifts of Illumination and Understanding

A key motif in the thought of Martin Luther (1483–1546) is that God remains hidden until God chooses to self-reveal. Correspondingly, the blessings of creation and the cross are not thoroughly apprehended unless the Holy Spirit makes plain what God is doing through them: "But because this grace would benefit no one if it remained so profoundly hidden and could not come to us, the Holy Spirit comes and gives himself to us also, wholly and completely."[26] The Spirit's self-giving makes possible all human knowledge, including awareness of God's goodness.

To receive the Spirit is also to receive the gift of coming to know God. This illumination is vital, as Paul argues, since the ways of God in former times were "a hidden mystery," but now,

> God has revealed to us through the Spirit, for the Spirit searches everything, even the depths of God. . . . No one comprehends what is truly God's except the Spirit of God. Now we have

24. Wang, "Holy Spirit Gives and nurtures Life," 207.

25. United Church in Jamaica and the Cayman Islands, *Our Church*, 84–85.

26. Luther, *Word and Sacrament III*, 366.

> received not the spirit of the world but the Spirit that is from God, so that we may understand the gifts bestowed on us by God.[27]

It is distinctively the work of the Spirit to teach and provide understanding. Jesus says as much to his disciples, "The Advocate, the Holy Spirit, whom the Father will send in my name, will teach you everything" and will "guide you into all the truth" (John 14:26; 16:13).

The very possibility of seeing God's presence within the life and work of Jesus is a gift of the Spirit. Even there, as the Evangelical Church in Germany remarks, "It is anything but self-evident to see God himself at work in Jesus' actions. For it is a 'seeing' that occurs through faith and is given through God the Holy Spirit."[28] The Spirit gives freely, for the Spirit's good pleasure. Jeffrey Paul Crittenden of The United Church of Canada notes that "it is crucial to remember that this gift [of the Spirit] is offered to any Christian believer regardless of status, gender, intellect, [or] geographical location."[29] All who were present received the Holy Spirit when Peter spoke in Caesarea—even gentiles, much to the astonishment of those who were Jewish believers in Jesus (Acts 10:44–46). It is not the role of human beings to decide or to limit the ways the Holy Spirit will be given.

The Gifts of Wisdom and Guidance

As Thayer and Jacobsen of the United Church of Christ (USA) put it, Christians are not taught that "we can resist the powers and temptations of evil unaided. Instead, Christ gives us the Holy Spirit as our comforter and help. The empowerment of the Holy Spirit is necessary for the transformation of our lives."[30] The notion of a person privately animating their moral advancement is foreign to Christian thought. It is again a distinctive gift of the Spirit to lead, guide, and give wisdom as we advance in maturity and grace. Ephrem sings,

> Your harbour looks for our ship to arrive.
> Your Spirit lovingly guides it with the rudder of your mercy.[31]

27. 1 Cor 2:7, 10–12.
28. Beintker and Philipps, eds., "Handeln Gotte," 60.
29. Crittenden, *Leisure*, 58.
30. Thayer and Jacobsen, *Christ, Creeds and Life*, 96.
31. Ephrem, *Hymns* 12.16.

Calvin teaches that the Holy Spirit is "the best guide in the right path."[32] The United Free Church of Scotland speaks of their "submission to the guidance and teaching of the Holy Spirit who is truth, and we shall ever seek of [the Spirit] enlightenment and grace both to unlearn our errors and also more fully to learn the mind and will of God."[33] According to the teaching of Jesus, those who bear witness to their faith in public will be guided by the Holy Spirit (Mark 13:11). For Samartha of the Church of South India, the Holy Spirit's guidance is directional and purposeful, but not coercive. The Spirit indicates, suggests, and inspires, but "does not appear as actively changing the human condition so much as being available to be tapped into as a resource for human beings in their daily lives."[34] The Spirit is given to the church, as the Uniting Church in Australia professes, "in order that it may not lose the way."[35]

The Gift of Remembering

One of the Spirit's actions is to remind the faithful of God's steadfastness to the covenant, and to preserve them in the living faith. The faith expressed in the creeds, for example, is "continuously confirmed by the Holy Spirit in the experience of the Church of Christ," as the Church of North India describes it.[36] In his farewell discourse in the gospel according to John, Jesus assures his disciples that the Paraclete will be active in and among them, to "remind you of all that I have said to you" (John 14:26).

GIFTS OF FAITH

The Gift of Hope

Speaking from the context of Chile's social and economic struggles, Juan Sepúlveda writes of the way the Holy Spirit brings hope to his people:

> We know we have a future because of the Spirit. . . . We rejoice in the signs of the Spirit among us, the new communities that are

32. Calvin, *Institutes* 4.8.13.
33. United Free Church of Scotland, "Statement of Faith," §12.
34. See Kim, *Mission in the Spirit*, 205–6.
35. Uniting Church in Australia, *Basis of Union*, 3.
36. Church of North India, *Constitution*, clause 3.

> coming up and the new impulses that move them. We feel the breath of the Spirit upon our dry bones and we wait in prayer for rebirth and renewal.[37]

Sepúlveda evokes here Ezek 37, the vision of the valley of dry bones. When all is lost for Ezekiel's people in the midst of their captivity and exile in Babylon, Ezekiel is brought "by the spirit of the Lord" into a vision. There, the dry bones, even when covered with flesh and sinew, have "no breath in them." God says,

> Prophesy to the breath.
> Prophesy, mortal, and say to the breath:
> Thus says the Lord God:
> Come from the four winds, O breath, and breathe upon these slain, that they may live.

Ezekiel obeys:

> I prophesied as he commanded me,
> and the breath came into them,
> and they lived and stood on their feet, a vast multitude.

Then the punch line comes:

> Then he said to me, "Mortal, these bones are the whole house of Israel. They say, 'Our bones are dried up, and our hope is lost; we are cut off completely.' . . . You shall know that I am the Lord when I open your graves and bring you up from your graves, O my people. I will put my spirit [*ruach*] within you, and you shall live, and I will place you on your own soil; then you shall know that I, the Lord, have spoken and will act, says the Lord."[38]

In the chaos and despair of any given moment, the Holy Spirit gives the gift of hope: to ancient Israelites in exile, to modern Chileans in their struggles, and to all people who long for deliverance. As the Evangelical Church in Germany says, "The Spirit testifies to believers that God's rule will prevail."[39] This is the foundation of hope.

37. Cited in World Council of Churches, *Come, Holy Spirit*, 23.

38. Ezek 37:1–14.

39. Beintker and Philipps, eds., "Handeln Gotte," 64.

The Gift of Trusting Faith

The gift of faith comes to each person in a unique way. For some, it is like a small seed that germinates and grows over time. For others, it is the result of a dramatic revelation that rapidly changes their minds and hearts. Still others find themselves living and breathing their faith long before they have words or even awareness of the feeling of trust in God that faith offers. In all cases, it is the work of the Holy Spirit to animate, confirm, nurture, and grow the faith of each person. Calvin calls faith "the principal work of the Holy Spirit."[40] The good soil of the Christian community and the word of God provide the basis for the growth and health of the seed of faith. The sacraments offer ongoing nurture for it. Again, the Spirit is at work in church, Bible, and sacrament to draw forward the faith of each one. Sahu of the Church of North India remarks, "Those who come to believe in Jesus through the words of Jesus do so through the work of the Paraclete."[41] Basil concurs: one cannot have faith in God the Father or God the Son "without the simultaneous presence of the Spirit."[42] The source of faith and hope for the first disciples was invariably the Holy Spirit.[43] This is her mysterious inner working that goes unseen and cannot be empirically observed or measured. But the rise of faith in any person comes as a gift, not as an achievement.

The Gift of Prayer

Like faith and hope, prayer is not a self-given gift. It arises through the action of the Holy Spirit to draw us closer to God and God's purposes. The Holy Spirit joins with human creatures in their prayer, and empowers them to pray. As Paul proclaims,

> Likewise the Spirit helps us in our weakness, for we do not know how to pray as we ought, but that very Spirit intercedes with groanings too deep for words. And God, who searches hearts, knows what is the mind of the Spirit, because the Spirit intercedes for the saints according to the will of God.[44]

40. Calvin, *Institutes* 3.1.4.
41. Sahu, *United and Uniting*, 66.
42. Basil, *On the Holy Spirit* 11.27.
43. World Council of Churches, *Come, Holy Spirit*, 7.
44. Rom 8:26–27.

This inhabitation of human prayer by the Holy Spirit is congruent with the steady, constant gifts of accompaniment and adoption that we discussed earlier in this chapter. It has the character of a loving parent who guides the steps of a child learning to walk into the parent's welcoming embrace. When Paul speaks of the Spirit praying in, with, and for human beings, he gestures toward the Spirit changing them "by prayer, not that they change themselves and earn the Spirit."[45] The Spirit is at work within them, transforming them, even when they are unsure how to pray. "Though prayer is a human activity," teaches the Uniting Presbyterian Church of Southern Africa, "at a deeper level it is the Spirit's activity within us."[46] God the Holy Spirit does not exact a high price, nor a measure of perfection, before interceding with "groanings too deep for words." It is precisely in our imperfections and inadequacies that God the Spirit is at work through our prayers.

An unresolved theological tension remains in the phenomenon of Jesus praying in Gethsemane, and on other occasions. To whom is Jesus praying? Does the Holy Spirit accompany and empower Jesus's prayers, as She does the prayers of other human beings? Although there is no consensus on the matter, I think it is helpful to consider that when Jesus is in prayer, we observe the Trinity in communion with the Trinity. There is a mystery here that human reason cannot entirely penetrate. But there is an analogy in any person who consults their "head, heart, and gut" when making a decision. The triune Self of God is a relational Someone. As an article of faith, it is coherent to trust that this Someone is in dialogue, for this Someone shares in mutual love.

GIFTS OF CHARACTER

The Gifts of Grace, Restraint, and Holiness

The Holy Spirit continually shapes individuals toward Christlike living. This process of sanctification will be discussed in greater depth in the next chapter. For now, we can note that Christoformity—living in the shape of Jesus Christ—is the goal. Jesus is Savior and Lord, but also the model for human conduct in this life. Accordingly, the Spirit spreads gifts among God's people to model and encourage the way of Jesus. The Holy Spirit's gift of grace is not a matter of making a person "nice." Grace is a gift that makes the human

45. Rogers, *After the Spirit*, 212.

46. Uniting Presbyterian Church of Southern Africa, *Manual*, 40.

creature able to live as God intends. Grace makes it possible for us to fulfill our human vocation and purpose. The fruit of the Spirit that Paul names as "patience, kindness, generosity, faithfulness, gentleness, and self-control" in Gal 5:22–23 are examples of this. When he is filled *with* the Holy Spirit, Jesus is led into the desert *by* the Spirit to face the devil's temptations of materiality, fame, and power (Luke 4:1–13). His restraint and holiness enable him to overcome these lures, and to fulfill his vocation as the Christ. These same gifts are offered by the Spirit to enable all human beings to adopt and embrace the way of Jesus.

GIFTS OF HUMAN THRIVING

The Gift of Being Alive

Jesus says, "It is the Spirit that gives life" (John 6:53). In this, the Spirit and the Son collaborate, for the Messiah has come "that they [human beings] may have life and have it abundantly" (John 10:10). "The Spirit is the source of life in all its fullness wherever it is found,"[47] write Thayer and Jacobsen. The creating and sustaining of all life, Ezekiel's vision of the dry bones, and the resurrection of Jesus all point toward this deep desire of God for human flourishing. Regarding the creation account in Gen 1, Luther writes, "As a hen broods her eggs . . . to bring them to life . . . the Holy Spirit brooded, as it were, on the waters to bring to life those substances which were to be quickened and adorned. For it is the office of the Holy Spirit to make alive."[48] The life-giving Spirit quickens the unlikely wombs of Mary and Elizabeth (Luke 1).

In the 1980s, an unnamed Argentinian contributed a personal reflection to *Come, Holy Spirit*, a book from the World Council of Churches. They write,

> At the height of the so-called "dirty war" in Argentina [1974–83], while the military junta was engaged in clandestine acts of violence against the civilian populace, those same rulers declared that it was henceforth a crime against the state to read or sing the Magnificat.[49]

47. Thayer and Jacobsen, *Christ, Creeds and Life*, 96.
48. Luther, *Lectures on Genesis 1–5*, 9.
49. World Council of Churches, *Come, Holy Spirit*, 38.

The joyful proclamation in the Magnificat contains a threat, in other words, to those who would diminish or destroy human life. In late 2025, United States immigration officials banned the offering of public prayers and the Eucharist outside the Broadview detention facility in Illinois. What is the threat posed by these acts of trust in the Holy Spirit?

The work of the Spirit is the antithesis of such death-dealing ways (see 2 Cor 3:6 and Ps 104:30). As Moltmann remarks, "The sending of the Holy Spirit is the revelation of God's indestructible *affirmation* of life and his marvellous *joy* in life. . . . Where the Holy Spirit is present there is life . . . [where] the Holy Spirit is, there is joy at the victory of life over death, and there the powers and energies of eternal life are experienced."[50] Michael Welker, of the German EKD union of churches, adds that the gift of peace which flows from the Spirit in this life "becomes an experience of great joy . . . [for we are] deemed worthy of being bearers of God's presence on this earth . . . [and have] a share in eternal life."[51] All of this coheres with the ancient testimony of the Christian movement, both in the Bible and in the creedal formulations. The Niceno-Constantinopolitan Creed describes the Holy Spirit as *to kyrion kai zōopoion*, "Lord and Giver of life." All life derives from and is knit together in the Holy Spirit, from the beginning and on an ongoing basis. "The Spirit," as Elizabeth Johnson says, "is the unceasing, dynamic flow of divine power that sustains the universe, bringing forth life."[52]

The Gift of Healing

As part of the gift of flourishing, the Holy Spirit seeks to repair and restore life when it is damaged. In the promised completion of the Spirit's work, all harms will be healed, and the whole of creation will be filled and delight in the goodness God intends. In the inward life, She renews human hearts: "I will give them one heart and put a new spirit within them; I will remove the heart of stone from their flesh and give them a heart of flesh" (Ezek 11:19). Basil likewise sees the Spirit's action in both inward and outward healing: "The working of miracles and the gifts of healing are all through the Holy Spirit. . . . The deliverance from sin is in the grace of the Spirit. . . . The resurrection of the dead comes by the working of the Spirit."[53] In the multiple healings performed by Jesus, the Holy Spirit collaborates with the Son to

50. Moltmann, *Source of Life*, 19–20.
51. Welker, *What Happens*, 166.
52. Johnson, *Women, Earth, and Creator Spirit*, 42.
53. Basil, *On the Holy Spirit* 19.48.

transform lives and bodies. In creation's capacities for cyclical renewal, we can see her at work to renew the earth (Rom 8:18–23).[54]

The Gift of Freedom and Liberation

"The Lord is the Spirit," writes Paul, "and where the Spirit of the Lord is, there is freedom" (2 Cor 3:17). The created and healed lives of human creatures are meant for freedom, not subjection. Jesus, who is one with the Holy Spirit, tells a crowd that "if it is by the Spirit of God that I cast out demons, then the kingdom of God has come upon you" (Matt 12:28). Freedom from demons—literal or metaphorical—is freedom from bondage and oppression. It means living within the realm of God, a location of justice, love, and peace, rather than a location of exploitation and manipulation.

Freedom means freedom from sin and eternal death, and freedom for service and eternal life. The United Protestant Church in France takes up the theme: "The Holy Spirit makes us free and responsible through the promise of a life stronger than death. He encourages us to witness to the love of God, in words and in actions."[55] Accordingly, no false powers can command our allegiance, for the Christian belongs to Christ. The Holy Spirit "works with us and through us as we struggle against injustice and to shake off the chains that bind us."[56] Harold Wells of The United Church of Canada writes that "resistance to domination . . . has to be seen as a movement of the Holy Spirit" and that "those (whether within the churches or outside of them) who strive to resist dominant, oppressive powers must be seen as gifted by the Spirit."[57] Moses's "prophetic resistance to the oppressive Pharaoh" is empowered by the Holy Spirit, enabling Moses to lead his people to freedom.[58] The Spirit who brings good news to the impoverished and sets the prisoners free (Isa 61:1) is embraced and embodied in the mission of Jesus Christ (Luke 4:18–21).

Leon Harris writes movingly of the experience of the Holy Spirit's liberation among the formerly enslaved black community in the United States: "The divine grace of the Holy Spirit freed the mind and affections of enslaved black Christians to recognize in the cross of Christ their restoration

54. Another study is warranted to address the complex question of why some individuals are healed and others are not.

55. Eglise Protestante Unie de France, "Nouvelle Déclaration de Foi."

56. World Council of Churches, *Come, Holy Spirit*, 10.

57. Wells, "Resistance to Domination," 170.

58. Wells, "Resistance to Domination," 173.

in a holistic manner," he notes. The embodied death of Jesus taught them that

> the black body is worth just as much as a white body. . . . The divine action of the Holy Spirit restored humanity to the slaves because they no longer saw themselves as alone; there is a God in Jesus Christ who is concerned with their struggle. This gave black Christians a sense of agency to cooperate with the Spirit in order to codetermine their own being in the world. Enslaved black Christians now felt a sense of agency and the divine right to resist the physical oppression.[59]

The profundity of this empowering liberation goes well beyond the symbolic and metaphorical to the existential, daily, embodied lives of real persons suffering under oppression. It is precisely them, and others like them, that the Holy Spirit is at work to liberate. The Spirit's work in this liberation often begins with the prophetic denunciation of injustice by the prophets of old and the prophets of today.

The work of liberation can be long, painful, and multigenerational. The sinful forces ranged against the purposes of God can be persistent and formidable. Within the complex, multireligious, colonized, and often violent context of the Philippines, Levi Oracion writes, "The Holy Spirit enables us to pursue the ministry of liberation and reconciliation. . . . The Pentecost experience does not take us out of the struggles of the world; it provides us with a spirituality that equips us for those struggles."[60] The Spirit is the source of hope for those who work toward and yearn for the day of liberation for all peoples (Rom 5:13).

~

To welcome and to receive the gifts of the Holy Spirit "is for us to participate in [the Spirit] and to be transformed by his indwelling presence."[61] The Spirit gives gifts in freedom and for freedom, enabling special skills and abilities, and in all cases seeking the good of the recipients and blessings for those around them. Relational gifts, as well as gifts of service, knowledge, ability, faith, character, and human thriving derive from the one Lord, the Spirit, who desires the wellbeing of the creation God loves. Such gifts are given to

59. Harris, "Holy Spirit as Liberator," 183.

60. Cited in World Council of Churches, *Come, Holy Spirit*, 23.

61. Ayres, "Holy Spirit as the 'Undiminished Giver,'" 69.

each one, for the sake of all. We turn now to the ways the Spirit continues to bless individuals through transformation and sanctification.

FOR REFLECTION OR DISCUSSION

1. If the Holy Spirit gives gifts for the common good and for the building of the realm of God, as you look around your church or community, what gifts to you see present?
2. Of the various types of gifts that the Holy Spirit gives (relational gifts; gifts of service; gifts of knowledge and ability; gifts of faith; gifts of character; gifts of human thriving), which does your church emphasize the most? Which does your church seem to neglect or de-emphasize? Why do you think this is so?
3. Of the many gifts listed in this chapter, which gift(s) do you think that you have been given? How do you share them?

Chapter 13

Transform, Sanctify, and Perfect

Inspired and guided by the Holy Spirit, and given a range of her gifts, what remains for human beings? In short, what remains is the completion and fulfillment of God's promised intentions for us. Toward this end, transforming, sanctifying, and perfecting are distinctively the work of the Holy Spirit.

Transformation is perhaps a familiar enough term these days, and there is an intuitive sense of what it might mean: to change the form of something. A human creature, or another aspect of creation, changes form under the influence of the Holy Spirit. To be transformed by the Spirit is to begin to correspond more and more closely to all that God longs for.

Closely aligned with this are the senses of sanctification and perfection. To be *sanctified* is to be made holy. This might make a modern person pull back a little. Do we really want to be *holy*? There is something a little suspicious about that, if the word is attached to negative connotations, as in the expression "holier than thou." But to be made holy is not a process of claiming to be better than anyone, nor to have an obnoxious shiny halo over our heads. It is to come into harmony with God's being, God's nature, God's character. (This is key when thinking about why the Spirit herself is called "Holy"—She is fully in harmony and one with God's being, nature, and character.) We don't *become* God, but God's ways are more and more reflected in our ways of being.

Similarly, *perfection* is not a claim to be superior to another person, but to draw closer to the ideal that God has in mind for human living: to live in freedom, with truth, goodness, peacefulness, gentleness, and faithfulness guiding every thought, word, action, and relationship. "Indeed," writes Chen Zemin, "without the Holy Spirit we cannot understand truth nor walk in truth."[1] This is not a human achievement, but the working of the Holy Spirit in the human spirit. To receive the Spirit, to have her indwell the human creature, is to begin these processes of transformation, sanctification, and perfection.

As the "Lord and giver of life," the Spirit is the source of transformation, sanctification, and perfection. She cannot be thought of as one who is created by God and then receives or participates in sanctification, as though from the outside. Basil notes that "holiness is the Spirit's nature," not given to her from an outside source.[2] The Spirit is herself God—God who transforms, sanctifies, and perfects the human creature. "All of us," writes Paul, "are being transformed into the same image [of Christ] from one degree of glory to another, for this comes from the Lord, the Spirit" (2 Cor 3:18). Transforming, sanctifying, and perfecting, then, are distinctively the work of the Holy Spirit.

Transformation

Nothing less than a complete reworking of the human creature, who has fallen under the influence of a sinful world-system (*kosmos*), is the Holy Spirit's goal. The Spirit is not content to impassively watch us suffer the harm we cause one another, nor to leave us in an unredeemed state. Instead, She works within us and through us to make us the people God would have us be. As Wang Weifen of the China Christian Council puts it, "The transformation of a person's worldview and values" occurs visibly, through the Spirit's actions.[3] Within her work of transforming, we find the gifts of conscience, awareness of guilt, and the desire for repentance. "We believe that the Spirit of God moves [people]," says The United Church of Canada, "to acknowledge their sins and accept the divine forgiveness and grace."[4] The World Council of Churches testifies that "as part of the process of liberation, the Spirit exposes and convicts the world of sin."[5] This is the language found in John 16:7–11. In that gospel passage, Jesus tells those who have gathered with him on the night before his crucifixion that the Paraclete, the Spirit of God, is coming. As John Wesley notes, "If I am troubled when I wilfully disobey God, it is plain his Spirit is still striving with me"—striving to call a

1. Chen, "Spirit, Please Come Upon Us," 250.

2. Basil, *Adversus eunomium* §3, cited in Ayres, "Holy Spirit as the 'Undiminished Giver,'" 65.

3. Wang, "Holy Spirit Gives and Nurtures Life," 204.

4. United Church of Canada, "Statement of Faith," art. 3.

5. World Council of Churches, *Come, Holy Spirit*, 9.

person to repent.[6] The United Free Church of Scotland testifies, "We believe that God through His Spirit is ever present in the lives of [persons], seeking them for Himself, rebuking their sinfulness, inspiring every right desire, and every effort after truth."[7]

But this coming of the Spirit is a complex and nuanced advent. It both blesses and challenges those who receive it. The Spirit comes not only to make persons feel happy and special, but also to move them powerfully in a Godward direction, sometimes with a sense of guilt or shame for their sin. But the repentance that follows opens the doorway to forgiveness and release from the heaviness of sin. This process of awakening to sin, repentance, forgiveness, and sanctification also brings about a change—a transformation—in a person's values and priorities. Selfishness, for example, gives way to a willingness to love and serve others, even without reward. "To transform," advises the World Council of Churches, "is to change the form as well as the substance and the character."[8] As persons liberated from sin and guilt, the redeemed are sent forth as agents of the mission of God in the world. This is what it means to be "a new creation" (2 Cor 5:17). It is no accident that the first Christian community's desire to ensure that everyone had enough to eat flows immediately after the Pentecost event (Acts 2:44–45). The Spirit enables the whole community to move toward economic transformation: goods and resources are shared so no one is left hungry.

To be in mission on God's behalf is to be caught up in the life of the Holy Spirit, who desires the good of all, and especially the lifting up of those who are oppressed, marginalized, and impoverished. "The one upon whom Yahweh's spirit rests," remarks Welker, "is described as one who executes justice and righteousness in favor of the lowly and the poor." He continues: "The servant [who receives the Spirit] preserves the endangered and the vulnerable."[9] The one anointed with the Spirit brings a message of liberation from enslavement. This is incredible news for anyone living under subjugation and tyranny.

On a macro scale, the Holy Spirit comes also to subvert and disrupt unjust power structures and systems of oppression by working through unexpected ways, people, and places. Not every movement of the Spirit is gentle and sweet. Pneumatology expressed in a liberationist key often focuses on

6. Wesley, "Means of Grace," 390.

7. United Free Church of Scotland, "Statement of Faith," §3.

8. World Council of Churches, *Come, Holy Spirit*, 85.

9. Welker, "Holy Spirit," 10.

> the action of the Spirit [that] arises within the very lives of communities whose experience is shaped by oppression, marginalisation, and exclusion . . . in the everyday lives and struggles of a people burdened, yearning for ethnic, social, economic, and racial freedom. . . . In a people broken by poverty, oppression, and death, the Spirit gives a new vitality and a hope of liberation.[10]

In contexts where oppression is resisted and overcome, where wars are ended, where justice arrives at last for a marginalized population, the Holy Spirit's divine disruptive transformation becomes visible. The very quest for survival and thriving in the midst of hardship is a sign of the Spirit at work in a people. Néstor Medina of The United Church of Canada relates that the "inspiring, energizing, and empowering activity of the Spirit" enables Latinas/os to persist through the multiple struggles of life. For those who, because of discrimination, abuse, exploitation, and marginalization, have lost their humanity," he says, "relationship with God implies being empowered by the Spirit to reclaim it."[11] Truly here the "Lord and Giver of Life" is at work.

The Spirit's power to help us see ourselves as God sees us (beloved, but in need of a changed heart and a new way of living) is part of the process of our transformation into the image of God and the uniting of our wills (individually and collectively) with the will of God. "I will take you," God says, in Ezekiel's prophetic overhearing,

> I will sprinkle clean water upon you, and you shall be clean from all your uncleanness. . . . A new heart I will give you, and a new spirit I will put within you. . . . Then you shall live in the land that I gave to your ancestors, and you shall be my people, and I will be your God.[12]

Because God remains faithful to the ancient and eternal covenant, and also desires that we should be faithful to it, this process of inward transformation continues.

The goals of the Holy Spirit's work of transforming the moral, ethical, spiritual, social, and economic aspects of life are not change for the sake of change. Rather, by renewing life and faith, She "restores our communion with God and one another," says the World Council of Churches. "We are built up through the gifts of the Spirit into a people empowered to do God's will. . . . We are carried beyond our narrow personal concerns to strive for

10. Schaab, "Liberation Pneumatology," 384–86.

11. Medina, "Theological Musings," 184, 185.

12. Ezek 36:24–28.

justice and peace in the world and to be in solidarity with the poor and oppressed."[13] Thus personal transformation is never for the sake of the individual alone, even though that transformation is surely a blessing to that person. It is also directed toward the community and the world in which each of us lives, so that our transformed selves may join in the Spirit's work of passionately transforming the world. The Holy Spirit's power "is a power that turns the world upside down."[14] This is a multi-millennial project for her, given the human tendency to sin. In our time, the systemic sin that has corrupted our stewardship and care for the earth is something that especially needs to be transformed and healed. The ongoing formation and transformation of the church is a Spirit-led process. Communities become increasingly Spirit-shaped by the quest for justice and peace for the whole of creation. Of course, communities of faith can resist this, and can descend into conflict and enmity, and can spurn the Spirit's leading. But She is nothing if not persistent, and returns again and again to transform and reform even the unwilling and hard-hearted.

Sanctification

Another distinctive work of the Holy Spirit is to *sanctify* believers. We could consider this as a still-deeper level of transformation. Following the theological principle of appropriation, as outlined in chapter 3, we can say that while redemption or salvation is the work associated mostly with Jesus Christ, it is the Holy Spirit who completes this action in the human creature by *sanctifying*.

"To sanctify" might sound rather grand (maybe too grand?) to a twenty-first-century person, especially if we think of it in the traditional way as a process of *being made holy*. "Sanctify" is related to *sanctus*, the Latin word for *holy*. We are rightly cautious about being seen to be (or thinking of ourselves as) "holier that thou"—better than our peers or indeed anyone. In this generation, there is a linguistic allergy to the term *sanctify*. Perhaps we can step down the high voltage of the term by thinking of it in terms of *preparation*—specifically preparation for participating in the life of God.

Sanctification is not an achievement, but the work of the Holy Spirit within a person to help them resist "the flesh," as Paul expresses it (meaning a tendency toward sin), and to live as God desires us to live (see Gal 5:13–21). Care must be taken here not to suppose that God dislikes bodies and materiality, as some Christians have concluded. After all, God made

13. World Council of Churches, *Come, Holy Spirit*, 8.

14. Dow, *This Is Our Faith*, 59.

our bodies and the whole of the material creation. God likes it, and redeems it. Paul's point in using the term "flesh" is to warn against the ways that we *misuse* our bodies and the physical creation to damage ourselves and others. Rather than following such pathways of harm, Paul reminds us to "be guided by the Spirit" (Gal 5:25). We know that the Spirit loves the world and people. When we love, in turn, we show signs of sanctification. The United Church of Canada refers to sanctification in terms of "grow[ing] in the likeness of Christ . . . growth in grace . . . [and] maturity and full assurance of faith whereby the love of God is made perfect in us."[15] It really is about loving, in the way that Jesus shows us how to love.

Obedience to the Spirit's purposes, in turn, means desiring what God desires—another sign of sanctification, together with love. This is not meek submission to an overpowering will. Obedience is about our readiness to cooperate with the Spirit to achieve God's purposes.

I want to caution here against supposing that by *sanctification* or *being made holy* we might mean *becoming God*. Rather, what is meant by "participating in the life of God" is a human life that is characterized by godly characteristics and dispositions, such as justice, kindness, generosity, and love. A direct link to the ancient words of Paul is useful here, when he speaks of the fruit of the Spirit. The fruit—the outward manifestation of the internal reality—of the Spirit's presence in a person are "love, joy, peace, patience, kindness, generosity, gentleness, faithfulness, and self-control" (Gal 5:22–23). These are characteristics that human creatures can outwardly reveal when their inward selves are united with the Spirit, precisely because they are characteristics that are true of God the Holy Spirit. Displaying those characteristics and dispositions are (in the old fashioned language) *evidence* of a person's sanctification or "holiness." In today's updated language, we can say that they are signs that *we are being prepared to participate in the life of God*. Other qualities that are believed to be of God are similarly shared, such as wisdom (yet even Solomon, said to be the wisest person ever, still erred). Further, the process of sanctification is ongoing. We don't "arrive" in such a way that the Spirit's work within us in no longer needed.

Sanctification is not a once-and-for-all flash, a single moment that instantaneously accomplishes its goal. Rather, it is lifelong, gradual, and usually incremental. It is an ongoing process, a dynamic interfusion of the Holy Spirit over a lifetime. Like much of the Spirit's work, which "functions slowly, as a time-consuming process,"[16] sanctification unfolds. Isaac of Nineveh, in the seventh century, compared the Spirit's activity to "a shell producing a

15. United Church of Canada, "Basis of Union," art. 12.

16. Seppälä, "Holy Spirit in Isaac of Nineveh," 139.

pearl."[17] Because the image of Christ in us is the ultimate goal (2 Cor 3:18), "the Spirit forms human beings into the shape of Christ."[18] Again, this is not instantaneous, but a process. Calvin suggests an organic metaphor: "By his secret watering the Spirit makes us fruitful to bring forth the buds of righteousness."[19] The Union of the Armenian Evangelical Churches of the Near East professes in their statement of faith that "by working on peoples' hearts . . . [the Holy Spirit] convicts them of sin, of righteousness, and of the coming judgement," and that due to the Spirit's "ministry a holy nature is granted to believers."[20] This reference to "a holy nature" is a gesture toward sanctification—being made holy. The process of sanctification might also involve a struggle to make us what we *ought* to be, not what we would *like* to be if left to our own choices and habits.[21]

To become holy is also to appreciate, love, and serve the holiness and goodness of all creation. It is to respect the sacred reality that is embedded by God within all that lives. The very life that is in each creature, each natural process, is a sign of God's presence. When we wonder at the mystery of creation, we are peering into the mystery of God. When we honor and protect creation, limit our use of natural resources, live more lightly on the land, reject violence, and strive not to pollute or to waste what is given by the earth, we honor God the Creator. When we find joy in the awesomeness of the stars, or the softness of a baby's skin, or the grandeur of the sunset, or the sound of the loon's cry across the lake, we are loving God. These are also holy acts, and forms of participation in the holiness of God. Sanctification "has nothing at all to do with getting out of the world," writes Douglas Hall of The United Church of Canada, "and everything to do with getting into it."[22] Such love and appreciation of the created order are empowered within us by the work of the Holy Spirit, the Sanctifier.

Perfection

One of the words used in the Second Testament for sin is *hamartia*. It is borrowed from archery, and suggests the idea of "missing the target." Sin, then, is something like missing the target of what is intended for human

17. Seppälä, "Holy Spirit in Isaac of Nineveh," 139.

18. Rogers, *After the Spirit*, 208.

19. Calvin, *Institutes* 3.3.3.

20. Tootikian, *Pastor's Manual*, 163.

21. "The conversion and renewal of the human will can only occur through an ongoing struggle at the core of our being." Hall, *Professing*, 249.

22. Hall, *Confessing*, 293.

life. It is an action that is misdirected—perhaps away from God's purposes or toward purposes that differ from what God desires. The teaching that the Holy Spirit is interested in perfecting human living is the contrast to this. Again, the process of *perfection* is not a process of becoming superior to other persons. It is the Spirit's response to *hamartia*—sin. It is her work in human beings who are learning to *hit* the target, rather than missing it. It is a process of learning to choose, with free will, that which God chooses. As we are perfected, God's will becomes the priority, rather than the grasping aims of the self. It is easy enough to act out of self-interest, self-centeredness, or selfishness. But the biblical ideals that are taught throughout Christian history are focused elsewhere. To live as we ought, we are meant to choose patterns that are God-centered, aiming for the target that God has in mind. Living in that way, willing what God wills by the Spirit's empowerment, is to enter the process of being perfected. This is a special role that the Holy Spirit plays in human life.

Again, perfection is not about being "better" than someone else. It is learning to live freely in agreement and joyful alignment with all that God intends for human life. We could even say that it is learning to be more fully human, more fully what we are meant to be. Like sanctification, it emerges slowly, over time. In fact, perfection is highly unlikely to be accomplished within the confines of this mortal life: "The perfecting of our here-and-now new birth in the Spirit will be completed only in the raising of the dead and the life of the world to come."[23] Most of the Christian tradition emphasizes sanctification and perfection as processes, not goals to strive after. To choose to receive and be open to the Spirit is to say "Yes!" to these processes, and to give our lives over to the Spirit's influence.

Vivification and Regeneration

Christian thought has also reserved a place for the work of the Holy Spirit under the terms *vivification* and *regeneration*. While they appear in historic creeds and theological writings, the terms are less common today. To *vivify* is to restore life passionately, especially after life has begun to decline, die, or decompose, morally or physically. The Holy Spirit can be seen, then, when life is flourishing and re-flourishing. Yet there can be a hiddenness to this work. For example, just as the mewling infant Christ does not immediately reveal the fullness of the incarnation, so also, we could say that in times of languishing, despair, or trouble, the Holy Spirit's work to comfort, sustain, and vivify are not necessarily evident at first glance. The Spirit's patient

23. Moltmann, *Source of Life*, 35.

promise unfolds in the Spirit's good time. Here, the Niceno–Constantinopolitan Creed's language of "all things seen and unseen" is helpful. The Holy Spirit is often at work in ways we don't see, perceive, imagine, or understand.

If the Holy Spirit is the Lord and Giver of Life (again in the language of the Creed), and is the One who hovers over chaos at creation and lends *ruach*, the Spirit-life-force to all that is, then the contrast to passionate living and flourishing is the reality that preceded creation: nothingness. Christian thought usually claims that the triune God created *ex nihilo*—"out of nothing." Nothingness is the near neighbor of creation, in that sense. The God who vivifies—that is, the Spirit who gives life—sustains and supports life throughout creation on an eternal, ongoing basis. Moltmann is helpful here:

> Life "according to the flesh" is a life that has miscarried, life that has strayed into contradiction with itself, life which suffers from the bacilli of death. Life "in the Spirit," on the other hand, is true life, which is completely and holy living, life in the divine power of life, life which has found the broad space in the marvellous nearness of God.[24]

This is the new and renewed life, the "new creation," to which Paul points so often in his letters in the Second Testament.

Regeneration is closely related to vivification: to once again (*re-*) bring people (*genos*) to life. "Where the Spirit is, Life also is," teaches Ambrose, "and where Life is, the Holy Spirit is also."[25] The encounter between Jesus and Nicodemus point in this same direction:

> Jesus answered him, "Very truly, I tell you, no one can see the kingdom of God without being born from above [or *born again/ born anew*]."
>
> Nicodemus said to him, "How can anyone be born after having grown old? Can one enter a second time into the mother's womb and be born?"
>
> Jesus answered, "Very truly, I tell you, no one can enter the kingdom of God without being born of water and Spirit. What is born of the flesh is flesh, and what is born of the Spirit is spirit. Do not be astonished that I said to you, 'You must be born from above.'"[26]

Traditionally, this passage is associated with baptism because of the reference to rebirth and water. But even apart from baptism, rebirth in the Spirit

24. Moltmann, *Source of Life*, 72.

25. Ambrose, *Holy Spirit* 1.15.

26. John 3:3–7.

is a powerful teaching. To *regenerate*—to bring the people to life again—transcends what human creatures can do on our own. It takes place thanks to "the gracious and mysterious operation of [the Spirit's] power."[27] In particular, to be redeemed and restored from a state of sin and to be "born anew" into a life of repentance and joyful service is a kind of re-creation. It is a *re*-generation, as we become (again) the people that God desires us to be. Here the power and promise of the Holy Spirit intersect, drawing us into the joyful, redemptive, and transformative purposes of God.

FOR REFLECTION OR DISCUSSION

1. How does the thought of being sanctified (made holy) or perfected make you feel?
2. What is your experience of being transformed by the Holy Spirit?
3. If one result of sanctification is a tendency to "appreciate, love, and serve the holiness and goodness of all creation," what are the practical implications for how you live your life?

27. United Church of Canada, "Basis of Union," art. 9.

Chapter 14

Human Participation in the Divine Life

WITHIN THE BIBLE AND Christian teaching, there is a thread that leads many thinkers and believers to affirm the concept that the Holy Spirit draws human creatures into the life of God. There is a continuum of ways to understand this idea. At one end of the scale, there is language of *participating* in the divine life (without becoming divine ourselves, e.g. as citizens of the kingdom or realm of heaven). At the other end of the scale, there is language of *becoming* divine (sometimes called *theosis* or *divinization*). So we have a range of views. There is no single consensus on this dynamic within Christian thought or experience.

The idea that God the Holy Spirit shares the divine life with us, and invites us into close companionship or participation in God's life, is well attested. In the Bible, we can see the following:

> But you are not in the flesh; you are in the Spirit, since the Spirit of God dwells in you.
>
> You are God's temple and . . . God's Spirit dwells in you.
>
> His divine power has given us everything needed for life and godliness, through the knowledge of him who called us by his own glory and excellence. Thus he has given us, through these things, his precious and very great promises, so that through them you may escape from the corruption that is in the world because of lust and may become participants of the divine nature.
>
> By this we know that we abide in him and he in us, because he has given us of his Spirit . . . God is love, and those who abide in love abide in God, and God abides in them.[1]

1. Rom 8:9; 1 Cor 3:16; 2 Pet 1:3–4; 1 John 4:13, 16.

Christianity has upheld this conviction (that we may be God's companions or share the divine life in some way) ever since the Second Testament writers articulated it. However it is understood—metaphorically, symbolically, spiritually, or literally—it has striking power. Christians' incorporation into the body of Christ through baptism and justification leads to a mystical but authentically real state of a life intertwined with the Holy Spirit.[2]

Paul's striking image of the human body as a temple of God, in which the Holy Spirit dwells (1 Cor 3:16) is delightful, but a little disturbing. Are human identity and autonomy retained in such a close living arrangement? Will cohabitation with the Spirit still allow us to be ourselves? Are we open to the possibility of the Spirit living and working through people quite unlike us, and whom we do not like? "The Spirit is much freer than we sometimes find comfortable," teaches the Uniting Church in Australia, "working through people who do not fit our neat categories."[3]

Moreover, Paul says that "God's love has been poured into our hearts through the Holy Spirit" (Rom 5:5). How far can this idea be taken? In his "Sermon on the Day of St. Peter and St. Paul" (1519), Luther says, "It is true that a man helped by grace is more than a man; indeed, the grace of God gives him the form of God and deifies him." His Christmas sermon for 1514 similarly echoes a phrase from Athanasius and several other Eastern theologians from the ancient period, claiming that "God becomes man so that man may become God."[4] John Wesley, commenting on 2 Pet 1:4, teaches that "ye may become partakers of the divine nature—Being renewed in the image of God, and having communion with them, so as to dwell in God, and God in you."[5] Does this mean more than receiving the gift of eternal life? In their further writings, neither Luther nor Wesley held to the idea of ontological change in the human creature such that we *become divine*. Rather, there is a kind of unity or union with God on the level of love or the will to love. A Christian may indeed be sanctified by the Holy Spirit—become holy—but not "become God."

The first creation story speaks of the breath of God's Spirit (*elohim ruach*) moving upon the surface of the deep waters (Gen 1:2). The Spirit here infuses herself, so to speak, within creation. Much later, in the incarnation, this bodily presence of the Spirit is prominent. In Mary the mother of Jesus, the "Holy Spirit does not avoid the body, but enters the body of a

2. Crittenden, *Leisure*, 59.

3. Uniting Church in Australia, "Report on Ministry," 272.

4. Luther, cited in Kärkkäinen, *One With God*, 47.

5. Wesley, *Explanatory Notes on the New Testament*, 621n4 (note for 2 Pet 1:4).

young woman who bears within her womb the life of the world."[6] Ephrem says it more poetically:

> It pleased [God] to make himself small, and bend down
> To show himself to us, mingle his Son with us,
> Mix his Spirit with us, and show his love for us.[7]

All this is echoed in the risen Christ's profound act of commissioning his followers: "Jesus said to them again, 'Peace be with you. As the Father has sent me, so I send you.' When he had said this, he breathed on them and said to them, Receive the Holy Spirit'" (John 20:21–22). From Christ comes the Spirit, with whom he is One, and that Spirit-breath [*pneuma*] moves from the body of Jesus to the bodies of those who follow him. From their terrified, secret huddle in an upper room, they are sent into Jesus's mission as apostles. It is in bodily form that they receive this breath. This isn't simply a metaphor. There is a physical interaction between the apostles' bodies and the Spirit-breath of God. They participate spiritually through a union of their lives with the Holy Spirit's will, thanks to a physical encounter.

From Soul to Body

Elsewhere, Christian writers have reversed the action, from the soul outward to the body. Ambrose writes that the Holy Spirit "is infused in our souls, and flows into our senses."[8] The author of 1 John celebrates that through the Spirit, God's life and love dwell within the human creature: "No one has ever seen God; if we love one another, God abides in us, and his love is perfected in us" (1 John 4:12). Here it is precisely the Spirit's work to draw human life into some kind of participation with God's life. *How* this takes place is not something that mechanics or physics can prove or explain. It is surely a theological claim that this is so.

But perhaps the effects of the Spirit-participation dynamic can still be discerned. Paul's metaphor of the fruit of the Spirit in Gal 5:22–23 (love, joy, peace, patience, and so on) gesture toward outward signs of the Spirit's work within an individual. These attributes can be detected via interpersonal interactions. When they are seen, Paul says, there the Spirit is at work. In one of his hymns, Ephrem sings,

> In a jar, the sun passes into water

6. Jensen, "Discerning the Spirit," 4.
7. Ephrem, *Hymns* 41.6.
8. Ambrose, *Holy Spirit* 1.4.

And produces hot fire inside the cold.[9]

In this way, Ephrem describes the interpenetration of the Divine Identities within the Trinity. The sun, the sun's ray, and the heat are all closely related, and together they cause the effect (fire). Can any one of them be removed from the equation without causing the effect to collapse? No. All are needed.

By extension—and again this is an analogy for the work of the Holy Spirit, and a thought experiment that I am suggesting—one could say that the Holy Spirit is given to persons (or *rests* on them, as the Bible often relates). This granting of the Spirit has an effect—in and through human lives—that cannot take place without the threefold collaboration of Holy Spirit, human creature, and the action of giving. The result is an interfusing that cannot be easily pulled apart without reversing or undoing the effect. Water mixed with salt stays salty, unless the salt is removed.

Freedom Is Still in the Picture

Throughout earthly human existence, the Holy Spirit works through individuals to draw all closer to God and God's purposes. However, a key aspect of being made in the image of God is that we are given a measure of autonomy. No one is ever coerced to cooperate with the Spirit. Even so, the perspicacity of the Spirit is gentle and relentless, forever trying to break through human sin and recalcitrance to soften hearts and align lives with the Divine will. Basil suggests that our goal is to be like God, "so far as is possible with human nature."[10] As that process accelerates, we are drawn more and more into the life of God, to the point where we participate in it.

From this perspective, "participating in the divine nature" should not be understood to mean that we *become God* or *become divine*. The China Christian Council helpfully notes that "Human beings are made in the image of God but cannot become gods."[11] For this reason, I am reluctant about the terms *theosis* and *divinization*. We remain thoroughly human, retain our human limitations, and are still liable to err. Even so, the Bible speaks of us being adopted through the Spirit, and the sacrament of baptism clearly gestures in that direction, as it ritualizes our inclusion within the body of Christ (the church) and the family of God. All this is the special work of the Spirit. She is fierce and gentle in trying to help human beings become loving, just,

9. Ephrem, *Hymns* 42.4.

10. Basil, *On the Holy Spirit* 1.2.

11. Joint National Conference, "Church Order," art. 6.

wise, and giving—more and more like Jesus, more and more like the one God who is all goodness, all love, all wisdom, all compassion.

Rogers speaks of fellowship with God as "the destiny of the human being."[12] Jesus Christ is the forerunner and model for all persons, because in his resurrection, through the power of the Holy Spirit, the human identity of God participates fully in the Divine identity. Moreover, Paul proclaims the union of human creatures with Christ "in a resurrection like his" (Rom 6:5). The pledge of resurrection to mortals is the promise of eternal life. That theme runs throughout Paul's letters. Eternal life is not a special resort destination for the exclusive enjoyment of human souls after death, but the full company of heaven delighting in human–divine intimacy. Or indeed, in the wideness of God's mercy and desire, eternal life is the fullness of divine intimacy with all creation.

All this is enacted through the power of the Holy Spirit, whose special vocation is to transform: mortal human life is transformed into an eternal life; the separations between God and human creatures are overcome; and the alienations among human individuals are healed (Eph 2:14–20). As Ambrose states, "Where the Spirit is, there is eternal life, for the Spirit himself . . . effects eternal life."[13] This vision and hope is anticipated in the church when believers are joined together in community (*koinonia*) through the Spirit, "having the same love, being in full accord and of one mind" (Phil 2:1–2).

The sign of this, in sacramental terms, is baptism. Baptism is the ritual action that embodies the rebirth that the Spirit brings about. But rebirth is not a process of restarting the engine of human life, or a reboot; it is "the eternal moment in which eternity touches time and puts an end to its transience . . . the moment of eternal livingness . . . it is something completely new in history."[14] The resurrection of Jesus Christ displays and continuously confirms this for Christians. Something new has happened; something new is happening; something new will happen. This newness that flows from the Spirit is eternal and cannot be halted. Indeed, it overcomes even the powers of evil and death.

An Even Greater Vision

Basil sees this in still grander terms:

12. Rogers, *After the Spirit*, 9.
13. Ambrose, *Holy Spirit* 2.3.
14. Moltmann, *Source of Life*, 30.

> Through the Holy Spirit comes the restoration to paradise, the ascent to the kingdom of heaven, the return to adopted sonship, the freedom to call God our Father and to become a companion of the grace of Christ, to be called a child of light, to participate in eternal glory, and . . . to have all fullness of blessing in this age and the age to come.[15]

The Holy Spirit is the pledge (*arrabon*—2 Cor 1:21–22) of all these blessings that will be fulfilled in due course, or that have already commenced. God does this, Basil says, because God desires "kinship" with us, rather than alienation.

Within the Christian community, especially when it is functioning in a healthy manner, we discover that we have been drawn into life with God. Through this communal encounter, and by learning from the Trinity's mutual self-giving, "human beings begin to participate already here below in the trinitarian life"[16]—that is, a life of mutual giving, joy, reconciliation, and justice. The Holy Spirit completes the action of redemption by bringing the redeemed into the family of God and the triune life. The Spirit works upon the human heart to make it open, "able and willing to receive" God; and thereby a person "participates in [the Spirit's] glory and therefore in the glory of God."[17]

Finally, to participate in the life of God is to share a portion of God's goodness and purposes, to will what God wills. To participate in the divine life is not to become divine, but to reflect the divine nature, by expressing the fruit of the Spirit, and loving as God loves.

Then Again . . .

Until now, I have proposed that one end of the continuum is preferable to the other—that is, understanding this dynamic as *participating* in the divine life without becoming divine, in contrast to claiming that humans can indeed become divine (theosis or divinization). But a word about this latter alternative is in order. Various authors within the Christian tradition do attest that the full trajectory of the Holy Spirit's work involves the *deifying* of human beings. In most Eastern Christian traditions, this is more commonly known as *theosis*. This teaching is not well attested in the United and Uniting Churches, nor in Protestantism generally. In fact, there often is silence about it.

15. Basil, *On the Holy Spirit* 15.35.

16. Rogers, *After the Spirit*, 145.

17. Barth, *Church Dogmatics* 2/1, 669–70, cited in Rogers, *After the Spirit*, 181.

Eugene Rogers (a Presbyterian from the United States) makes the distinction that "deification does not mean that human persons become trinitarian persons. They become deified human persons, not persons of deity."[18] I am not sure that this distinction is helpful or convincing. In any case, the threads of this teaching are not taken up by the United and Uniting denominations. The Roman Catholic tradition, in broad terms, is more open to the idea. The closest that Protestants usually come to it is in the language of sanctification (a distinctively Methodist emphasis) or perfection. These terms perhaps suggest a lower-voltage theological claim than deification, but it is authentic to United and Uniting perspectives, and is better suited to it.

Elsewhere, however, deification is deeply felt and believed as a theological truth. Basil expresses it in powerful and somewhat stark terms. From Basil's perspective, the illumination and perfection brought about by the Spirit finally results in

> foreknowledge of the future, understanding of mysteries, apprehension of secrets, distribution of graces, heavenly citizenship, the chorus with angels, unending joy, remaining in God, kinship with God, and the highest object of desire, becoming God.[19]

It could be argued that the root of this teaching about divinization lies in the Second Testament. Second Peter 1:3–4 teaches as follows:

> [God's] divine power has given us everything needed for life and godliness, through the knowledge of him who called us by his own glory and excellence. Thus he has given us, through these things, his precious and very great promises, so that through them you may escape from the corruption that is in the world because of lust and may become participants of the divine nature.

Here, "lust-corruption" (*epithumia phthoras*) might point toward distorted sexual behavior, but it is just as likely to point toward any craving for the wrong things. Freed from that craving, the author says, we can become participants (*koinōnoi*) in the divine nature (*theias physeōs*). The Greek root word is *physis*, meaning the distinctive inward essence of something—in this case, the "God-essence." This is strong, convicted language. The letter writer couches it in the context of Christ sharing his glory with believers.

18. Rogers, *After the Spirit*, 47.

19. Basil, *On the Holy Spirit* 9.23 .

If indeed, through God's gift, humans can share in the God-essence, the implications are intensely significant. Does this mean that we become more-than-human? Or become divine and are no longer human? A major difficulty with this line of inquiry is that there is little in the Bible to supplement this teaching. The ten other uses of *physis* in the Second Testament refer to human nature, or the nature of non-human animals. The term is only used in relation to *theos* (God or the divine) here in 2 Pet 1:4. Furthermore, nowhere else does the Bible speak of this human participation in the divine nature. Nevertheless, it is a theme that appears from time to time in Christian writing. Those more convicted of its truth will need to make the case for believing in true divinization. The closest I think we can fairly come—and consistent with the doctrinal tendencies of the United and Uniting Churches—is a lower-voltage claim to sharing or participating in God's life, much like one participates in the immediacy of a family relationship.

EXCURSUS: QUANTUM ENTANGLEMENT

In a rather different idiom, we could explore the question of human participation in the divine life through the phenomena of quantum entanglement. Quantum entanglement was first described in the 1930s by persons such as Albert Einstein and Edwin Schrödinger. While it is a relatively recent discovery, much of what it describes resonates with many Christian accounts of the Holy Spirit's influence upon and presence within the human creature. I am far from an expert on the subject, but a brief summary is worthwhile, even if it is imperfect.

The core idea of quantum entanglement is that two subatomic particles, like electrons, are extremely closely interrelated and affect one another; and "they remain connected even when separated by vast distances." They have similar or even identical properties, to the extent that when looking at them, it is impossible or nearly impossible to distinguish them from each other. The particles also exchange information and are highly mutualistic in their relating. Perhaps most astonishingly, "entanglement can also occur among hundreds, millions, and even more particles. . . . When hundreds of particles become entangled, they still act as one unified object."[20]

In light of this, there is a possibility of describing human participation in the divine life in a way that correlates with a naturalistic phenomenon. Just as two subatomic particles—or indeed, millions—communicate and impact one another; are connected even at a distance; have nearly identical

20. Caltech Science Exchange, "What Is Entanglement?"

properties; and are virtually impossible to distinguish, so also the Holy Spirit's life and the life of human creatures can be seen as deeply, mutually interrelated. The quantum description of particles as "together-in-separation" is an attractive way to speak (at least analogously) of the free and sovereign Holy Spirit in relation to a human self, or to creation as a whole.[21] They are together, mutually impactful, yet remain distinct realities.

A key difference in my proposal about quantum entanglement as an analogy for the human–Holy Spirit relationship is that in quantum entanglement, the phenomenon arises when a single particle is duplicated and has a "twin," as it were. What was once single is now a dyad. In contrast, I suggest that in the dynamics of a human life participating with the Holy Spirit (living in agreement and alignment with the will of God), these two realities (human and divine) live in harmony with one another only *after* having been misaligned or even striving in opposition to each other. We do not begin in alignment, especially if we factor in the reality of sin. A traditional way to speak of this, then, would be in terms of repentance from sin, redemption by Christ, and sanctification by the Spirit. Alignment is not automatic and natural, as in quantum mechanics. A correlating teaching is found in Ephesians:

> You were dead through the trespasses and sins. . . . For by grace you have been saved through faith, and this is not your own doing; it is the gift of God. . . . Remember that you were at that time without Christ . . . having no hope and without God in the world. But now in Christ Jesus you who once were far off have been brought near by the blood of Christ.[22]

The possibility that human life can participate in the divine life (without "becoming divine") is deeply appealing. It is the promised climax of what traditional theology calls sanctification and perfection. But unlike a "dance of entanglement" which "materializes not from any one particle but from the connections between them,"[23] any divine–human inter-participation arises because *it is the will of God* to bring about the transformation of the human creature and indeed all creation. The Holy Spirit desires, empowers, and enacts this transformation. In Kenneth Bakken's words, "Conformity with the will of God is the work of the Holy Spirit, not the result of the struggling of the [human] will."[24] The human creature learns and grows through the process, but is not its originator. Nor are the two selves (human

21. See Polkinghorne and Welker, *Faith in the Living God*, 53.

22. Eph 2:1, 8, 12–13.

23. Caltech Science Exchange, "What Is Entanglement?"

24. Bakken, "Holy Spirit and Theosis," 413.

and divine) merged into a single reality. As Hall writes, participation in the life of God is not "destructive of our individual personhood. . . . The Spirit remains God's Spirit [and is not] ontologically amalgamated with our spirits."[25] Two "someones" in covenant remain distinct, and do not absorb each other. The quantum model might help to shed light on the problem of theosis, as described earlier in this chapter.

Curiously, I believe that this dynamic of quantum entanglement is attested in ancient Christian authors, though of course in different terms. Paul favored language that suggested that the Holy Spirit can live in a person, or in one's heart. "But you are not in the flesh," he advises the Christian community in Rome.

> You are in the Spirit, since *the Spirit of God dwells in you*. . . . If the Spirit of him who raised Jesus from the dead *dwells in you*, he who raised Christ Jesus from the dead will give life to your mortal bodies.[26]

Gregory of Nyssa (c. 335–95) perhaps builds on Paul in saying, "All things are in Him, and He is in all things."[27] Isaac of Nineveh tells the reader that when aware of the Spirit in moments of prayer, "One's heart becomes 'full of him' [the Spirit], and the Holy Spirit excites in one the things that one prays, as if co-mingling himself with the praying human mind."[28] This notion of *comingling* sounds similar to quantum entanglement. John of Dalyatha (c. 690–780) "urges his reader to 'breathe the Spirit of life' . . . so that Life may mingle with one's material substance."[29]

The initiative God takes toward human beings to bless, forgive, restore, and recreate them in the Holy Spirit leads ultimately to this kind of "mingling" or "entanglement." Michael Ramsey writes, "The response of the believers to God's action towards them is enabled by God's action within them. God within responds to God beyond, as the Spirit prays within them and mingles his prayers with theirs."[30] All these expressions have resonance with quantum entanglement.

While modern scientific work on entanglement is principally focused on subatomic realities, and rarely makes mention of God or spiritual matters, there is merit in exploring quantum theory to better understand how it

25. Hall, *Professing*, 164.
26. Rom 8:9–11.
27. Gregory of Nyssa, "On What it Means to Call Oneself a Christian."
28. Seppälä, "Holy Spirit in Isaac of Nineveh," 139.
29. Seppälä, "Holy Spirit in Isaac of Nineveh," 141.
30. Ramsey, *Holy Spirit*, 56.

is that human life or indeed the life of all creation can participate in the life of God. "The very life energy of the Eternal has flowed into the lives of the believers," teaches the United Church in Jamaica and the Cayman Islands. "That is the meaning of the power of the Spirit."[31]

FOR REFLECTION OR DISCUSSION

1. Whether talking about baptism or Jesus breathing the Holy Spirit into his followers, both body and soul seem to be involved in our participation in the divine life. How do you understand the connection between body and soul when it comes to our participation in God?
2. How would you describe the difference between participating in the divine life and becoming divine?
3. What is your response to the section on quantum entanglement and human participation in the divine life?

31. United Church in Jamaica and the Cayman Islands, *Our Church*, 82.

Chapter 15

For the Sake of All: Universal and Unifying

In chapter 7, to introduce Part Two, I noted that the Holy Spirit acts in a purposeful and personal way toward and within creation as a whole; toward and within individual human creatures (for the sake of each one); and toward and within humankind as a collective, both in the church and beyond it (for the sake of all). In the next three chapters, we will focus on the Spirit's actions in the last of these categories: toward and within humankind as a collective, in the church and beyond it. As described in the last five chapters, the personal, individual dimensions of the Holy Spirit's presence and activity are the ways that people most often experience the Holy Spirit. We turn now to the ways She works for the good of all through collective presence, power, and action in the Christian community, the church. *For the sake of all*, the Spirit is at work.

With profound care and love, the Spirit's deeply relational orientation draws humankind as a whole into the life of God. "I will put my spirit [*ruach*] within you," says God to the people—the collective nation—in Ezekiel's hearing (Ezek 36:27). This prophecy comes in Ezekiel's narrative immediately before his astonishing vision of the valley of the dry bones (Ezek 37). Here, the overwhelming power of goodness and life sweeps through a valley of dry, lifeless bones through the *ruach* (breath-wind-Spirit) of God. Filled with *ruach*, the bones rise to new life, knit together with sinews and flesh. Then Ezekiel hears God say, "Mortal, these bones are the *whole* house of Israel . . . [and to them I say] I will put my Spirit with you, and you shall live" (Ezek 37:11, 14). Life, transformed life, is the will and desire of God. God the Holy Spirit enacts these good ends, for the sake of all.

On the day of Pentecost, as it is related in Acts 2, the Holy Spirit rushes in upon the gathered apostles and the thousands of others who have gathered in Jerusalem for this religiously significant harvest festival. Many nations have gathered. They are there to worship, celebrate, give thanks, connect, and renew their faith. No doubt family bonds are renewed and strengthened, and commercial ties are made and remade. Perhaps there is a little sightseeing going on. In the midst of this, the disciples of Jesus, who are now his apostles and specially commissioned to carry the news of his life, death, and resurrection (Matt 28:19–20), have also remained in Jerusalem to worship and discern their next steps. They have witnessed the ascension of Jesus (Acts 1:6–11). They have chosen Matthias as a new member of their group, to replace Judas (Acts 1:12–26). And now, "suddenly," the sound of "a violent wind" comes from heaven, and "divided tongues, as of fire, appeared among them . . . all of them were filled with the Holy Spirit." This exciting and life-altering day is often understood as fulfilling Jesus's promises that the Holy Spirit would be sent upon his followers:

> The Advocate [*paraklētos*], the Holy Spirit, whom the Father will send in my name, will teach you everything and remind you of all that I have said to you.[1]

> But you will receive power when the Holy Spirit has come upon you, and you will be my witnesses in Jerusalem, in all Judea and Samaria, and to the ends of the earth.[2]

From that room "upstairs" where they had gathered, the apostles spill out into the street. They are amazed to see that the manifestations of the Spirit continue among the international crowds gathered in Jerusalem (Luke, the author, is careful to point out the international character of those who were present). The visitors are delighted and perplexed to hear the proclamation of the Christian gospel in their own languages. In the midst of the joyful chaos, Peter stands up to proclaim that all this is the fulfillment of a prophecy of Joel: "I will pour out my Spirit upon all flesh" (Acts 2:17/Joel 2:28). Among other consequences of that day's manifestations of the Spirit, Luke reports that three thousand persons were converted and baptized (Acts 2:41). The Spirit is at work, for the sake of all—not just a special elite class or nationality. "At Pentecost, the church became a diverse, intercultural, polycentric, polyvocal, Spirit-filled body," writes Graham Hill of the Uniting Church of Australia. "Pentecost exemplifies the Spirit's vision of inclusion, where no culture, language, or nation holds exclusive claim

1. John 14:26.

2. Acts 1:8.

to the gospel. . . . [It] symbolises breaking barriers, borders, divisions, and exclusions and the call of God's Spirit for the church to join in the universal mission of God in Jesus Christ."[3] This day of Pentecost, with its powerful manifestations of the Holy Spirit, is often described as the "birthday" of the church. On this day, She calls together and animates the whole Christian movement in a significant and public way, empowering and commissioning them for their unique ministry in the world.

Following the day of Pentecost, her work and presence transforms the whole Christian community. The Spirit alters their way of life. They develop a kind of voluntary poverty for the sake of the common good (Acts 4:32–35). They worship together and serve others (Acts 2:43–47). More and more conversions take place (Acts 2:47, 9:31), and the Holy Spirit continues to move among all the gathered community, not just a select few (Acts 4:31). As Ramsey notes, the "Holy Spirit comes upon the company of believers in a way which affects profoundly their subsequent life as a community: prophetic speech, joy, fellowship, conversions. . . . A new age is here."[4] The ongoing life of the Christian movement, ever since, has been shaped in monumental ways by this collective action by the Spirit. The very identity of the church catholic (universal), the gift of unity, the sacraments, the ministries of preaching and teaching, and other forms of service are all empowered by the One Spirit—for the sake of all.

The Church Catholic (Universal)

The Niceno-Constantinopolitan Creed speaks of the "one, holy, catholic, and apostolic church." Catholic with an uppercase "C" often refers to the Roman Catholic Church in English usage. But here, *catholic* means more than only the "Roman Catholic" tradition. Rather, *catholic* is rooted in the Greek word for *universal* or *worldwide*. The nature of the church as worldwide or "catholic" arises from the action of the Holy Spirit to call the church into existence, because the Spirit has a worldwide mission. The Spirit commissions the church to participate in her mission, which takes all of creation into view (thus "universal"). As the Uniting Presbyterian Church in Southern Africa notes, "The Church has been called into being by the will of God, who gathers all people into a fellowship in Christ, which is created and sustained by the power of the Holy Spirit."[5] This is a crucial distinction. The church exists because God the Spirit wills it to exist, to fulfill the divine

3. Hill, "Contemporary Issues," 41–42.

4. Ramsey, *Holy Spirit*, 37.

5. Uniting Presbyterian Church in Southern Africa, *Manual*, 15.

purpose, not because of "our enthusiasm, our 'involvement,' our activities."[6] Indeed, the church is always highly reliant on the Holy Spirit to guide and empower it. In the words of the Uniting Church in Australia, the church "has the gift of the Spirit in order that it may not lose the way."[7]

The old saying "The church doesn't have a mission, the mission has a church" points to the *missio dei*—the mission of God. It is the mission of God to redeem and transform all creation. That mission is undertaken in and through the church (and beyond it), by the power of the Holy Spirit. In other words, the Christian movement is called into being, from the day of Pentecost onward, for the sake of the purposes of God's mission. Zizioulas writes, "The Spirit is not something that 'animates' a Church which already somehow exists. The Spirit makes the Church *be*."[8] The church is not the result of a few well-meaning people sitting around a campfire or meeting table and coming up with the idea of a community of faith. The church exists because through it, the Holy Spirit intends something good: the divine mission. Her many gifts to individuals throughout all epochs are always intended *for the common good*, as Paul says in 1 Cor 12:4–7. Whatever gifts may be found among individual members of the church are never given only for their personal benefit. They are given so that all may be built up and together strengthened for the mission of God in the world.

Testimony and Service

To accomplish her mission, the Spirit first makes possible the sharing of the gospel—the "good message"—about Jesus Christ throughout the world. This is not an argument for "Christianizing" all creation, as if non-Christians play no role in the mission of God. Indeed, I would argue the contrary: God is able to work through all religions and all peoples, even atheists! The Holy Spirit is *free* to work where, how, and through whom She wills, including non-Christians. Still, it is a distinctive action of the Holy Spirit to bring the Christian movement into being and to sustain its life, so that Christians may serve together as an instrument of God's will and purposes. The first move in that direction is the work of proclamation (*kerygma*): sharing the gospel. The Holy Spirit empowers preaching first of all. Peter's public proclamation on the day of Pentecost is a sign of this.

The Spirit was at work through the ancient prophets, calling the people to repentance and renewal. The Spirit was at work through the apostolic

6. Hall, *Confessing*, 60.

7. Uniting Church in Australia, *Basis of Union* §3.

8. Zizioulas, *Being as Communion*, 131.

witness of the Second Testament, in people like Paul, Peter, Aquila, Priscilla, and Lydia. The Spirit is at work among contemporary prophets and apostles today. Irenaeus remarks that God "promised, that in the last times He would pour [the Spirit] upon [God's] servants and handmaids, that they might prophesy."[9] The gift of speaking and teaching (*didachē*), to guide God's people, assists them to overcome injustice, to work for the common good, and to share the news of Christ's redemptive promises. In the Holy Spirit, the dividing line between Jew and gentile—and divisions between any groups—can be set aside as unity emerges (Eph 2:18–22). The proclamation of the gospel, as the church bears witness to Christ in the wider world, is meant to bring reconciliation to all persons. The message of the church is meant, above all, to be the good news of God's desire to provoke peace and to overcome division among the peoples of the world.

Ultimately, the whole Christian movement, all God's people, in all places and times, are drawn into the mystery and power of the resurrection of Jesus by the power of the Holy Spirit. This is in accord with the will of God, who does not desire that anyone be excluded from redemption and the divine eternal blessing.[10] Because it is the will of God, the Holy Spirit (the "Spirit of adoption") is at work to draw all persons together as "children of God," "heirs," "citizens," and "members of the household of God."[11] To this end, followers of Christ are "marked with the seal of the promised Holy Spirit; this is the pledge of our inheritance towards redemption as God's own people" (Eph 1:13–14). The "holy temple of the Lord" is found in Christ, but the building of it and the human inhabitation of it are the work of the Spirit (Eph 2:21–22).

On this basis of inclusion across all times and places, by the Holy Spirit, God calls the church into existence. As the United Church of Christ (USA) celebrates,

> You bestow upon us your Holy Spirit,
> creating and renewing the church of Jesus Christ,
> binding in covenant faithful people of all ages, tongues, and races.[12]

This Christian vision of an inclusive Spirit is in turn grounded in the prophets of the First Testament, like Joel, who overheard God say, "I will pour out

9. Irenaeus, *Against Heresies* 3.17.1.

10. See Eph 1:9–10. See also Anselm, *Cur Deus Homo*: God "created [human beings] holy that [they] might enjoy a state of blessedness" (1.9). Anselm (c. 1033–1109) further writes that human beings were "made for [eternal] happiness" (1.10).

11. Rom 8:14–17; Eph 2:18–19.

12. United Church of Christ [USA], "Statement of Faith (1981)."

my spirit on *all* flesh" (Joel 2:28; emphasis added). This is the precise passage Peter remembered when he got up to preach on the day of Pentecost, as the Spirit rushed mightily upon him and thousands of others. Peter recognized the global, inclusive Spirit in this moment. On that day of profound revelation, ecstatic experience, and international representation, the church of Jesus Christ found its birth.

The existence of the church relies, then, upon the will and purposes of God, as expressed through the Holy Spirit. Indeed, without the Spirit, there is no church. As Irenaeus said, "Where the Church is, there is the Spirit; and where the Spirit of God is, there is the Church."[13] The Holy Spirit calls the church into being, finally, for the sake of God's passion: the transformation of the world. There is a cosmic and mystical understanding of the church at play here. But the constituting of the church always also takes concrete form. It is also always local, taking its form among real people in real time. This might be a local congregation, parish, house church, or prayer group. It might exist online. The mystical body of Christ, the church, is invariably united with locally situated communities of believers and their physical bodies. The physical presence of believers also transcends space and time, and is united mystically with the person of Jesus Christ. The phrase "the communion of saints" in the Apostles' Creed gestures toward this transcendent reality: that *communion* is local, personal, interpersonal, global, historical, and mystical.

The idea of the *mystical* body of Christ is not strongly emphasized in United and Uniting Churches, but neither is it rejected. The real presence of the Holy Spirit within a local community of faith tends to have a stronger emphasis in United and Uniting thought. As Rogers remarks, "The Spirit does not float free from concrete human bodies, but rests upon, inspires, and takes embodied life from them."[14] The same can be said of relationships within the community of a local church—it is precisely in and through the concreteness of those embodied relationships that the Spirit acts. Through *koinonia* (community or fellowship) as well as acts of worship (*leitourgia*) and social action and service (*diakonia*), the Spirit is active in real bodies and real relationships, in real times and places.

The Gift of Unity

The unity of the church is also an aspect of the Spirit's work, enabling effective, collective witness and mission by Christians. Once again, the phrase

13. Irenaeus, *Against Heresies* 3.24.1.

14. Rogers, *After the Spirit*, 191.

in the Niceno-Constantinopolitan Creed—"one, holy, catholic, and apostolic church"—implies a singleness to the Christian movement. However, it would be naïve and shortsighted to claim that the church is *one* today, at least in terms of its outward forms, such as worship, governance, and unified theological perspectives. Alas, there are many differences and divisions, from one sect critiquing another, to two large bodies like Protestantism and Roman Catholicism who still cannot share the Eucharist together. These and so many other barriers to full fellowship are a blight upon Christianity that require continual dialogue, humility, repentance, insight, and wisdom from the Holy Spirit. The Armenian Evangelical Church prays that "by your Holy Spirit we may, with the saints of all ages, come into full communion with you and with one another."[15] The motto of The United Church of Canada since its beginnings in 1925 has echoed Jesus's prayer in John 17:21, "that all may be one."

For many Christians, unity is symbolized in the episcopal leadership of an office, such as bishop, metropolitan, patriarch, or pope. For others, that episcopal function is distributed through a collective, such as synod, presbytery, conference, or regional structure. Unity can also be expressed as a spiritual reality that does not rely upon institutional structures or linkages. The World Council of Churches and other interchurch organizations work toward this goal, as they enact multilateral collaboration on a great range of themes and priorities.

In all cases, the Holy Spirit is at work. Underlying every form of "church" is the unity expressed in shared membership in the Body of Christ, made real through the Holy Spirit in the act of baptism. The one Body of Christ who together share in baptism are sustained "in a web of belonging, or mutual accountability and support."[16] Personal union with Jesus Christ is also envisaged. "The Spirit unites us to Christ," teaches the Uniting Presbyterian Church in Southern Africa, "and to one another in his Body."[17] A still greater future unity is also anticipated by the Uniting Church in Australia, which testifies that "God in Christ has given to all people in the church the Holy Spirit as a pledge and foretaste of that coming reconciliation and renewal which is the end in view for the whole creation."[18] This reflects Paul's teaching that the Holy Spirit is an *arrabon*—a foretaste of what is to come (2 Cor 1:21–22).

15. Tootikian, *Pastor's Manual*, 135.
16. World Council of Churches, *Nature and Purpose*, 50.
17. Uniting Presbyterian Church in Southern Africa, *Manual*, 26.
18. Uniting Church in Australia, *Basis of Union* §3.

The Holy Spirit is keen to foster life and unity among Christians. The mission of Peter to Cornelius and his household in Acts 10—11 illustrates this. It is a story of overcoming divisions. As Priscille Djomhoue of the United Protestant Church of Belgium and the Evangelical Church of Cameroon reflects,

> Acts 10.1—11.18 is the story of the breaking of geographical and ethnic barriers. Divisions that exist among different Christian confessions are due to traditions that people have developed over time and which today are part of their identity. . . . [They can create] separations and prejudices and are not able to promote the flourishing of all Christians. By asking Peter to kill and eat impure animals, the Holy Spirit, whose role is to unite . . . invites Christians to transcend their structural differences and to work with the common aim of promoting the Kingdom of God . . . without confessional distinction.[19]

Learning to set aside differences requires effort and humility, trusting the Spirit rather than our own preferences and favorite ideas.

Adrian Jacobs also testifies to the gift of Christian unity from the Spirit in his lifetime: "I have worked in Indigenous interdenominational settings for thirty years and rarely, almost never, have I been in a theological debate. There were strongly held positions, but respect—not rancour—marked people's attitude toward different opinions. This is the unity of the One Spirit."[20] Jacobs says that, in contrast, an emphasis on denominational differences and distinctiveness is indeed contrary to the unifying work of the Spirit. Unity, then, does not require uniformity. Diversity is often a hallmark of the Spirit. This desire of the Spirit for life and unity is acutely perceived by those in the United and Uniting traditions. As Sahu of the Church of North India writes, "It is the living Spirit which can and does give life to bodies which lack in some measure the fullness of the church's true teaching and order. It is grace that defines and determines the relation."[21] Paul lifts up the diversity within the body of Christ and also affirms that "in the one Spirit we were all baptized . . . and we were all made to drink of one Spirit" (1 Cor 12:13). The one Spirit longs for the unity of her people.

Luther cherishes the oneness of the body of Christ as well—even though he was at the heart of one of its main fissures. The Holy Spirit, he says, "calls, gathers, enlightens, and sanctifies the whole Christian church on

19. Djomhoue, "Manifestations of Ecumenism in Africa," 366.

20. Jacobs, "Holy Spirit," 163.

21. Sahu, *United and Uniting*, 63.

earth, and keeps it with Jesus Christ in the one true faith."[22] The unity of the church, then, is in Christ, and is *mystical* more than it is a matter of single forms and approaches. Some traditions might use wine at communion, and others grape juice. Some will have bishops, and others have presbyteries. Some will emphasize full independence of each congregation, and others will value connectivity though dioceses or synods. But diversity, in itself, is not necessarily problematic. K. H. Ting of the China Christian Council notes that in Rev 2 and 3, "The Spirit did not want to make all seven churches conform to a single pattern. . . . The Spirit was apparently willing for all the churches to share the guidance they received with each other and multiply the grace all the more through sharing."[23] Diversity is not a barrier to unity, but seems in fact to be part of God's intention. It's not a defect, as the saying goes, but a feature of the divine purposes.

The Grace of Difference

How Christians respond to their differences is crucial. In the past (and sometimes in the present), terrible conflict over differences, including great violence, has overtaken the church, whose vocation should be peace and reconciliation. This can unfold despite the Christian calling to "signify, participate in, and anticipate the new humanity God wants."[24] Responding to difference cannot be merely a matter of out-arguing or out-muscling other voices. Rather, as Ennis Macleod of the Uniting Church in Australia teaches, "It is the whole church that discerns the way when it is alert to what the Holy Spirit is saying. . . . Recognizing and valuing the movement of the Spirit . . . requires the church to listen to the diverse voices of the people in the church."[25] The Church of North India has similarly adopted a principle of discernment in the face of significant diversity: "Those of diverse convictions will be led together in the unity of the Spirit to learn what is his will in these matters of difference."[26]

Unity is often proclaimed as a desirable goal for the church. Some long for organic unity, in which a single Christian entity or denomination can emerge by combining previous, smaller denominations. This has been the vision of many United and Uniting Churches. The existence and life of these "union" churches all around the world is a beautiful testament to the

22. Luther, *Small Catechism*, art. 3.

23. Ting, "What the Spirit Is Saying," 394.

24. World Council of Churches, *Nature and Purpose*, 16.

25. Macleod, "On Not Losing the Way," 98.

26. Church of North India, *Constitution*, clause 5.

power and reality of that goal. Those who advocated for the formation of the Church of South India, for example, "had the conviction that the Holy Spirit was definitely leading them toward unity."[27] The unity of the United Church of Christ in Japan is also received as the gift of the Holy Spirit.[28] The Church of North India likewise sees itself as the result of the Spirit's work amid many prior, divergent prior Christian groups. The Church of North India calls itself "the fruit of the continuous working of the Holy Spirit in the church from apostolic times down to our own day."[29] Similarly, T. Valentino Sitoy Jr. writes that the overcoming of differences by the founding denominations that formed the United Church of Christ in the Philippines "can perhaps only be the work of the Holy Spirit."[30]

The unity of the church, even in its great diversity, is always in view for the Holy Spirit. Yet differences do not need to be hidden, harmonized, or eradicated. The persistent existence of differing nations in the "end times" foreseen in the book of Revelation indicates that all peoples are welcome in the vision of God's final purposes. Cultural and religious eradication, in the name of assimilation (which was for so long the goal of European colonizers in many parts of the world), "is not the inevitable end" or purpose of the Holy Spirit.[31] Rather, the biblical vision is one of embracing diversity, even rejoicing in it. God's realm is not monochrome.

On a smaller scale, the Spirit also enables unity within and between congregations, parishes, and individuals. When a family experiences reconciliation after a period of strife and division, the Holy Spirit has been at work. When fractures and pains that endure over a period of time within a local congregation are gradually healed, the Holy Spirit is at work. One such story comes from Leslie Boseto of the Solomon Islands. Boseto was the first indigenous moderator for the United Church of Papua New Guinea and the Solomon Islands.[32] He tells of an episode in which the people of Liuliu village had been in an extended conflict:

27. Burnabas, "Theological Vision," 48. Consider also the Church of South India's *Constitution*, 2.3: "[We believe] that the Holy Spirit has guided those Churches into this union in order that this same work of evangelization may be the more effectually fulfilled, in accordance with the prayer which Christ prayed that by the unity of His disciples the world might know that He had been sent to be its Saviour."

28. United Church of Christ in Japan, "Constitution."

29. "An Affirmation of Faith and Commitment: A Statement for Use in the Church of North India," §I, in Sahu, *United and Uniting*, 97.

30. Sitoy, *Several Springs*, ch. 6.

31. Jacobs, "Holy Spirit," 164.

32. Moore, "Boseto, Leslie."

> On Sunday, 20 September 1985, at about 8 a.m. I began to feel the presence of the Spirit. At 10 o'clock in the morning I preached on the subject, "Let God transform you." The message was very simple and yet very powerful, the announcement of the message of the Lord's transforming power. At the end of my sermon, I made an appeal. Most of the people were standing up; they were not moving towards the front where I was standing, but moving towards their neighbours and enemies, embracing one another. They were weeping! We could not hear anything but singing and crying![33]

Boseto's story illustrates in a concrete and local context how essential reconciliation is, and how reconciliation is possible within the power and guidance of the Holy Spirit. Her work draws human beings toward one another in peace, and draws all of creation toward God in harmony. God is not satisfied to leave the world alienated by sin, and so Jesus Christ comes and through his death and resurrection forgives us. God the Spirit is not content to leave communities unreconciled, and so She comes to transform and build unity.

Recalling Augustine's phrase "the bond of love," Kärkäinnen writes that "the Spirit unites us with the rest of the church, and as the eschatological gift, with the purposes of God's coming new creation. . . . [The Spirit] inspires us to transcend ourselves and reach out to others to receive and to give."[34] The fullness of unity remains elusive on earth. It may well be an eschatological hope rather than a practical hope for any given lifetime. There is indeed a mystical dimension to the unity of the church that exceeds human capacities to live and act in unity. But by the grace of God, the unity of the church exists within its "common partaking in God's own life whose innermost being is communion."[35] Some things do practically unite Christians, however, such as regard for the Bible; claiming and proclaiming the centrality of Jesus Christ and his saving work; desiring the wellbeing of all people; working to transform the world in accordance with God's realm; and seeking to love as God has loved us. "A central role of the Spirit in Christian community," says Pauw, "is to bind believers to God and to each other in loving union."[36] This union founded in love is perhaps the greatest of the Spirit's gifts, for in love and in unity the church can do far more than it is ever able to do in division and hostility.

33. Cited in World Council of Churches, *Come, Holy Spirit*, 65.

34. Kärkäinnen, *Pneumatology*, 184.

35. World Council of Churches, *Nature and Purpose*, 10.

36. Pauw, "Holy Spirit and Scripture," 28.

FOR REFLECTION OR DISCUSSION

1. "It is precisely in and through the concreteness of embodied relationships that the Spirit acts." Can you describe an example of the Holy Spirit acting in and through relationships in your local church, family, or community?
2. The Holy Spirit brings unity but not uniformity. She gives us grace to build relationships despite differences. Balancing unity and difference can feel like a monumental task! What are some ways that we can create space for the Holy Spirit to build and maintain relationships, even as we leave room for diversity?
3. This chapter refers to the universality of the Holy Spirit's action: "The Holy Spirit is free to work where, how, and through whom She wills, including non-Christians." How does this concept relate to what you understand (or were previously taught) about the Holy Spirit?

Chapter 16

Sacraments and Service

In this chapter, the theme of the Holy Spirit's work "for the sake of all" continues, focusing now on the sacraments and Christian service, including ministry. These reflections sharpen our attention toward the specifics of the Spirit's actions. Outlining as clearly as possible all that She does will help us get away from the unhelpful vagueness of supposing that She does "something" or "everything" (see chapter 8).

THE SACRAMENTS

Just as the Holy Spirit acts through the church universal and through the gift of the Bible, She acts through the sacraments for the sake of all. To be sure, the sacraments bless individuals—and thank God for that! Receiving the sacraments does indeed encourage individuals and draw them closer to the heart of God: "The Spirit makes our sacraments deep moments of connection with the life of heaven."[1] But the sacraments are given in the first instance to bless the whole community of the body of Christ, to strengthen, build up, and commission God's people for mission. "True worshipers," says Jesus in the Gospel according to John, "will worship the Father in spirit [*pneuma*] and in truth . . . God is spirit [*pneuma*]" (John 4:23–24). Such "spiritual worship" is, nevertheless, enacted with the material frame of human existence. It is in that materiality—saturated by the Holy Spirit—that Christians can discover the work and presence of the Holy Spirit through the sacraments. Protestant Christians, such as United and Uniting Church people, hold that there are only two sacraments: baptism and communion (also called the Lord's Supper or the Eucharist). Accordingly, my reflections

1. United Reformed Church [UK], *What Do We Believe*, 4.

will be focused here on baptism and communion. A broader treatment of the sacraments (as understood in the Roman Catholic or Orthodox traditions, for example) would rightly consider more than these two.

It is a distinctive task of the Holy Spirit to animate the sacraments, giving them power to awaken and strengthen faith, and to draw believers closer to Jesus Christ. "The sacraments," writes Calvin, "properly fulfill their office only when the Spirit, that inward teacher, comes to them, by whose power alone hearts are penetrated and affections moved and our souls opened for the sacraments to enter in."[2] Apart from the Holy Spirit, the sacraments would be pointless rituals. "You do not receive mere water at the washing [of baptism], but spiritual grace with the water," suggests Cyril of Jerusalem. "When you are about to descend into the water, look for salvation not from the water's ordinary properties, but from the action of the Holy Spirit."[3] Without the Spirit, the material substances of wine, bread, and water would be nothing more than collections of molecules and compounds.

Accordingly, prayers for the Holy Spirit normally accompany sacramental celebrations. For example, the *epiclēsis* is always properly part of the communion liturgy. Such a prayer to invite the Holy Spirit can be found within The United Church of Canada's communion settings:

> Loving God, pour out your Holy Spirit upon us and upon these gifts,
> that they may be for us the body and blood
> of our Saviour Jesus Christ.
> Grant that we may be for the world the body of Christ,
> redeemed through his blood,
> serving and reconciling all people to you.[4]

Similarly, at baptism, the faithful pray for the Spirit to come:

> Send, O God, your Holy Spirit upon us and upon this water,
> that all who are gathered under this sign,
> being one in Christ,
> may be nurtured by the bread of life.[5]

The presider continues, after placing water upon the head of the baptized person:

> [Baptisee's name], the power of the Holy Spirit work within you,

2. Calvin, *Institutes* 4.14.9.

3. Cyril of Jerusalem, *Catechetical Lectures* 3.3, 3.4, cited in Day, "Cyril of Jerusalem," 79.

4. United Church of Canada, *Sunday Liturgy*, 18.

5. United Church of Canada, *Baptism and Renewal*, 13.

that being born of water and the Spirit,
you may be a faithful witness of Jesus Christ.[6]

Gathered Christians cannot take for granted that the Spirit will be present, nor can the congregation rightly expect that She will "appear" if the right words are uttered. This would be an act of magic, like an incantation—not the action of the free and sovereign Spirit of God. Rather, She comes of her own free will, choosing to bless and inhabit the sacramental celebration, elements, and worshipers. The Spirit can and will come, indeed, quite apart from the holiness or worthiness of the sacramental presider, who is the Spirit's instrument, but not the source of the blessing.

This endowment of the Spirit transforms the people and enables them to live and love more faithfully in the Way of Jesus: "By means of the sacraments the Spirit confirms our faith, binds us to Christ, and incorporates us in one body."[7] This collective transformation is the point: All who gather in worship ask for and are given whatever the Spirit ordains. In harmony with the Spirit's intentions for creation, the sacraments point to an alternative world order, where *all* are equal; where *all* get fed and washed; where grace is distributed to *all* without regard for status, color, height, age, size, economic power, gender, sexual identity, or political ideology. The sacraments model the realm of God in microcosm. They are signs of another way, another path through this world, where Christ alone is Lord—not Caesar, not the market, not the Self, nor any other false claimants to our allegiance. This communal reorientation to the way of Jesus is distinctively the work of the Spirit in the sacraments.

Baptism

Often, baptism is observed as a ritual of welcome that celebrates the birth of a child. Parents present their infants to the gathered community and to God, seeking blessing and, through their own faith, the incorporation of the child into the Body of Christ. For older children, teens, and adults, it can take on a more direct meaning when a person chooses for themselves to be part of the Christian community. But it is also saturated with deeper, broader, and more powerful meanings in Christian thought. If being "born of water and the Spirit" refers to the ritual of baptism in John 3:5, then baptism is the action that draws persons into the realm of God.

6. United Church of Canada, *Baptism and Renewal*, 14.

7. Uniting Presbyterian Church in Southern Africa, *Manual*, 30.

The sacramental action of transformation is again the keynote in this moment. In baptism, Basil says, "the Spirit infuses life-giving power, renewing our souls from the death of sin to their original life. . . . Thus, if there is some grace in the water, it is not from the nature of the water, but from the presence of the Spirit."[8] Even at the baptism of Jesus, the model for the rest of humankind, the Holy Spirit's presence is vital. She is the power of God to commission Jesus to ministry. Through the action of baptism, the Spirit both incorporates the baptized person into the family of God and signifies God's work to overcome sin and its power. This is perhaps what Baptizing John was thinking of when he spoke about his cousin, Jesus the Messiah, saying, "He will baptize you with the Holy Spirit and fire" (Matt 3:11).

As the active presence of God in the sacrament of baptism, the Holy Spirit is the gracious power that unifies, creating anew a dynamic life in God for each individual and the community they share with others. The significance of this always unfolds within the whole body of Christ—when the Spirit acts in the sacraments, it is always for the good of the whole. "At baptism we receive the Holy Spirit," teaches the World Council of Churches, and "we are admitted to the community of faith and we become heirs of a hope for today and for hereafter. But baptism has also ethical and social implications."[9] Those implications draw the baptized person well beyond their personal objectives and interests. In this sense, the power of the Holy Spirit to sanctify the baptized individual moves through them to sanctify the whole community, and through that community, to sanctify the whole world.

It is the norm for Christians everywhere to baptize with water after invoking the power of the Holy Spirit. Consistent with nearly all Christian communities, it is characteristic of United and Uniting Churches to baptize in the name of God the Father, Son, and Holy Spirit. Sahu notes that baptism signifies "a renewal by the Spirit, a liberation into a new humanity, an act of justification, God's gift of anointing and the promise of the Holy Spirit, a sign and seal of common discipleship, [and] a bond of Christian unity."[10] Baptism is loaded with significance that is bound up in the gracious gifts of the Spirit.

At a somewhat superficial level, baptized persons receive the blessing of welcome, to be sure. In my tradition (The United Church of Canada), they often receive a certificate, a candle, and a cake. Deeper still, however, all who are baptized are engrafted forever into a splendid, complex, and

8. Basil, *On the Holy Spirit* 15.35.

9. World Council of Churches, *Come, Holy Spirit*, 93.

10. Sahu, *United and Uniting*, 72.

living reality called the church, the Christian movement. That movement welcomes new members and recognizes that they, by virtue of their baptism and the gifts of the Spirit, will now join in her work to transform the world: "Baptism is our introduction to a life of discipleship and to our participation in the ministry of the whole people of God."[11] It is not a magical change, however, regardless of the age of the baptized person. All Christians "need to claim again and again the help of the Spirit so as to grow in Christ."[12] It is a lifelong process.

Part of the way that God provides for the needs of this world and continues to influence it is to motivate persons to present themselves and their children for baptism. Pulsing with the Spirit's power, and through baptism, the vocation to be agents of the mission of God will be animated and (we pray) will fill them with conviction. As the World Council of Churches says, "Those who are born of water and the Spirit become part of God's redemptive work in history. . . . They are part of the 'new creation'; they are also agents of the 'new creation.'"[13] It is a tall order! It is far more than a little water sprinkled on the head. Every Christian has a calling to be part of changing the world for the better.

Not everyone perceives these layers of meaning, or allows themselves to be taken up into this high calling. Not everyone receives sufficient teaching to understand the significance of baptism. But this does not seem to stop the Holy Spirit from showing up again and again, making use of the water, the minister, the baptized, and the community. The Holy Spirit is endlessly optimistic! Still, "not all the baptised grow into the promised faith. The baptised person, whether baptised in infancy or adulthood, may reject the gift of life and stifle the voice of the Spirit."[14]

Yet rather than overpowering us with divine force to insist on change, the Holy Spirit passionately desires to work through each limited human life to draw all creation into a community of redeemed holiness and grace. Ephrem communicates a glimpse of this power in a hymn:

> Behold the fire and the Spirit in the womb which bore you.
> Behold the fire and the Spirit in the river in which you were baptized.
> Fire and Spirit are in our baptism.[15]

11. "United Church of Canada," 2:277.

12. Uniting Church in Australia, "Understanding the Church's Teaching on Baptism," 541.

13. World Council of Churches, *Come, Holy Spirit*, 46.

14. Uniting Church in Australia, "Response to *Baptism, Eucharist and Ministry*," 214.

15. Ephrem, *Hymns* 10.17.

Baptizing John, the cousin of Jesus, told the crowds who came to him that Jesus would baptize "with the Holy Spirit and fire" (Matt 3:11). The fire here is a metaphor of God's purifying love. It is the power of God to transform and to burn away all that keeps us apart from God's purposes. This can be slow, patient work for the Spirit. The baptized followers of Jesus are indeed meant to be the pioneers of the new creation, even when they are imperfect in their response to the gifts of grace.

Communion

As in baptism, the Holy Spirit is active in the sacrament of communion to transform individuals and also the whole gathered community of worshipers. Communion—in its materiality, its physical presence, in its words, music, and gestures—serves the community by making real the presence of the Holy Spirit, enabling us to delight in her and to be receptive to her. In the actions of communion, the outpouring of the Holy Spirit is revealed, "who continuously indwells and inspires the church."[16] The word *communion* suggests unity: *com* (together) + *union*. In the sacrament of the table, the gathered body of Christ is united and their differences are set aside. The Holy Spirit is invoked and (as we seek through prayer) fills the space, wine, and bread to make the gathered worshipers fully Christ's own people. In the celebration around the table, the Holy Spirit "makes the crucified and risen Christ really present to us in the eucharistic meal."[17] John Wesley teaches that "the eating of that bread, the drinking of that cup [are] the outward, visible means whereby God conveys into our souls all that spiritual grace, that righteousness, and peace, and joy in the Holy Ghost."[18]

In the first instance, this is the nourishment of human faith, without a doubt. But it is also a binding together of a people with their Lord. Ephrem captures the movement of the Spirit in the elements of the Eucharist in his distinctive poetic style:

> In your bread is hidden the Spirit which cannot be eaten
> In your wine dwells the fire that cannot be drunk.
> Spirit in your bread, fire in your wine:
> It is a distinct wonder that our lips have received![19]

16. Sahu, *United and Uniting*, 73.
17. World Council of Churches, *Baptism, Eucharist and Ministry*, 13.
18. Wesley, "Means of Grace," 389–90.
19. Ephrem, *Hymns* 10.8.

In the celebration at the table of the Lord, the Holy Spirit is present and at work. She inhabits the bread and wine so that we who are mortal may take into ourselves (both physically and spiritually) the presence of God. All this occurs so that we may be transformed and progressively sanctified—together and for the sake of all. Just as baptism makes a new people for the sake of the realm of God, communion reinscribes that people into the unity of the Spirit and commissions them to be the agents of the *missio dei*—God's worldwide mission of service, renewal, and love.

As noted above, Christians call upon the Holy Spirit in the *epiclēsis* prayer within a communion liturgy. If the Spirit wills it, the elements of the sacraments—water, bread, and wine—are able to convey the presence of Christ to us. "The whole action of the eucharist," writes the World Council of Churches, "depends upon the work of the Holy Spirit."[20] The Spirit's action enables human interaction with the eternal Christ at the table. Protestants, such as those in the United and Uniting Churches, do not adhere to the doctrine of *transubstantiation*, as the Roman Catholic Church teaches. In transubstantiation, the bread and wine upon the table of the Lord become the actual physical body and blood of Christ in their substance (deep inner reality), and are bread and wine only in their outer form. This is not a conviction widely shared by Protestants. However, there is room in Protestant thought and practice for *consubstantiation*, in which the presence of Christ is truly revealed in the bread and wine. Consubstantiation can also be understood to mean that the bread and wine remain bread and wine while also becoming Christ's body and blood—neither form is obliterated.

The overarching doctrines to consider are Christ's ubiquity and divine sovereignty. If Christ is *ubiquitous*—that is, present everywhere, in the power of the Holy Spirit—who is any one of us to suggest he cannot be present in the bread and wine? If God is truly *sovereign*, how can a celebrating minister or congregation declare that God is *not* present in the sacrament? To proclaim the freedom of the Holy Spirit is to declare that through her, Christ's presence and indeed the fullness of the triune God can indeed be present in the sacraments, in the elements, in the room, in the gathered people of God. The transformation of the people, indeed, might begin with the transformation of the elements into Christ-infused realities, by the power of the Holy Spirit. That transformation propels the church—the people of God—into the world God loves.

Welker argues that in communion, the Holy Spirit "gathers, builds up, and sends the churches of all times and regions of the world, binding all these churches together in a way that far exceeds the capacity of our

20. World Council of Churches, *Baptism, Eucharist and Ministry*, 13.

sense perception."[21] In other words, the commissioning that is embedded within the sacrament is both a reminder of transnational and transtemporal Christian unity, as well as the communal vocation to be about the business of God's mission in the world. "In the power of the Holy Spirit," writes Moltmann, the church at the eucharistic table "experiences itself as the messianic fellowship of service for the kingdom of God in the world."[22] The unity of the people around the table is translated into unity of purpose in God's will, for the world's sake.

The Ministries of Preaching and Teaching

The Holy Spirit inhabits and empowers the ministries of preaching and teaching for a similar purpose: to bless the wider circle who receive the word through the preacher and teacher. Wise preachers and teachers invite the Holy Spirit into the processes of developing the message they will offer, from the initial pondering, to searching the Scriptures, to further research, then inward to the writing and thinking-through of what will be spoken to the assembled believers (or not-yet believers). In the proclamation that follows, the Holy Spirit will act as She sees fit, to inspire, move, motivate, instruct, chasten, or bless the hearers.

These acts of transmission and reception of the Spirit do not rely on the holiness of the preacher or teacher, just as the holiness of the presider is not the guarantor of the sacraments' effectiveness. Within the Christian community, the Spirit instructs believers and not-yet-believers through the witness of preachers and teachers. The preachers and teachers in turn learn from those they serve. It is a reciprocal process of speakers forming the church, and the church forming speakers. As Luther has it, through the church's preaching, the Spirit first "creates, calls, and gathers the Christian church." Then the Spirit "leads us into his holy congregation, and places us in the bosom of the Church, whereby [the Spirit] preaches to us and brings us to Christ."[23] All this occurs under the Spirit's care and direction. But it always requires human cooperation and intention, for the Spirit does not force minds and hearts to be receptive to instruction. She is free, and She honors the freedom of her people. Even the advanced theological work of academic theologians is, at best, diligent attentiveness to what the Spirit is saying into the present moment of the faithful, trying to "think God's

21. Welker, *What Happens*, 123.
22. Moltmann, *Church in the Power of the Spirit*, 289.
23. Luther, *Large Catechism*, 3.37, 3.45.

thoughts after God has spoken," to borrow an old expression from Johannes Kepler. Advanced knowledge in not necessarily advanced wisdom.

Many biblical episodes reveal the Holy Spirit's work and presence among those who teach in the name of God. Stephen, the first martyr, was noteworthy for "the wisdom and the Spirit with which he spoke" (Acts 6:8–10). When Phillip is sent to meet an Ethiopian official heading home from Jerusalem, the Spirit empowers Phillip to teach the official and to lead him to Christ (Act 8:26–39). In Acts 18:24–28, Apollos from Alexandria is gifted for preaching, and he is taught by elders of the way of Jesus so that his preaching may be more effective and accurate. This is again a sign of the Spirit's work among the whole people, as mutual teaching and learning are part of Christian communal life.

When he is imprisoned with other apostles, Peter's address to his captors is "filled with the Holy Spirit" (Acts 4:8). After they are released, they return to the new Christians congregating in Jerusalem. After praying together, "they were all filled with the Holy Spirit and spoke the word of God with boldness" (Acts 4:31). Centuries later, Ephrem the Syrian modestly celebrates the gift of the Spirit as empowering his preaching:

> Who has given me a little breath of the Spirit?
> It is not for prophecy—this would be a request for death—
> But that I might be able to proclaim the glory
> Of him who is greater than all, with my poor tongue.[24]

By the gracious gifts of the Spirit, those who preach and teach the gospel are given courage, boldness, clarity, and passion so that the message they offer will transform the people of God, and (it is hoped) will even reach those who are unsure or unconvinced of the gospel. Those who serve in these ways "are lifted up and carried, enabled, and infused by the Holy Spirit. We do not cease to be ourselves, yet we are not only ourselves, and certainly not [acting] only for our sakes."[25] This work of building up the community is characteristic of the Spirit, who gives gifts—for the sake of all.

Other Forms of Christian Service

The calling of some Christians to lead as the shepherds (pastors, ministers, priests, bishops, and so on) is a well-attested understanding in Christian thought. Acts 13:1–3, among other biblical passages, suggests that this calling arises from the work of the Holy Spirit. In the language of the United

24. Ephrem, *Hymns* 25.1.

25. Long, *Worshipping Body*, 119.

Church in Jamaica and the Cayman Islands, "God, through the Holy Spirit, consecrates or sets the apart those who express their readiness to be available for participating in the work [of ministry leadership]."[26] The World Council of Churches teaches, "As Christ chose and sent the apostles, Christ continues through the Holy Spirit to choose and call persons into the ordained ministry."[27] Alongside ordination, many other forms of designated ministry are equally Spirit-led and Spirit-filled.

Beyond such designated ministries, many more expressions of the Spirit's power can be found throughout the life of the church, working for the sake of all. There is no hierarchy in the forms of service. All are Spirit-breathed and blessed. In the words of the United Presbyterian Church of Brazil,

> Accepting the multifaceted operation of the Holy Spirit in the lives of God's people . . . [means that] ministry to the whole Church cannot be reduced to pastoral ministry, but that the diversity of gifts and callings of the Spirit is granted to all members of God's people, without excluding any of them on account of sex, color, culture, or social position.[28]

The broad category of mission—by which the church participates in God's work—is undoubtedly made possible by the Holy Spirit. To John and Charles Wesley and the early Methodists, to be moved inwardly by the Holy Spirit is necessarily to be drawn into an outward ethical life of service to others and their needs. They are inseparable aspects of "inward and outward holiness."[29] The acts of service, care, mercy, love, and healing that the gathered community of Christians extend to one another and to the wider world do not arise simply because a handful of people thought it would be "nice." The Spirit is continually calling the church forward into mission, drawing God's people into the greater purposes of the Trinity to transform the world, helping the world to agree and align with God's vision for healing, justice, and perfection. "To bring humanity and all creation into communion,"[30] the Spirit is constantly commissioning all Christians for service and witness.

In biblical terms, this understanding can be anchored in the sending of the seventy-two (Luke 10:1ff); the breath-Spirit blown upon the disciples by the risen Christ (John 20:22); and the commission of the apostles in Matt 28:16–20. The promise of Jesus to send the Spirit (John 16:7) to guide and

26. United Church in Jamaica and the Cayman Islands, *Our Church*, 80.

27. World Council of Churches, *Baptism, Eucharist and Ministry*, 21.

28. Igreja Presbiteriana Unida do Brasil, "Declaração de Atibaia," art. 3, 4.

29. Outler, "Focus on the Holy Spirit," 11.

30. World Council of Churches, *Nature and Purpose*, 15.

empower the church (the whole church) is embodied day by day among those who receive and welcome the Spirit's leading and gift-giving as they follow Jesus into the world. As Thayer and Jacobsen of the United Church of Christ (USA) observe, "The same Holy Spirit sent from Jesus is in the world today, comforting us in our times of trouble and empowering us to proclaim good news and do good to all those who cross our paths."[31] The Uniting Church in Australia concurs: "The whole body of the Church [i.e. every member] . . . is called to participate in the ministry of Christ and to carry out . . . its true service and witness in the world."[32]

The work of the Holy Spirit is emphasized in many Christian movements of justice-seeking and social transformation. The social gospel movements that coalesced in the United Kingdom, the United States, and Canada in the late nineteenth and early twentieth centuries channelled the Holy Spirit's gifts in seeking social justice for those who were impoverished by the political and economic conditions of that era. The many liberation theology movements in Latin America and elsewhere have undertaken sociopolitical engagement, theological critique, and passionate action to emphasize "that salvation is not only an otherworldly anticipation but also a this-worldly experience, manifest in the material, economic, social, and political dimensions of human existence."[33] This desire for a "world made new" is characteristic of the Spirit's drive toward liberative release from bondage and reconciled relations among all persons.

The Spirit is at work in many forms among the nations of the world. The Korean Methodist Church, among others, has articulated its desire for the reunification of the Korean peninsula and its peoples:

> We express our longing for unification of the nation in any form possible through peaceful means . . . through establishing a democratic political structure based upon freedom and human rights . . . by working toward the establishment of a just society built for the sake of the people. . . . [We] disavow any form of war or the taking of life, and commit the whole strength of the Korean Methodist Church to the peaceful reunification of our country.[34]

Following the genocide in Rwanda, the Friends Peace House was established with a mission "to promote peace, unity, and reconciliation among the people of Rwanda and to holistically contribute to the development of

31. Thayer and Jacobsen, *Christ, Creeds and Life*, 89–90.
32. Uniting Church in Australia, "Church," 172.
33. Yong, *Spirit Poured Out*, 82.
34. Cited in United Methodist Church [USA], "Korea."

the Rwandan society."[35] These movements, and tens of thousands of others, illustrate the outward movement of the Holy Spirit, through the church and toward the world, for the sake of renewal, healing, and transformation.

~

The work of the Holy Spirit "for the good of all" is broad ranging. The Spirit calls the church into being, giving it a mission and continually bolstering its life and courage. The Spirit gives the people of God the gift of unity, so that their life and work may be harmonious and all the more powerful in service to God's purposes. Through Scripture, the sacraments, and preaching and teaching, the Spirit freely shares gifts that empower and lift up the community, Christ's body, to be and to become all that God desires it to be. Through a broad range of shared work, the whole church embodies the Spirit as it tries to fulfill the ambitious and generous desire of God to transform the whole creation. The flow of the Spirit in and through the church continually seeks the common good. We turn now to see how the Spirit is at work beyond the limits of the church.

FOR REFLECTION OR DISCUSSION

1. This chapter presents many layers of meaning to baptism, then goes on to note that "not everyone receives sufficient teaching to understand the significance of baptism. But this does not seem to stop the Holy Spirit from showing up again and again, making use of the water, the minister, the baptized, and the community." Which of the many meanings of baptism were already familiar to you? What layers of meaning might be new for you?
2. What is your understanding of how the Holy Spirit works in the bread and wine of the sacrament of communion?
3. "Through Scripture, the sacraments, and preaching and teaching, the Spirit freely shares gifts that empower and lift up the community, Christ's body, to be and to become all that God desires it to be." How would you describe God's vision for the church? How do you see the Holy Spirit working to make this vision a reality?

35. Friends Peace House, "About Us."

Chapter 17

Beyond the Church

ON MANY OCCASIONS, I have told my students the most important thing I learned in theological school. It was the chiastic axiom I mentioned in chapter 15: "The church doesn't have a mission; the mission has a church."[1] In other words, the church is the instrument of the Holy Spirit, who has called it into being to enact God's good purposes. In humility, Christians have to accept that God might well be at work beyond the church too. The Holy Spirit is radically free, after all, and not subject to human limits or control. Amy Plantinga Pauw, paraphrasing Stanley Samartha, remarks that "the mission of the Spirit in the world is broader and deeper than the mission of the church."[2] The worldwide and history-encompassing purposes of God the Holy Spirit transcend the limitations of the church, its people, and its work. John Dow of The United Church of Canada indicates that "we must acknowledge that God is at work beyond ecclesiastical frontiers" given that the Spirit's work can at times be seen so clearly in persons who are not Christian.[3]

This should come as no surprise. Up to this point, this book has intentionally focused on a Christian account of the Holy Spirit. However, it would be hubris-filled, stubbornly narrow, and jingoistic to think that Christianity can claim her as its own property or domain. The vital teaching of Jesus that is so frequently repeated—that "the wind [*pneuma*, Spirit] blows where it chooses" (John 3:8)—demands at the very least that we respect the freedom and sovereignty of the Spirit to be active wherever and to do whatever She

1. Prof. Harold Wells taught my classmates and me this expression in an introductory theology course at Emmanuel College, Toronto, in the early 1990s. I do not know the original source for the saying.

2. Pauw, "Holy Spirit and Scripture," 35.

3. Dow, *This Is Our Faith*, 65.

desires. United Church of Christ (USA) theologian Roger Shinn points out that "the Spirit is not a possession of the church."[4] The United Church of Canada notes that Jesus "says nothing about it [the Holy Spirit] blowing only among Christian people."[5] As Harold Wells of that same denomination writes, "If the Spirit of God, whom Christians also name Spirit of Jesus Christ, is present and at work in all creation and with all people, we must eagerly expect to find truth and wisdom in many places."[6]

With that conviction in mind, it is not hard to discover that lived experience, personal reflections, the testimony of a variety of religious and spiritual traditions, as well as academic research, all reveal that the Holy Spirit is surely at work beyond the church and Christianity. One of the key learnings for those of European descent is to recognize (and celebrate) the presence and work of the Holy Spirit among other peoples long before European settlement/invasion in places like Turtle Island (the North American land mass), India, and Oceania. "Indigenous people had their own theology of the Spirit from time immemorial," writes Adrian Jacobs. "The Holy Spirit has always spoken to us."[7] The Uniting Church in Australia has expressed a similar teaching, thanks to their increasing integration of Aboriginal Australian wisdom: "The First Peoples had already encountered the Creator God before the arrival of the colonisers; the Spirit was already in the land revealing God to the people through law, custom and ceremony."[8]

Jacobs names creation care, mutual respect, peace-making after war, creating balance, treaties, ceremonies, communal life, and honoring the spiritual power of God within the created order as part of the work of the Spirit among human creatures. Moreover, the "Holy Spirit's work . . . is extended to the whole of the Indigenous creation family: the rock people, the tree folk, the fish family, our Elder Brother the Son, our Mother Earth, our Grandmother Moon, our Grandfathers the Thunders."[9] Many others attest to similar Indigenous or non-European awareness and interaction with the divine *Someone* whom Christians from these communities identify as the Holy Spirit. It is important to clarify that this authentic identification and claiming of the Holy Spirit is by Indigenous persons themselves, in contrast to a Western, colonial imposition of Christian concepts.

4. Shinn, *Confessing Our Faith*, 79.
5. United Church of Canada, *Mending the World*, 14.
6. Wells, "Holy Spirit," 490.
7. Jacobs, "Holy Spirit," 153, 166.
8. Uniting Church in Australia, "Revised Preamble," §3.
9. Jacobs, "Holy Spirit," 153–54, 169.

Rather than imposing Western notions, or erasing cultural and religious differences, as colonialism has often done, those of European descent and those they live alongside are better off to share and to listen carefully in a spirit of mutual respect. In the words of Kirsteen Kim, "The first act of mission is discernment, to discover the way in which the Spirit is moving in the world in order to join in."[10] Or, as Joseph Comblin teaches, "The Spirit leads peoples and religions in directions we cannot know in advance. All we can do is observe the signs of the Spirit at work and go along with it."[11] To this charge to "observe" we might add, *rejoice* and *give thanks!* Care must be taken at this point not to suppose that all religions are the same, somehow, or that all religious truth claims can be harmonized. Some are indeed in contradiction to each other. Even so, the Spirit's power, imagination, and scope of activity far exceeds what any one group of humans (in the church or otherwise) might conceive and dream. She, always One with the Trinity, will decide the nature and location of her actions and purposes, without being subject in any sense to Christianity's directives or limitations. At the very least, this ought to provoke theological humility.[12] Harry Oussoren of The United Church of Canada writes, "The Church cannot and may not claim to limit or control the Spirit's work of showering gifts and generating spiritual fruits upon the entire human family."[13]

Honoring the Integrity of Others

Indeed, it is essential that Christians not impose Christian paradigms and assumptions about the Holy Spirit on other religious, faith, and non-faith traditions and movements. They have their own integral convictions, logic, and grammar. In other words, it would be irresponsible and colonialistic to look upon "Religious Tradition X" in "Country Y" and conclude, "Oh well, when they use such-and-such a term, they just mean what I mean when I say 'Holy Spirit.'" That might be remotely possible, but it is more likely to be a presumptuous imposition and indeed a distortion or misunderstanding. Everyone is better off if all parties respect how others speak from within their own traditions, experience, and faith. Authentic encounter and listening are more human and (dare I say) more Spirit-led forms of exchange

10. Kim, *Holy Spirit in the World*, 165.

11. Comblin, *Holy Spirit and Liberation*, 161.

12. "In seeking to discern the work of the Holy Spirit we best do so with humility and openness to being corrected." Uniting Church in Australia, "Discerning the Work of the Holy Spirit," 13.

13. Oussoren, "Scope."

than the dominant-nation and dominant-religion colonial attitude that has plagued many centuries of human interaction. In a statement of faith called simply "An Affirmation," The United Church of Canada attests, "We believe that God calls the Church . . . to discern and celebrate God's Spirit in people of other religions and ideologies."[14] This is a laudable ideal, but still runs the risk of that ignoble imposition. How can Christians, instead, come with openness and humble appreciation, asking adherents of other traditions to speak *for themselves?*

Genuine and humble encounter promises to enrich Christian self-understanding without overtaking, erasing, or subsuming the differences between traditions, which are often irreducible and cannot be expressed by a common denominator in any language. Where true confluences emerge between or among religions, then sincere celebration can occur. But the patient, slow, sometimes difficult, and often illuminating interaction of waiting and listening offers great promise. Christians are indeed often able to understand better their own convictions when clarified and placed side by side with those of others.

The World Council of Churches urges, "The transformation wrought by the Spirit impels us to overcome divisions and confirms in us the search for the renewal of the whole human community."[15] These are the Spirit-led impulses that we have begun to identify in this book. The work of liberation, transformation, and the affirmation of abundant life for all of creation (including human creatures) are some of those impulses. The purposeful work of the Holy Spirit, who is One with the triune God, can be found and should actively be sought among many religious communities and other movements in this world. Anything and anyone who lifts up, restores, values dignity, cherishes creation, and enables a more genuinely human existence should be welcomed and embraced, even across lines of difference and division that might otherwise separate the human family. As Patricia Wells of The United Church of Canada writes,

> Though we would like to package it up neatly in our own faith (or even our own denomination), the Spirit . . . will continue to work within people of other religions and people of no religion. . . . Wherever there is a true striving for justice and peace, the evidence of love and wholeness, there the Spirit of Christ is at work.[16]

14. United Church of Canada, *Mending the World*, 5.
15. World Council of Churches, *Come, Holy Spirit*, 11.
16. Wells, *Welcome*, 6.

This awareness is an occasion for awe and wonder, praising the Spirit's creativity and scope.

This does not mean that Christians should abandon the specific ways that their faith is articulated. Christianity will always consist, in part, in the proclamation of Jesus Christ as one who was filled with the Holy Spirit and who incarnated the very presence of God in history. Relativizing or diminishing the importance and significance of Jesus as a way of honoring other religious traditions is a dead end. Harold Wells is right in saying that "the claim of Christians—that God is uniquely present and disclosed in the utter powerlessness of the obscene event of crucifixion—was contemptible and laughable [in ancient times], and it is increasingly incredible today in a culturally and religiously pluralist society."[17] But it is also true, as Wells notes, that Christian faith cannot set aside Christological claims as irrelevant. In chapter 2, we saw that there is no coherently trinitarian, Christian account of the Holy Spirit in the absence of the Son. The task is not to dismiss Jesus when noticing the work of the Spirit throughout the world, but simply to give thanks for it, and to join in the Spirit's passionate action whenever possible. Christians are still Christ's people.

A Challenge to Christian Exclusivity

If it is true that the Holy Spirit is present in and active through many other non-Christian peoples, can Christians claim any kind of exclusivity or preferential status? "God in Christ has given to *all people in the Church* the Holy Spirit," testifies the Uniting Church in Australia.[18] The United Church of Canada at one time nodded in this direction as well, saying that the Spirit dwells "in every *believer* as the spirit of truth, of power, of holiness, of comfort and of love."[19] In an absolute sense, these claims do not exclude the Spirit's work in others, but they do imply it. A corrective to such exclusive notions is needed. Nearly a century later, The United Church of Canada endorsed the "explicit claim that the Spirit is active in *all* peoples, not merely in those who call themselves Christian, and that the church is challenged to recognize and celebrate the holy in all its expressions."[20]

To think and live as if the Spirit could be restricted "to certain people, places, and religions is to claim that she is Lord of some lives but not all."[21]

17. Wells, "Holy Spirit," 477–78.

18. Uniting Church in Australia, *Basis of Union*, §3; emphasis added.

19. United Church of Canada. "Basis of Union," art. 8; emphasis added.

20. United Church of Canada, "Song of Faith," appendix A.

21. Jensen, "Discerning the Spirit," 7.

But as we have seen, the Spirit has a global, universal, creation-wide mission to heal, redeem, and restore. Or as Shinn writes, "The activity of the Holy Spirit cannot be confined within any human boundaries . . . Christians must be alert to the moving of the Spirit outside churches and even against them."[22] Shinn is plainspoken in naming the conviction that God the Spirit is at work beyond the limits and boundaries of the Christian movement.

Shinn's further prophetic claim that the Spirit might even work *against* churches is at first glance rather alarming. At a minimum, there is vulnerability and contingency in this. No one can be certain that God is on "our side." The perplexing spectacle of opposing sports teams, or opposing armies, both praying for victory through God's interceding, puts this into stark relief. God does not desire the flourishing of one people at the expense of another. Thus no group of Christians can rightly and unquestioningly declare that God is "theirs," as if God could be claimed and colonized. Nor can Christians as a whole claim that their ways are necessarily blessed by God. As Schweitzer and Kwon of The United Church of Canada have noted, "The Holy Spirit may at times address the church *through the world*, leading it to repentance and conversion."[23] The Spirit critiques the church when needed, to draw it to toward greater faithfulness.

It is the brilliant insight of the Barmen Declaration (1934) to renounce the false doctrine that was proclaimed in that generation by the so-called German Christians—that is, the party within the Protestant German church that had entirely conformed itself to Nazi distortions and heresies. Among those who composed and adopted the Barmen Confession against these heretical *Deutsche Christen* were many United Church pastors and members in Germany. The Barmen Synod was a movement of the Spirit "against" the church, in the sense of a small voice crying out against the errors of the majority state church. To those who gathered at the Barmen Synod, the truth of the gospel "is threatened by the teaching and actions of the ruling church party of 'German Christians' and of the church leadership exercised by them."[24] The Holy Spirit compelled them to protest, to denounce the distortions and heresies of a fascism-infected church, and to work actively against it: "In opposition to attempts to establish the unity of the German Evangelical Church by means of false doctrine, by the use of force and by insincere practices," write the Barmen theologians, "the Confessional Synod insists that the unity of the Evangelical Churches in Germany can come only

22. Shinn, *Confessing Our Faith*, 80.

23. Schweitzer and Kwon, *Hope Peace Unrest*, 17; emphasis added.

24. Confessional Synod of the German Evangelical Church, "Barmen Theological Declaration."

from the Word of God in faith through the Holy Spirit."[25] Human customs, societal trends, and political ideologies will never be an adequate substitute.

A similar protest arose among some Christians in South Africa who denounced the Dutch Reformed Church's support for the racially oppressive system of apartheid. Their efforts were strengthened through the active resistance of Muslims and persons from Traditional African Religions in the anti-apartheid movement.[26] Again, the Holy Spirit reveals her active engagement with the world among all those who are not part of the Christian movement, but who—just as authentically—seek the restoration of human dignity and thriving. The same could be said of countless other movements and groups, both religious and secular: Amnesty International, Greenpeace, Médecins Sans Frontières, United Nations Children's Fund (UNICEF), Indigenous Friendship Centres, Jewish Family Services, twelve-step groups, the Red Crescent Society, the Institute for Islamic, Christian, and Jewish Studies, BAPS Swaminarayan Sanstha, food and clothing banks, and many thousands more all over the world. As Moltmann puts it, "The Holy Spirit's wave of salvation embraces the whole of life and everything living, and cannot be confined to religion and spirituality."[27] The traditional Lauru peoples of the Solomon Islands professed their confidence in the Spirit's presence throughout creation in a way that has found resonance within the United Church in the Solomon Islands, which shares the Lauru prayer:

> The power of God is here,
> In land, sea and sky
> We can never escape it
> The Spirit of God in all places.[28]

The same omnipresent Spirit is at work among all peoples who seek justice, love, and freedom for all.

The final consummation of God's purposes—the realm of God—is also the work of the Holy Spirit in concert with the whole of the Trinity. "The Spirit moves in mysterious ways," writes Oussoren, "to bless and accompany the one [human] family towards the universal reign of God."[29] Indeed, all of creation is implicated. The Holy Spirit power that raised Jesus from the dead is the same power that will accomplish all that God intends for creation, from individual atoms to humankind to the whole universe. This testimony

25. Confessional Synod of the German Evangelical Church, "Barmen Theological Declaration."

26. See Musuku, "Prophetic Mission."

27. Moltmann, *Source of Life*, 22.

28. Pitakaji, *Theo-Cultural Exploration*, 44.

29. Oussoren, "Scope."

of hopeful anticipation is itself empowered by the Holy Spirit, who awakens faith in believers, animating their trust in God, and inspiring their collective work in this life toward accomplishing what God desires. The Uniting Presbyterian Church of Southern Africa professes,

> The Spirit moves us to respond to God's grace not only with faith but with love and glad obedience that seeks to serve God both in our private lives and in public life. . . . True faith always issues in action.[30]

Acts of service, love, inclusion, feeding, housing, empowering, dignifying, liberating, alleviating suffering, fostering community and compassion, and preventing violence are precisely the work of the Holy Spirit through the church, but also well beyond it. Millions, billions of persons all over the world work toward these same ends—persons within all religious traditions and none. All human activity that aligns with God's purposes is the embodiment of the mission of God, through the power of Holy Spirit. The theological recognition of the Spirit's activity in these ways does not require the imposition of Christianity on anyone, nor its abandonment. It can simply be a joyous recognition that the Source of our hope is real.

SUMMARY OF PART TWO

In the fullest terms, the Holy Spirit acts in a purposive and personal way toward and within creation as a whole; toward and within individual human creatures (for the sake of each one); and toward and within humankind as a collective, both in the church and beyond it (for the sake of all). It is in these actions that we are best able to see what the Spirit does. Guiding, inspiring, transforming, and renewing, the Spirit is constantly on the move, like a restless wind. The Holy Spirit does not stand still so that we can capture and contain her movements. The best that theology can do is to glimpse how and where She is at work, and begin to describe what we have seen. The mighty power of the triune God self-reveals in countless ways, and is always purposefully directed toward the consummation of God's purposes—the realm of God. The adventure for human creatures is to lift the sails of our lives and let the Spirit propel us onward in the direction She intends. This is the great divine promise that we can joyfully trust.

30. Uniting Presbyterian Church of Southern Africa, *Manual*, 38.

FOR REFLECTION OR DISCUSSION

1. The Holy Spirit works outside the Christian church, but it's important to try not to fit experiences from outside of the church into Christian patterns and assumptions. What are some ways (or attitudes) we can adopt for being alert to the Holy Spirit's movement beyond the bounds of the church?
2. This chapter notes two examples of the Holy Spirit working *against* the church (through the Barmen Declaration and in working to overturn apartheid). What do you think about that idea? Can you think of any other examples of the Holy Spirit working against the church?

PART THREE

Features of United and Uniting Approaches

Chapter 18

Seven Features of United and Uniting Church Approaches

THIS NEXT TO LAST chapter considers several of the distinctive ways in which United and Uniting Churches articulate their doctrine—that is, their theological understandings. Here I want to be cautious not to set these denominations apart from other Christian communities in a radical way. Indeed, the ecumenical unity desired by all United and Uniting Churches directly contradicts such a move. United and Uniting Churches are not separatists or sectarians. They are inherently ecumenical bridge builders. Moreover, in a "fundamental sense, the identity of United and Uniting churches is no different from the identity of any other church."[1] Apart from being entirely Protestant in their configurations (so far), United and Uniting Churches make no claim to significant ontological, doctrinal, or sociological differences from any other Christian community. The matters of nuance and emphasis in theological approaches, however, are worth identifying, even though it would be impossible to present a single "United–Uniting" form of theology.

It is indeed difficult to make a definitive, absolute statement about how theology is done in a United or Uniting Church key, given at least four factors: (1) each United or Uniting Church emerged and exists within a specific, layered cultural context; (2) each has distinctive originating denominational partners that formed their respective union and that continue to shape their approach; (3) since their original union, each one has had a unique history and development following trajectories that have sometimes been parallel, and sometimes divergent, from their international counterparts; and (4) there is no consistent global forum in which all United and

1. Thompson, "Earthen Vessels," 76.

Uniting Churches as a distinct denominational family are able to confer and seek consensus on a regular basis, as is common for others, such as the Anglican, Lutheran, and Roman Catholic traditions. Despite those four factors and the limitations they present, here we shall make an effort to consider a few features of the theological work that typically characterizes United and Uniting approaches.

Feature 1: Drawing on Scripture, Tradition, Reason, and Experience

Among the many aspects of theological work in the United and Uniting Churches, it is crucial to note that these churches are not doctrinaire, in the sense of rigidly clinging to specific formulations that must be adhered to by all members. Rather, flexibility and compromise are often seen in the practical outworking of theological conversation and documentation. As L. Nishan Bakalian, coordinator of church relations for the Union of the Armenian Evangelical Churches in the Near East remarks, "Armenian Evangelical Churches throughout the world express their faith and doctrine fairly loosely."[2] Nevertheless, it is characteristic of most United and Uniting Churches to make use of four elements in articulating their doctrinal statements: the Bible, tradition, reason, and experience.

Albert Outler, of the United Methodist Church (USA), once called this cluster of four elements "the Wesleyan Quadrilateral," although he later regretted coining the phrase.[3] As Outler notes, John Wesley himself never correlated these four elements in a coequal relationship. The Bible was always uppermost, the "pre-eminent norm" that interacted freely with the other three but was never overruled by them.[4] Although Wesley rarely put these four elements into direct conversation in a single passage of his writing, they do function in his theological work to organize and moderate what he says. It is also worthwhile to emphasize that Wesley's use of reason was closer to the medieval sense of *ratio*—that is, a process of carefully thinking things through, rather than a non-religious, anti-supernatural reliance on *reason* as pure objectivity, as most modern science tends to favor.

With those caveats, we can safely say that many United and Uniting Churches freely and openly draw from and appeal to these four elements in doing their theological work, even if they themselves are not Wesleyan in their origins. The Church of North India, for example, lifts up the centrality

2. Personal correspondence with author, Sept. 29, 2023.

3. Outler, "Wesleyan Quadrilateral," 16.

4. Outler, "Wesleyan Quadrilateral," 9.

of the Bible. While recognizing the value of ongoing change and development in theological work in any era, the Church of North India cautions that such revisions are only legitimate "provided always that such statements are agreeable to the Holy Scriptures."[5] This aligns with Wesley's perspective. The Uniting Church in Australia "acknowledges that the Church has received the books of the Old and New Testaments as unique prophetic and apostolic testimony, in which it hears the word of God."[6] As Michael Owen of that denomination writes, "Faith grounded in Jesus Christ is nourished and regulated by the witness of the prophets and apostles in the Scriptures." Moreover, its members are charged with the "serious duty of reading the Scriptures."[7]

Tradition can be understood broadly as the consensus-bearing formulations of doctrine that the Christian movement and its branches have offered, such as the prayer and hymn traditions, creeds and statements of faith, and the witness of accredited and widely received theologians. Reason, once again, should not be understood as an anti-faith or post-faith perspective that is hostile to spiritual conviction. Rather, reason as it is used in the Wesleyan model is a tool for careful, interconnected thought about a given subject. Finally, experience is a category of theological reflection that does not operate with the same degree of authority as the other three elements. Nevertheless, it is deeply valued, especially among the denominations that are Western in their orientation.

In sum, Scripture, tradition, reason, and experience play a consistent part in the theological work produced in many of the United and Uniting Churches. "God's Spirit is active in all four sources of faith," attests The United Church of Canada, "heritage, understanding, experience, and the Bible."[8]

Feature 2: Grounded in the Creeds

As a crucial subset of the category of tradition, it is vital to see that most United and Uniting Churches name and claim their grounding in the historic creeds of Christianity, especially the Apostles' Creed, the Nicene Creed (or Niceno-Constantinopolitan Creed, to be more precise), and the testimony of the Council of Chalcedon (451). These creedal contributions from ancient Christianity are not, as a rule, set aside or renounced by the

5. Church of North India, *Constitution*, clause 6.
6. Uniting Church in Australia, *Basis of Union*, 5.
7. Owen, "Place and Nature of Doctrine," 290.
8. United Church of Canada, *Authority and Interpretation of Scripture*, 33.

United and Uniting Churches. Rather, they are either assumed to remain effective and faithful witnesses to the gospel, or they are explicitly identified as part of a church's theological convictions. "The Christian church does not originate a new faith in each age," write Roger Shinn and Daniel Day Williams of the United Church of Christ (USA). "It confesses the faith of the prophets, apostles, and martyrs in its past" in dialogue with the present and in anticipation of the future.[9] The China Christian Council and the Chinese Christian Three-Self Patriotic Movement of Protestant Churches in China jointly declare a similar adherence to ancient Christian testimonies: "The Chinese Church takes the Bible, the Apostles' Creed and the Nicene Creed as the foundation of our faith."[10] The United Presbyterian Church of Brazil endorses a broad range of historic documents as authoritative, including the Apostles' and Niceno–Constantinopolitan Creeds, as well as the Heidelberg Catechism, Second Helvetic Confession, Westminster Confession of Faith, Shorter Catechism, and the Barmen Declaration.[11]

Some United or Uniting Churches have added new statements alongside the historic creeds. In the case of the Church of North India, the adoption of a new *Affirmation of Faith and Commitment* (1986) "is not a substitute for the classical Creeds but a faith-response to the contemporary Indian context."[12] Indeed, the Church of North India's *Constitution* forthrightly states that it "accepts the Creeds commonly called the Apostles' and Nicene as witnessing to and guarding the faith, which is continuously confirmed by the Holy Spirit in the experience of the Church of Christ."[13] The Church of North India adopts the Nicene Creed's language for the church (one, holy, catholic, apostolic) in its own statements without reserve. Similarly, the Uniting Church in Australia

> enters into unity with the church throughout the ages by its use of the confessions known as the Apostles' Creed and the Nicene Creed. The Uniting Church receives these as authoritative statements of the Catholic Faith. . . . It commends to ministers and congregations their use for instruction in the faith.[14]

The Uniting Presbyterian Church in Southern Africa, for its part, "shares the faith that the one, holy, catholic and apostolic Church has always held. . . .

9. Shinn and Williams, *We Believe*, 19.

10. Joint National Conference, "Church Order of Protestant Churches in China," art. 6.

11. Igreja Presbiteriana Unida do Brasil, "Princípios de Fé e Ordem."

12. Sahu, *United and Uniting*, 67.

13. Church of North India, *Constitution*, clause 3.

14. Uniting Church in Australia, *Basis of Union*, 9.

It accepts the ecumenical creeds commonly called the Apostles' Creed and the Nicene (Niceno–Constantinopolitan) Creed."[15] Similarly, the Armenian Evangelical Church gladly claims and prints the Apostles' Creed and the Nicene Creed in its *Pastor's Manual.*[16] The United Church of Canada reprints both creeds in *Voices United*, its most-used liturgical resource. The United Church of Christ in the Philippines includes these two creeds in their 2015 constitution, and the United Reformed Church (UK) also claims them. Many more United and Uniting Churches do the same.

Certain United or Uniting Churches have rejected the use of creeds, whether in doctrinal statements, liturgy, or personal devotion. However, these are the exception. Given the historic and contemporary importance of the ancient creeds, United and Uniting Churches do not try to rewrite or replace them, but sometimes add supplemental confessions of faith. The United Church of Christ (USA), for instance, "chose to develop a Statement of Faith rather than a creed . . . [because] 'statement of faith' suggests a less rigid, less authoritarian document than 'creed.'" For this denomination, such a faith statement functions as "a testimony, and not a test, of faith."[17] Although this denomination acknowledges the ongoing importance of the ancient creeds, its contemporary Statement of Faith is encouraged for use "'in congregational worship, in private devotions, and for the purposes of study. But the United Church of Christ nowhere requires its use."[18] The United Church of Canada similarly endorses the use of a contemporary creed-like statement ("A New Creed," 1968) and a poetic expression of doctrine ("A Song of Faith," 2006) in non-binding ways.

Whatever contemporary expressions of faith might be developed by United and Uniting Churches, they do not have the authority of the historic, ecumenical creeds. Rather, these denominations aim to be *in continuity* with the ancient testimonies via more contemporary language. For its part, the Church of North India confirms that "it accepts the Creeds commonly called the Apostles' and Nicene as witnessing to and guarding the faith" and at the same time proclaims that "it shall be competent for the Church of North India to issue its own statements."[19] Such statements are not seen as substitutes for the historic creeds, but as contextually helpful adjuncts.

15. Uniting Presbyterian Church in Southern Africa, *Manual*, 19.
16. Tootikian, *Pastor's Manual*, 160.
17. Shinn, *Confessing Our Faith*, 7.
18. Shinn, *Confessing Our Faith*, 8.
19. Church of North India, *Constitution*, clause 3 and 6.

Feature 3: Embracing the Reformers' Wisdom

The United and Uniting Churches often locate their theological work in relation to Protestant antecedent sources, such as magisterial Reformers (Luther and Calvin), as well as later church renewers and reformers, such as John Wesley, and documents arising from those eras. This positioning is self-consciously chosen. The Church of North India attests to its confidence in the "confessions of faith adopted at the time of the Reformation and subsequently."[20] The Uniting Church in Australia explicitly names several historical sources as vital to its theological understandings, including the Scots Confession of Faith (1560), the Heidelberg Catechism (1563), the Westminster Confession of Faith (1647), and the Savoy Declaration (1658).[21] For some other United and Uniting Churches flowing along the streams of the Reformed tradition, the Westminster Confession can also be a core source, even if it is not cited. Of this seventeenth-century confession, Graham Duncan of the Uniting Presbyterian Church in Southern Africa notes, "Though not specifically mentioned [in the *Manual of Faith and Order*], it has had an enormous influence throughout the years and has given impetus to the concepts of conscience and 'liberty of opinion.'"[22]

The statement of faith of the Armenian Evangelical Church explicitly "affirms the legacy of the Reformation."[23] Within this legacy, for example, is Luther's conviction that it is the work of the Holy Spirit to animate faith within the Christian's heart. For Luther, the road to salvation begins when the Spirit convicts a person of sin. Salvation cannot be earned through good works. The Holy Spirit is needed, because "we cannot come by our own reason of strength to believe in Jesus Christ or to come to him."[24] Luther's emphasis on two sacraments, rather than seven; on the essential role of preaching; and on the work of the Holy Spirit to animate faith in the believer remain influential for United and Uniting Churches.

The United and Uniting Churches similarly draw on the teaching of John Calvin. The Union of Protestant Churches of Alsace and Lorraine cites Calvin approvingly when describing its understanding of faith: "Faith is a firm and certain knowledge of the benevolent will of God towards us, based on his gratuitous promise in Jesus Christ, revealed to our understanding

20. See "Section III: The Doctrines of the Church" in Church of North India, *Constitution*, clause 7.

21. Uniting Church in Australia, *Basis of Union*, 10.

22. Personal correspondence with author, Nov. 3, 2023.

23. Tootikian, *Pastor's Manual*, 161.

24. Luther, *Small Catechism*, 126.

and confirmed in our heart by the Holy Spirit."[25] Among other legacies, Calvin's emphasis on the role of the Holy Spirit in interpreting the Bible remains influential.

John Wesley's emphasis on an experiential encounter with the Holy Spirit is appealing to many in the United and Uniting Churches. In late modernity and postmodernity, especially, the experiential has once again become highly valued, as it was in the Romantic era (counterbalancing the then contemporary high rationality of the Enlightenment). Experience, as a way of focusing on subjective individual encounters and therefore on personal autonomy, is similarly prized. Today, it would be difficult to argue that this is quite what Wesley had in mind, as a priest and theologian who cherished the collective body of Christ, the church. In another key, Keith Rowe of the Uniting Church in Australia helpfully notes the appeal of Wesley's contribution to those who are United and Uniting:

> His sensitivity to the interaction between theology and contemporary culture, his concern for the spiritual and theological formation of his people, his identification with the poor and his use of Eastern as well as Western, Roman as well as Protestant insights in the development of his theology mark him out as a practical and ecumenical theologian.[26]

Rowe describes Wesley's approach as one in which "differences could be held within a larger and Christ-focussed love and where no group was required to reject what was important to them as a price of acceptance."[27] Such ecumenical breadth is characteristic of United and Uniting Churches, who are typically open to other Christian traditions and eager to exchange wisdom with them.

Since, as Wesley maintained, all are sinners and yet still receive God's grace, the Calvinist idea of predestination finds no foothold in Wesley's thought. Although it would be a distortion to suggest that Wesley was entirely a universalist (the teaching that *all* persons are saved), his openness to seeing that the Spirit was at work among all peoples has influenced United and Uniting attitudes, which often tend toward universalism. As the United Protestant Church in France professes, "God welcomes each human being as he is, without any merit on his part. In this gospel of grace, at the heart of the Bible, the Spirit of God is manifested."[28] God is able, as the sovereign

25. Union of Protestant Churches of Alsace and Lorraine, "Ce que nous croyons."
26. Rowe, "Wesleyan Heritage," 49.
27. Rowe, "Wesleyan Heritage," 50.
28. Eglise Protestante Unie de France, "Nouvelle déclaration de foi."

Holy Spirit, to reach and to transform every heart. Human judgment cannot predetermine who is included in or excluded from God's economy of grace. To Wesley, grace of the Spirit works throughout one's lifetime to bring about sanctification, or holiness of living. "Goodness is not a quality we can attain by pulling upwards on our own moral and ethical shoelaces," according to the United Reformed Church (UK). "It needs to be a gift from God."[29]

At the same time, the Spirit gives free will to all, to choose or to reject God's purposes—we are not God's marionettes. While discussion of sanctification is rare among United and Uniting Churches today, it is usually understood in relation to Wesley's sense that the Spirit brings about holiness in cooperation with human will. Sanctification, while an historically significant doctrine, is more commonly encoded in United and Uniting teaching as God's work to *transform* us.

Feature 4: Open to Their Local and Global Contexts

Vitally, most United and Uniting Churches seek actively in their faith and witness to engage with the contemporary societies in which they live and serve. They are not separatist nor sectarian. In the multilayered and complex religious environment of India, the Church of North India proclaims, "We rejoice in this our rich religious and cultural heritage and are one with the generations of the people of our land [India] who have developed with it."[30] Those who combined to form the Church of South India express their confidence that "the united Church, conserving all that is of spiritual value in its Indian heritage, will express under Indian conditions and in Indian forms the spirit, the thought and the life of the Church Universal."[31] The Church of South India saw their role explicitly as part of the wider, layered culture and society and world, not apart from it.

In a similar vein, Stanley J. Samartha of the Church of South India was renowned for his pneumatologically based ecumenism, in which he celebrated the common mission of the Spirit in and through all Christian traditions. This perspective has been influential in the World Council of Churches. But even more radically, Samartha affirmed the Spirit's inhabitation of other religions, in that the "truth" that is specially borne by the Spirit may be found in them as well. The universal mission and presence of the

29. United Reformed Church [UK], *What Do We Believe*, 4.

30. "An Affirmation of Faith and Commitment," 98.

31. Church of South India, "Basis of Union," 88.

Spirit provides Christians a way to "recognise truth and goodness in the lives of neighbours of other faiths."[32]

This conviction is still a growing edge for United and Uniting Churches. Not all would affirm it. However, their membership and participation in the World Council of Churches does reveal a readiness to influence and to be influenced by interchurch encounters, as well as to participate in the projects of social, ecological, and political transformation that the World Council of Churches pursues. Interfaith encounters are also part of this readiness, as seen in The United Church of Canada's work in studies such as *Mending the World: An Ecumenical Vision for Healing and Reconciliation* and *That We May Know Each Other: United Church-Muslim Relations Today.* The Union of Protestant Churches of Alsace and Lorraine has also made a special study of its faith in dialogue with Jewish and Muslim believers. In the great variety, range, and depth of religious life and belief in the Indian context, the Church of North India testifies that "we believe that Christ calls us to affirms this [broad, shared Indian] heritage with the people of diverse religions and cultures."[33] United and Uniting Churches are fully immersed in their societies and the wider world, responding creatively to them, and desiring the wellbeing of all.

Feature 5: Oriented Toward Liberation, Inclusion, and Diversity

A common feature among many United and Uniting Churches is a theological commitment to emphasize a Christ-centered mandate to participate in the work of liberation and inclusion, and to embrace diversity. In some cases, this is expressed through theological statements that (for example) denounce modern slavery, elevate the status of women, advocate for the genuine inclusion of sexual minorities, or work toward overcoming racism. Beyond making statements, United and Uniting Churches frequently work passionately for these and related causes in civil society and within government policy.

The diversity of theological articulations and various practices within any given United or Uniting Church at the time of its union became a template, in most cases, for welcoming diversity within that denomination. The United Reformed Church (UK), for example, blended prior traditions regarding infant or adult baptisms in a way that varying "convictions were

32. Kim, *Mission in the Spirit*, 31–32, 71.

33. See §IV, "An Affirmation of Faith and Commitment," in Sahu, *United and Uniting*, 98.

respected . . . [and] there is a greater sense of freedom" for families to choose the manner and timing of baptism.[34] Similarly, flexibility about who may receive communion, and how often the sacrament is celebrated, has been negotiated with grace in the United Reformed Church. At their best, local United and Uniting Church congregations are robustly diverse in terms of ethnicity, national origin, sexuality, gender identity, and economic class. However, that is not always the cases, despite best wishes and concrete actions toward that end.

Another example of a commitment to diversity was the development of a statement of faith for the United Church of Christ (USA). The denomination intentionally drew together a broad range of persons to study and deliberate. The commission charged with this work was "a commission of thirty men and women . . . [that] included biblical scholars, theologians, pastors, and lay people from various walks of life."[35] The important theological work of the denomination was not left only to authorities who would hand down a decision. Indeed, a broad ecumenical and public conversation resulted in many changes to the wording of the statement, as did extended conversation and debate at their general synod meetings.

Yearning for a society characterized by liberation, the Church of North India, in its "Affirmation of Faith and Commitment," has carefully interpreted the Bible. The conclusion of this study is that the Bible

> reveals that God has a special concern for the liberation of the powerless, the poor and the oppressed from all that hinders their full development as God's free children. We believe that at the present time God calls us to strive for justice and freedom to multitudes of the poor and oppressed, the outcasts and the powerless in our own country and in the world.[36]

In the cause of liberation, The United Church of Canada has made headlines, domestically and internationally, for its public and vocal support of LGBTQ+ persons within its congregations, structures, and streams of ministry since the 1980s. This denomination, as well as the Uniting Church of Australia, is also undertaking multi-decade efforts to encourage repentance and healing for their part in Indigenous boarding schools (residential schools) and the harm they caused. These acts of public repentance, inclusion, and bridge building are premised on a theological understanding of God's desire for liberation and inclusion of all persons.

34. Thompson, "Earthen Vessels," 85.

35. Shinn, *Confessing Our Faith*, 22.

36. Cited in Sahu, *Church of North India*, 328.

Feature 6: Ecumenically Eager

It is characteristic of nearly all United and Uniting Churches to be ecumenically engaged and unfailingly open to continuous ecumenical dialogue and cooperation. This is deeply embedded in the "DNA" of these churches, given that they themselves are unions of previously divided Protestant denominations that have wrestled, prayed, and sometimes struggled their way toward deep unity. This makes them predisposed to collaborate and consult with other traditions. Some have explicitly named the desire to continue to unite with still more branches of the Christian family over time, and some have indeed achieved this. As David M. Thompson of the United Reformed Church (UK) says, "The main thing which United churches have to offer in their relation to other church is themselves, as they are. They offer commitment to the unity of the church and a readiness to be renewed in the interest of wider unity."[37] A good example of this is the willingness of The United Church of Canada to adopt a church structure that included bishops when they were contemplating union with the Anglican Church in Canada in the early 1970s, even though The United Church of Canada did not originally favor having bishops.[38] Twenty years later, this same denomination expressed their conviction that "listening to others and examining our assumptions in the light of theirs brings us to a new understanding and appreciation of both." Genuine mutual encounter can be deeply rewarding, but also risky: "When we truly enter into conversation with others, we know that we risk being changed by the power of God's spirit."[39]

Even in articulating distinctive faith formulations, these churches do not seek to distinguish themselves as unique or discontinuous from the wider Christian movement. "A final quality of the Statement [of Faith] is its ecumenical purpose," write Shinn and Williams.

> It does not intend to state the peculiar faith of the people who came together in the United Church of Christ; it aims to state the Christian faith as this church, in conversation with other groups of Christians, apprehends that faith. . . . [It is] certainly not the only way to declare the Christian faith.[40]

The United and Uniting Churches warmly embrace the conviction that no single denomination or tradition has privileged insights that exclude the validity of other views and experiences. Each branch of the Christian

37. Thompson, "Earthen Vessels," 92.

38. Alas, this union did not come to fruition.

39. United Church of Canada, *Authority and Interpretation of Scripture*, 18.

40. Shinn and Williams, *We Believe*, 28.

ecumenical tree has fruit worth sharing. Dialogue, shared studies, and joint action among denominations and other groupings through the World Council of Churches, the World Communion of Reformed Churches, the Anglican Communion, and many other transnational groups, as well as in bilateral church-to-church efforts, United and Uniting Churches reveal a desire for unity and reconciliation within the body of Christ.

"We are agreed," wrote the Church of North India, in their 1965 Plan of Church Union, "in seeking a united church which will be an integral part of the universal church and yet develop the special and distinctive gifts which God has given the people of India and Pakistan in the expression of their worship, their faith and their common life."[41] This clearly expresses the Church of South India's original intention to remain one with the whole Christian movement around the world and not to become sectarian. Yet they also wanted to embrace the local features of the faith that exist within the region. The approach to ecumenism in the Church of North India looks beyond "a mere fusion of denominations" in order to "seek for truth that corrects and reconciles the partial insights" of those who have come into the union. "It is wrong," says Sahu of his denomination, "to contend that one of the denominations has the exclusive expression of the Christian faith."[42] Rather, the Church of North India recognizes that "a genuine appreciation and admiration for traditions other than one's own and sharing each other's experience is the basis" for their ability to unite as one church.[43] This ecumenical mode of doing theology and being the church also allows for ongoing learning and receptivity to the Holy Spirit's instruction, rather than stagnating or becoming theologically immobilized. In other words, interchurch efforts ideally promote the development of greater wisdom and faithfulness to God's call.

This ecumenical impulse is seen as a significant asset in the Uniting Church in Australia. In its *Basis of Union*, we find this remark: "The Uniting Church lives within a worldwide fellowship of Churches in which it will learn to sharpen its understanding of the will and purposes of God by contact with contemporary thought."[44] One Uniting Church in Australia scholar, Michael Owen, writes, "Helpful doctrine will emerge from continuing work on the connections and tensions between the united traditions and teachings grounded in the experiences and insights of other traditions."[45]

41. Church of North India, *Plan of Church Union*, 9.

42. Sahu, *Church of North India*, 148, 150.

43. Sahu, *Church of North India*, 160.

44. Uniting Church in Australia, *Basis of Union* 11.

45. Owen, "Place and Nature of Doctrine," 292.

The United Reformed Church (UK) echoes that spirit of openness to ongoing exchange and learning:

> We affirm our intention
> to go on praying and working,
> with all our fellow Christians,
> for the visible unity of the Church
> in the way Christ chooses
> so that people and nations
> may be led to love and serve God
> and praise him more and more for ever.[46]

Likewise, the Union of Protestant Churches of Alsace and Lorraine expresses clearly its ongoing commitment to ecumenical dialogue and cooperation. But it goes further:

> In a world undergoing religious, social and ecological tensions, ecumenical dialogue is more than ever an act of faith and hope. It allows the Churches to witness together, to carry common commitments and to respond in a united manner to major contemporary challenges, in connection with other religions and currents of thought.[47]

The ecumenicity of the United and Uniting Churches is one of their most salient features. It continues to hold great promise in the Christian movement's vocation, guided by the Holy Spirit, to reconcile with all peoples.

Feature 7: Unfinished and Constantly Reforming

Finally, it is characteristic of United and Uniting Churches to assume that they will always continue to develop and refine their theological understandings. This refinement is itself the work of the Spirit: "The church must always be ready to correct and reform itself in accordance with the teaching of [the] Scriptures as the Holy Spirit shall reveal it."[48] This conviction is an echo of the Reformed theological principle of *ecclesia reformata, semper reformanda* ("the church is reformed, and is always being reformed"). Christians cannot claim with finality (or hubris) that their understandings are complete and perfect. This side of eternity, the Holy Spirit will always

46. United Reformed Church [UK], "Statement Concerning the Nature, Faith, and Order of the URC."

47. Union of Protestant Churches of Alsace and Lorraine, "Dialogue Interreligieux/Dialogue Œcuménique."

48. Church of North India, *Constitution*, clause 2.

be at work to refine and vivify the church toward greater wisdom and sanctification. Consequently, United and Uniting Churches acknowledge their imperfections and claim no superior status over any other Christian communion. Still, they long for unity within and between the churches. This is a special grace and charism (spiritual gift) they carry for the worldwide Christian movement.

Denominational faith statements often embed this assumption of continuous development and refinement. As Shinn concludes, the statement of faith of the United Church of Christ (USA]) "was never meant to be everlasting. But in this interim it is a point of reference, perhaps a banner as the United Church of Christ guides its own life and enters into ecumenical conversations, looking for more light to break forth from God's holy Word."[49] The Uniting Presbyterian Church of Southern Africa affirms "its right to formulate, adopt, modify, and interpret its doctrinal statements, always subject to the Word of God, under the promised guidance of the Holy Spirit."[50] The United Church of Canada declared in its "Statement of Faith (1940),"

> The Church's faith is the unchanging Gospel of God's holy, redeeming love revealed in Jesus Christ. . . . But Christians of each new generation are called to state it afresh in terms of the thought of their own age and with the emphasis their age needs. This we have attempted to do . . . aware that no statement of ours can express the whole truth of God.[51]

Many other United and Uniting Churches strike a similar tone. It is a consistent theme around the world.

> The United Church in Papua New Guinea and the Solomon Islands: "Always be ready to correct and amend [this] constitution as God's will becomes revealed by the Holy Spirit through the Scriptures and in the continuing life of obedience."[52]
>
> The United Protestant Church of France: "The truth by which [this church] lives always surpasses it."[53]

49. Shinn, *Confessing Our Faith*, 32.

50. Uniting Presbyterian Church of Southern Africa, *Manual*, 19.

51. United Church of Canada, "Statement of Faith (1940)."

52. United Church in Papua New Guinea and the Solomon Islands, *Basis for the Union*, art. 1.

53. Eglise Protestante Unie de France, "Nouvelle déclaration de foi."

> The United Reformed Church (UK): "Readiness, if the need arises, to change the Basis of Union and to make new statements of faith in ever new obedience to the Living Christ."[54]

Indeed, the United Reformed Church (UK) "acknowledges its *duty* to be open at all times to the leading of the Holy Spirit and therefore affirms its right to make such new declarations of its faith and for such purposes as may from time to time be required by obedience to the same Spirit."[55]

> The Uniting Church in Australia: "[The church] will not pretend to have captured the truth, but teach about it as truth that it will itself never to be able fully to grasp or comprehend."[56]

The Uniting Church in Australia's *Basis of Union* concludes with the humble confession that it needs the Holy Spirit so that "God will constantly correct that which is erroneous in its life."[57]

It is worth noting that the nature of United and Uniting Churches tends to exclude totalizing or magisterial proclamations about Christian teaching. Structurally, and due to the diversity of their membership, there are limitations on consensus that are intrinsic to these union churches. To be sure, respective constitutions or basis of union documents often set down the best wisdom available to the members undertaking the original organizational and theological work of a United or Uniting Church. Yet there is nearly always an accompanying disclaimer that their work is not expected to last for eternity nor to be perceived as perfectly stated. Ongoing illumination from the Holy Spirit, new learning, and responsiveness to context might well provoke nuances and reconsiderations.

Correspondingly, differences within a United or Uniting Church are not to be feared or suppressed outright, for unity and truth are to be found in the Spirit, through whom the church receives its life, not in human wisdom. In its constitution, we read that

> the Church of North India is keenly aware of the fact that divergence of conviction on certain other matters of faith and practice is something which can only be borne within one fellowship by the exercise of much mutual forbearance and charity. . . . [We have] confidence that in brotherly converse within one church those of diverse convictions will be led together in the

54. United Reformed Church [UK], "Statement Concerning the Nature, Faith, and Order of the URC."

55. United Reformed Church [UK], "Basis of Union," §18; emphasis added.

56. Owen, "Place and Nature of Doctrine," 292.

57. Uniting Church in Australia, *Basis of Union*, §18.

> unity of the Spirit to learn what is [God's] will in these matters of difference.[58]

In this vein, the United and Uniting Churches tend to embrace interaction with other denominations, communities, the World Council of Churches, other Christian assemblies, and other religions for mutual sharing and growth in grace. There is a humble assumption in this that no single expression of the body of Christ knows all there is to know or can state it perfectly.

FOR REFLECTION OR DISCUSSION

1. This chapter outlines seven features of how United and United Churches tend to do theology. In your own experience of your own denomination, which of these seven are you able to see at play? Which (if any) seem less emphasized by your denomination?
2. Take one idea or teaching about the Holy Spirit in one of the previous chapters and explore it through the lens of the "Wesleyan Quadrilateral" (Feature 1 of United and Uniting Churches' theological work). What do Scripture, tradition, reason, and experience tell you about this aspect of the Holy Spirit?

58. Church of North India, *Constitution*, clause 5 and 6.

Chapter 19

Postlude: Unfinished Business

No single book of theology will fully address all the issues it raises. It is the nature of the Holy Spirit to be reaching ever outward, opening, encouraging growth and "greening." Reading and writing about the Spirit is the same—it provokes new thinking and restless imagination. As this book ends, a few items remain that I would like to include briefly:

- The doctrines of procession and spiration
- The "unforgiveable" sin
- The thorny problem of the Spirit withdrawing or withholding her gifts
- The Spirit's ecstatic or charismatic gifts to people
- The experience of baptism in the Holy Spirit

I will address each of these, then conclude with a word of encouragement.

Procession and Spiration

Some Christian theological contribution says a great deal about the "processions." Much is developed in writers such as Augustine and Thomas Aquinas along the lines of the Son "proceeding" from the Father, and the Spirit "proceeding" from the Son or from the Father and the Son together. Terms like *filiation*, *generation*, and *spiration* are also used.[1] The Son eternally *filiates* or is *generated* from the Father (rather than being created).[2] The way the

1. See Thomas, *Summa Theologica* 1.28.4.
2. See Sanders and Swain, *Retrieving Eternal Generation*.

Spirit specifically proceeds from the Father (or from the Father and the Son) is through the action of *spiration*.

There is no single consensus about these matters. Even the ancient Christian writers could be uncertain. Ambrose says in one place, "The Holy Spirit proceeds from the Father, and bears witness to the Son."[3] But later he notes that "He [the Spirit] proceeds from the Son."[4] Still later in the same work, he teaches that "both the Father and the Spirit sent the Son; also, the Father and the Son sent the Spirit."[5] This could be understood to accord with Gal 4:6—"God has sent the Spirit of his Son into our hearts, crying, 'Abba! Father!'" It also accounts for the "sending" language in John 15:26—"When the Advocate comes, whom I will send to you from the Father, the Spirit of truth who comes from the Father, he will testify on my behalf." Anything that might be said about procession, spiration, or filiation occurs outside of time, Augustine teaches, or happens eternally—it is "timeless . . . one must not think of any time in this matter . . . because there is absolutely no such thing as time there [within the Trinity] at all."[6] Even the otherwise rather modern United Church of Canada attests, like the Niceno-Constantinopolitan Creed, that the Holy Spirit "proceeds from the Father and the Son" in the simple present tense—not a past event, nor one that is complete.[7]

These technical treatments of the relations among the Trinity have their place. Another, more complete and exacting book of pneumatology would need to address these concepts, and those books exist. They are elements essential to the full complexity of trinitarian theology. However, I will neither refute nor develop these concepts here, because they are very rarely mentioned or prioritized within the United and Uniting Churches. I will note only that spiration almost inevitably demotes the importance of the Holy Spirit in relation to the Father and the Son, suggesting a derivative, less important status—something against which I cautioned in chapter 2.

The Unforgivable Sin

In Matt 12:31–32, Jesus utters a difficult teaching:

> Therefore I tell you, people will be forgiven for every sin and blasphemy, but blasphemy against the Spirit will not be forgiven.

3. Ambrose, *Holy Spirit* 1.1.
4. Ambrose, *Holy Spirit* 1.11.
5. Ambrose, *Holy Spirit* 3.1.
6. Augustine, *Trinity* 15.6.47.
7. United Church of Canada, "Basis of Union," art. 8.

> Whoever speaks a word against the Son of Man will be forgiven,
> but whoever speaks against the Holy Spirit will not be forgiven,
> either in this age or in the age to come.

Christians have wrestled with this perplexing statement ever since. Some are certain that they have identified what this unique sin might be—anything from lying to theft, from disrespecting God to a specific sexual behavior. Kirsteen Kim suggests that it is related to a kind of idolatry: "It is a serious matter to substitute another spirit for the Holy Spirit . . . mistaking the Holy Spirit for an unclean spirit is described as blasphemy against the Holy Spirit, a sin which cannot be forgiven . . . because the sinner is cut off from the very means God has given of seeing the truth."[8] John Dow, of The United Church of Canada, suggests as follows: "What is this unforgivable sin? It is to see [the Spirit's] good deeds and call them the work of Satan—the sin of deliberate resistance to the truth as we know it in our souls, a stubborn obstinacy that calls good evil and falsehood truth rather than acknowledge our defeat."[9] Others have been less certain about pronouncing a clear interpretation. Scripture itself does not give a precise solution to the question.

If we understand God as graciously forgiving, by virtue of the cross and resurrection of Jesus Christ, and especially in a framework of universalism (the teaching that everyone, in the end, will be saved by God's grace and mercy), the notion of an unforgivable sin is deeply problematic. United and Uniting Churches rarely touch the matter—John Dow was an exception. The assurance of John the apostle—"If we confess our sins, he who is faithful and just will forgive us our sins and cleanse us from all unrighteousness"—also influences what we might say.[10]

I suggest two conclusions. The first is to do all we can to avoid sin, and to live in alignment with Jesus's emphasis on loving God and loving others.[11] Easy to say, harder to accomplish! The second is to remember Paul's dual teaching in Rom 3. First, he says, "All have sinned and fall short of the glory of God" (3:23). Then he follows up immediately with, "they are now justified by his grace as a gift, through the redemption that is in Christ Jesus" (3:24).

The great German theologian Dietrich Bonhoeffer, famous for his resistance to Nazism in the Second World War, was confronted with a terrible, protracted crisis of conscience. He had become involved in a conspiracy to assassinate Hitler, which ran counter to his deep Christian conviction that murder is always wrong. Bonhoeffer refused to explain away his guilt

8. Kim, *Holy Spirit in the World*, 167.

9. Dow, *This Is Our Faith*, 57.

10. 1 John 1:9.

11. Matt 22:34–40.

in this situation. He concluded that we must do what we think to be right (without claiming to be right), and then throw ourselves on the mercy of God. Our own goodness will never save us, and God's grace is never cheap. But the Spirit invites us to rely upon God's grace and mercy when seeking forgiveness, rather than our ability to be perfect and to earn salvation. No matter how the unforgivable sin is defined—or remains undefined—salvation flows from God's grace, not our achievement of private righteousness.

Can the Holy Spirit Be Withdrawn?

No less problematic than a sin that cannot be forgiven is the idea that the Holy Spirit might withdraw her presence or gifts from a person or a community. Most Christian authors rejoice, in contrast, in the unfailing omnipresence of the Spirit, even to the point of expecting an automatic, natural, and necessary endowment. It is a pleasant and reassuring thought that the Spirit of God is always and everywhere present, especially when the blessings and gifts of the Spirit are emphasized. The contrary idea—that She might withdraw—is subjectively and intuitively distressing.

In a passing reference, we see in Gen 6:3 that God resolves not to allow the Spirit (*ruach*) to live within the human race forever, but to limit their lifespans. But within a single lifetime, is the Spirit given permanently? Most notoriously, we find that the accompaniment of the Holy Spirit with King Saul is not guaranteed. He begins his kingship with a sense of humility and the assurance of God's presence in his life. Yet Saul's reign is marked by constant warfare with the Philistines as well as his own temperamental violence. At two decisive points, Saul's unfaithfulness leads to his rejection by God. But later, the Spirit returns. Despite his murderous and mercurial ways, his successor, David, still calls him "the Lord's anointed" and spares his life more than once. Towards the end, Saul consults a psychic medium for guidance, for "when Saul inquired of the Lord, the Lord did not answer him, not by dreams or by Urim or by prophets." His uneven and often sad saga ends when he dies by falling on his own sword and he is humiliated by the Philistines.[12] Another famous Israelite leader, Samson, also loses his connection with the power of the Spirit, though he had enjoyed it for many years. When Samson falls asleep beside Delilah after revealing the secret of his strength, she calls the Philistines, who cut off his hair. Samson rouses himself to fight, but "he did not know that the Lord had left him."[13]

12. See 1 Sam 9:21; 10:7, 10; 11:6; 16:14; 18:12; 19:23; 26:9, 16, 23; 28:3–25; 31:1–10.

13. Judg 16:15–20.

The gifts that the Spirit gives to each individual are closely linked, both to that person's vocation and to the purposes of God that are meant to be enacted through them. Basil writes,

> As an art is *in* the one who practices it, so the grace of the Spirit is *in* him who receives it: it is always present but not always acting. As an art is potentially *in* the artist but becomes so actually when he acts according to it, so also the Spirit, who is always present to those who are worthy, acts when there is a need, whether in the prophecies, or healings, or some other acts of power.[14]

According to Basil, however, this Spirit-endowment can be lost if the acts of grace that the Spirit desires are not exercised, or if a person's sin is too great. Yet—contrastingly—Jesus's teaching in John 14:16 indicates that the Spirit's coming to believers is "for ever."

There is no specific reference to this problem in the teaching of the United and Uniting Churches, who most often affirm the constancy and continuity of the Holy Spirit with and for human beings. The best solution might be to begin by recognizing once again the Holy Spirit's freedom and sovereignty to give or withhold her presence and gifts. That might give us pause when assuming that the Holy Spirit is always and necessarily with us. But our human response should not be fearfulness or hesitation about divine freedom. Instead, we can boldly pray for and seek the blessing of the Spirit, so that we can fulfill our vocation as God's people. It might well be that the Spirit will empower a person with certain gifts for a certain time, then alter that gifting in another season of life. Through it all, God is trustworthy. Our task is to remain faithful and open to sharing in the good work God does, knowing that God's ways are wiser than our own.

Ecstatic or Charismatic Gifts

We looked at the wide range of gifts the Holy Spirit gives to human beings in chapter 12. Each of these empowers the individual and serves the greater good. Beyond these, there are gifts that are considered "ecstatic" or "charismatic"—such as speaking in tongues (glossolalia), words of wisdom, prophecy, exorcism, and performing miracles. These are not emphasized by most United and Uniting Churches, though other Christian traditions value them highly. Generally, there is silence about them in United and Uniting Church writings.

14. Basil, *On the Holy Spirit* 26.61 (italics original to this edition).

Alternatively, we can find suspicion, distrust, or even dismissal of such manifestations of the Spirit. Richard Roberts, of The United Church of Canada, expresses his disdain this way:

> The "speaking with tongues" at Pentecost must be identified with those ecstatic but unintelligible utterances which frequently accompany outbreaks of religious excitement. Their significance is psychological rather than religious . . . it is safe to say that glossolalia was only a passing phenomenon.

Roberts continues, asserting that by the time of Paul's later letters

> the church had outgrown the phase in which transient aberrations and extravagances were regarded as the marks of the spiritual life and had reached the normal plane of a rational spirituality.[15]

Roberts's terms—*outgrown, aberrations, normal, rational*—are telling! Luther and Calvin, in their time, were also hesitant about the gifts of tongues, healing, and visions. The trust that Anabaptists (and perhaps Roman Catholics) placed in such gifts challenged the magisterial Reformers' insistence that the word and sacraments must govern the Christian life.[16]

I would suggest that the hesitation (and disdain) seen in Roberts, Luther, and Calvin continues to inform the trajectories of United and Uniting Churches, who tend to distance themselves from ecstatic experiences of the Spirit. Perhaps even more significant for these contemporary denominations, which are deeply influenced by Western rationalism, the United and Uniting Churches are also shaped by modernist skepticism, making them suspicious or even hostile to these gifts. The rationally oriented, science-informed, and largely disembodied northern European and British theological and ecclesial approaches that have shaped many United and Uniting Churches are not friendly toward ecstatic, "emotional" expressions of faith. As Thayer and Jacobsen argue, "Other traditions, the [United Church of Christ (USA)] among them, tend to focus less on the spectacular and more on the ways the Spirit affects us as persons," such as developing the fruit of the Spirit within us (Gal 5:22–23).[17] From this same denomination, Shinn and Williams claim that "today we tend to distrust emotionalism and exaggerated religious behavior. . . . Most of us [distrust] excessive

15. Roberts, *Spirit of God*, 23, 25–26.
16. Kärkäinnen, *Holy Spirit*, 50.
17. Thayer and Jacobsen, *Christ, Creeds and Life*, 96.

emotionalism."[18] Of course, this is highly determined by cultural norms, as Shinn and Williams acknowledge in passing.

Who is "us"? Who determines what constitutes "excessive"? And what makes emotionalism untrustworthy? In some cultures, emotion is a sign of authenticity, not insincerity. The United and Uniting Churches (especially those in the North Atlantic) can be narrow-minded about this aspect of human religious expression.

In contrast, Pentecostal and other charismatic movements have revived an embrace of ecstatic gifts in the last century, in all countries, and especially in the global South. As Ruthven notes,

> The salient characteristic of Pentecostalism is its belief in the present-day manifestation of spiritual gifts, such as miraculous healing, prophecy and, most distinctively, glossolalia [speaking in tongues]. Pentecostals affirm that these spiritual gifts (charismata) are granted by the Holy Spirit and are normative in contemporary church life and ministry.[19]

While the United and Uniting Church orientation to these manifestations might be skeptical, there is still something to learn from and respect in our siblings in the Christian family. There are insights here to which United and Uniting Churches are typically less alert.

At the same time, there are warnings about the misuse of ecstatic gifts. Meehyun Chung cautions as follows:

> Yonggi Cho [founder of the Yoido Full Gospel Church in South Korea], who has the charismatic power to control exorcism and healing, underlines the disturbance of the Holy Spirit's work. . . . Because of the expectation of prosperity, his message and prayers for wellbeing have been very influential. Personal cults are the logical outcome of this process. If the pastor is identified as a messenger of the Holy Spirit . . . people are not allowed to comment or criticize. Those who dare to raise their voice could easily be accused of possessing evil power and disturbing the Holy Spirit's work. Thus, a lack of democratic discussion on administration and management reinforced the authoritarian congregation system. The monopoly of power and dominance in one person causes frequent financial opacity and sexual harassment. . . . [But] the monopolization of power and dominance is not a work of the Holy Spirit.[20]

18. Shinn and Williams, *We Believe*, 89.

19. Ruthven, *On the Cessation*, 14.

20. Meehyun Chung, "Inquiry of Pentecostalism," 52, 57.

Such misuse of spiritual gifts is a dire distortion of God's purposes. Care must be taken to assess and to consult wisely in community to discern the authenticity and integrity of any gift's deployment. Christians are no less likely to err in their use of resources than any other group.

In biblical terms, the ecstatic gifts include seeing visions, speaking in tongues, interpreting tongues, physical healing, casting out demons, prophecy, being slain in the Spirit, auditory communication from God, performing miracles, and dreams. Paul lists some of these in 1 Cor 12:4–11. To understand these gifts as the actions and influence of the Holy Spirit is consistent with other biblical testimony about the Spirit "filling" or "coming upon" individuals and groups. Despite modernist rejection of such gifts, Western skepticism, and healthy cautions about their misuse, these gifts are well attested throughout Christian history and are once again broadly celebrated and observed around the world today.[21]

It remains, then, to discern the value and appropriate use of the ecstatic gifts. They are not fading into history. It is helpful to think of the ecstatic gifts in the same way that Luther regards the gifts of the Holy Spirit in general. According to him, they are

> bestowed for the good of the entire Church. . . . [The Spirit] would have the Spirit's gifts used in the service of others, and admonishes Christians to consider all they have as given of God. . . . [Thus] let Christians know they are under obligation to serve God with their gifts; and God is served when they employ them for the advantage and service of the people—reforming them, bringing them to a knowledge of God, and thus building up, strengthening and perpetuating the Church.[22]

As with any gift of the Spirit, the church must certainly test and verify the ecstatic gifts, lest a false spirit inhabit them. The Holy Spirit's work of liberating, transforming, and healing, while drawing persons and communities into harmony with God's purposes, ought to be a visible result of the exercise of these gifts. Any other outcome should be rejected or at least critically examined. But they ought not to be rejected outright without such testing. To paraphrase Gamaliel, who called for patience when Peter and other apostles were examined before the Sanhedrin (Acts 5:27–39), I suggest that it is not for any of us to dismiss *in advance* what the Holy Spirit might do. Is there in her an element of mystery, or do we have her completely figured

21. See Dodson and Yong, "Charismatic Gifts."

22. See "Ascension Day—Stewards of God's Gifts" in Luther, *Sermons on Epistle Texts*, 278.

out in advance? Is She truly free, or is She subject to the conditions we place upon her? Who are we to "hinder God?"[23]

There are important exceptions to the "no thanks" attitude of many United and Uniting Churches with regard to ecstatic gifts. The United Church in Jamaica and the Cayman Islands, for example, acknowledges the gift of tongues while placing various cautions around its use.[24] The Uniting Church in Australia has communities of faith in which the ecstatic gifts and charismatic experiences of the Holy Spirit are welcome and normative. Djiniyini Gondarra, a minister and former moderator of the northern synod of the Uniting Church in Australia, provides an important example. He describes a period of charismatic Holy Spirit revival in Galiwin'ku, a small community on Elcho Island, 640 km east of Darwin in Northern Australia. In the midst of much social upheaval and turmoil on the island, Gondarra relates the following events during a Bible study session:

> I then asked the group to hold each other's hands and I began to pray for the people and for the church, that God would pour out his Holy Spirit to bring healing and renewal. . . . Suddenly we began to feel God's Spirit moving in our hearts . . . and everybody began to pray in the Spirit and in harmony. And there was a great noise going on in the room and we began to ask one another what was going on. . . . In that same evening the word just spread like the flames of fire and reached the whole community in Galiwin'ku. Gelung and I couldn't sleep at all that night because people were just coming for the ministry, bringing the sick to be prayed for, for healing. . . . Next morning the Galiwin'ku Community once again became the new community. The love of Jesus was being shared and many expressions of forgiveness were taking place in the families and in the tribes. . . . Before then I would have expected to hear only fighting and swearing and many other troublesome things that would hurt your feelings and make you feel sad. . . . The spirit of revival has not only affected the Uniting Church communities and the parishes, but Anglican churches in Arnhem Land as well, such as in Angurugu, Umbakumba, Roper River, Numbulwar and Oenpelli. These all have experienced the revival, and have been touched by the joy and the happiness and the love of Christ.[25]

Note here the genuinely Spirit-led effects of these events: communal impact ("for the good of all"), healing, unity, love, and reconciliation. Experiences

23. Acts 11:16–17.

24. United Church in Jamaica and the Cayman Islands, *Our Church*, 84–89.

25. Gondarra, "Pentecost for Australian Aborigines," 37–38.

such as these transcend and are unconcerned with the Enlightenment skepticism of the modern West.

Paul's caution is always helpful: We should test that using any spiritual gifts truly benefits the community, as they did in Galiwin'ku on Elcho Island. Love comes first and serving others follows quickly after:

> Pursue love and strive for the spiritual gifts. . . . Those who prophesy speak to other people *for their upbuilding and encouragement and consolation.* Those who speak in a tongue build up themselves, but those who prophesy *build up the church.* Now I would like all of you to speak in tongues but even more to prophesy. One who prophesies is greater than one who speaks in tongues, unless someone interprets, *so that the church may be built up.* . . . So with yourselves: since you are striving after spiritual gifts, seek to excel in them *for building up the church.*[26]

I would argue that as Pentecostal and charismatic expressions of Christianity continue to spread throughout the world, those of us in the mainline denominations would do well to listen carefully and respectfully to the spiritual experiences of those who are unlike us. A fundamental commitment to the freedom of the Holy Spirit to do as She wishes among her people ought to inform that careful listening. The free and sovereign Spirit will act in ways that accord with her nature and serve the greater (and sometimes inscrutable) goals of the triune God. That might indeed include actions that surprise and astound us, or cause us to doubt: "Of one thing, however, we can be sure: God's Spirit regularly has surprises in store for us."[27] I also want to listen attentively to those (like Djiniyini Gondarra) who testify to how these gifts have blessed them, as well as the legitimate warnings of others (like Meehyun Chung). The two essential guides in assessing the legitimacy of all spiritual gifts must be love and building up.

Baptism in the Holy Spirit

Baptism is most often considered a sacramental act that involves water. Still, some Christians prize "Holy Spirit baptism" as a distinct phenomenon. While the Second Testament refers occasionally to "baptism in the Holy Spirit" (see Matt 3:11; Acts 1:5 and 19:6), this expression of faith and practice is rarely mentioned by the United and Uniting Churches. The United

26. 1 Cor 14:1–5, 12; emphasis added.

27. United Reformed Church [UK], *What Do We Believe*, 7.

Church in Jamaica and the Cayman Islands offers the following helpful assessment:

> It would seem that the "Baptism of the Holy Spirit" refers to a special outpouring of the Spirit on an individual or group of individuals. . . . Baptism of the Holy Spirit takes place in some dramatic or supernatural form. . . . [But it] may not be outwardly dramatic.

At the same time, the experience of such a Spirit baptism should not be mistaken for advanced spiritual status:

> Christians who have never had such a dramatic experience must not assume that they do [not] have the Holy Spirit or that they are "second-rate" Christians. . . . Rom 8:9 clearly states that all who believe in Christ are "His" [and] have the Holy Spirit.[28]

The United Church in Jamaica and the Cayman Islands provides useful guidance here. Like other ecstatic or charismatic gifts, described above, baptism in the Holy Spirit remains a significant experience for many Christians.

Others disagree about the significance of this phenomenon. The Uniting Church in Australia argues that Spirit baptism does not complete or fulfill something that was absent from water baptism, as if that "first" baptism was insufficient, or as if the Spirit was only partially present: "Those who speak of one Baptism that makes us new creatures spiritually, and another Baptism by which we receive the Holy Spirit with power, are making a division which is not found in the New Testament."[29] Ephesians 4:4–5 is a good reminder: "There is one body and one Spirit . . . one Lord, one faith, one baptism."

At its best, baptism in the Spirit is understood as a blessing to both an individual and to the community. But it should never be understood to elevate the status, importance, or authority of one Christian over another. All baptized Christians are beloved in the Lord and are commissioned for meaningful service and ministry. Although United and Uniting Churches are mostly silent on the question, once again, there are worthwhile things to learn from those who have closely assessed this experience.

28. United Church in Jamaica and the Cayman Islands, *Our Church*, 88–89.

29. Uniting Church in Australia, "Understanding the Church's Teaching on Baptism," 544.

CONCLUSION: A WORD OF ENCOURAGEMENT

In these final considerations, the unfinished business of this book, there are many threads that could be pulled. These subthemes of pneumatology are worthy of further study. I will leave them for another day, or for another researcher to pursue.

At the outset of this study, I noted that accounting for the Holy Spirit will always be partial and incomplete, given the nature of the subject matter. The well-respected Methodist scholar Albert Outler reassures me when he writes that "any attempted focus on the Holy Spirit is bound to be blurred."[30] Theological study is not so much the quest for the perfect formulation of the divine mystery in words, but the development of virtues such as humility, temperance, justice, and love within those who study theology.[31]

My final word to you, dear reader, is to encourage you to be bold in asking for, seeking out, noticing, and embracing the presence and gifts of the Holy Spirit. She who is One-with-the-Trinity desires your wellbeing. She comes to liberate, transform, and heal. She longs to empower your life and service for the sake of the realm of God and the health of the communities and world in which you live. Learning about the Spirit's gifts and how they manifest in your life, and in the life of your community and God's beloved world, is a dynamic and enriching process. Learning to see and to embrace the presence of the Holy Spirit in everyday life is a pathway that brings much joy and fulfillment. The *promise* of the Holy Spirit is that, in the end, no sin or trouble will prevent the triune God from bringing about the loving redemption, joy, and transformation of all creation.

Above all, the fruit of the Spirit—"love, joy, peace, patience, kindness, generosity, faithfulness, gentleness, and self-control" (Gal 5:22–23)—are truly the graces that make life in God's world of nature and people an exhilarating and fulfilling journey. I will conclude by joining Ambrose of Milan in this prayer, hoping that you will share it also:

> Let the water of your Holy Spirit come into my soul and my body, that by the moisture of this rain, the valleys of our minds and the fields of our inmost hearts may grow green. Amen.[32]

30. Outler, "Focus on the Holy Spirit," 3.
31. See Rogers, *After the Spirit*, 14.
32. Adapted from Ambrose, *Holy Spirit* 1.16.

FOR REFLECTION OR DISCUSSION

1. Two of the pieces of unfinished business—charismatic gifts of the Holy Spirit and baptism in the Holy Spirit—are much more developed in denominations beyond the United and Uniting Churches. What could you share about your experiences or thinking about these phenomena?
2. At the end of the book, what unanswered questions are you left with? What would you like to learn about next?

Appendix

United and Uniting Churches Affiliated with the World Council of Churches as of 2026

WHAT ARE THE UNITED and Uniting Churches? The World Council of Churches offers the following information:

> United churches are those which have been formed through the fusion of two or more separate churches, of different or the same confession. They have arisen over the past two centuries as churches have sought to make the unity given them in Christ fully visible. In union, churches move beyond cooperation and partnership to a degree of mutual accountability which can adequately be expressed only by life within a single ecclesial structure. . . .
>
> The United churches form probably the most diverse family of churches worldwide. . . .
>
> To this point the United and Uniting churches have not formed their own Christian World Communion, not wanting to become "another denomination" and perhaps fearing that such a move would lessen their zeal for further union. . . .
>
> With their commitment to making unity fully visible, and their practical experience of union, the United and Uniting churches continue to make a distinctive and important contribution to the ecumenical movement.[1]

1. World Council of Churches, "United and Uniting Churches."

The denominations considered part of the United and Uniting Churches of the World Council of Churches are as follows:

China Christian Council
Church of Bangladesh
EKD—Bremen Evangelical Church
EKD—Evangelical Church Berlin-Brandenburg-Silesian Oberlausitz
EKD—Evangelical Church in Baden
EKD—Evangelical Church in Rhineland
EKD—Evangelical Church of Anhalt
EKD—Evangelical Church of Kurhessen-Waldeck
EKD—Evangelical Church of the Palatinate
EKD—Evangelical Church of Westphalia
EKD—Protestant Church in Hesse and Nassau
Evangelical Church in Germany
International Council of Community Churches
Union of Protestant Churches in Alsace and Lorraine
Union of the Armenian Evangelical Churches in the Near East
Union of Welsh Independents
United Church in Jamaica and the Cayman Islands
United Church in Papua New Guinea
United Church in the Solomon Islands
United Church of Canada
United Church of Christ—Congregational in the Marshall Islands
United Church of Christ in Japan
United Church of Christ in the Philippines
United Church of Christ (USA)
United Church of Christ in Zimbabwe
United Church of Zambia
United Congregational Church of Southern Africa
United Free Church of Scotland
United Presbyterian Church of Brazil
United Protestant Church of Belgium
United Protestant Church of Curaçao
United Protestant Church of France
Uniting Church in Australia
Uniting Church in Sweden
Uniting Presbyterian Church in Southern Africa
Uniting Reformed Church in Southern Africa
Waldensian Church

About the Author

Robert C. Fennell is professor of historical and systematic theology and past academic dean of Atlantic School of Theology. He is also an ordained minister of The United Church of Canada. His previous books, as coeditor or coauthor, include:

The Rule of Faith and Biblical Interpretation: Reform, Resistance, and Renewal

31 Short Spiritual Practices

Following Jesus Today: Stories and Reflections

Living Traditions: 500 Years of Re-Forming Christianity

The Other Side of the Wardrobe: C. S. Lewis and Everyday Discipleship

Three Ways of Grace: Drawing Closer to the Trinity

Turning Ourselves Inside Out: The Thriving Christian Communities Project

Bibliography

"An Affirmation of Faith and Commitment: A Statement for Use in the Church of North India." In Dhirendra Kumar Sahu, *United and Uniting: A Story of the Church of North India*, 97–98. Delhi: ISPCK, 2001.

Ambrose of Milan. *The Holy Spirit*. In *Saint Ambrose: Theological and Dogmatic Works*, 29–214. Translated by Roy J. Deferrari. The Fathers of the Church 44. Washington, DC: Catholic University of America Press, 1963.

Anselm. *Proslogium; Monologium; An Appendix in Behalf of the Fool by Gaunilon; Cur Deus Homo*. Translated by S. N. Deane. La Salle: Open Court, 1926.

"The Apostles' Creed." Creeds of Christendom. https://www.creeds.net/ancient/apostles.htm.

Aquinas, Thomas. *Summa Theologica*. New York: Benzinger, 1947.

"Athanasian Creed." Creeds of Christendom. https://www.creeds.net/ancient/Quicumque.html.

Augustine of Hippo. "Letter 169 (415 CE): Bishop Augustine to Bishop Evodius." In Vol. 1 of *The Nicene and Post-Nicene Fathers*, First Series. Edited by Philip Schaff. Translated by J. G. Cunningham. New York: Christian Literature, 1887.

———. *Of Faith and the Creed*. In Vol. 3 of *The Nicene and Post-Nicene Fathers*, First Series. Edited by Philip Schaff. Translated by S. D. F. Salmond. New York: Christian Literature, 1887.

———. *The Trinity*. Vol. 5 of *The Works of Saint Augustine*. Edited by John E. Rostelle. Translated by Edmund Hill. New York: New City, 1991.

Ayres, Lewis. "The Holy Spirit as the 'Undiminished Giver': Didymus the Blind's *De spiritu santo* and the Development of Nicene Pneumatology." In *The Holy Spirit in the Fathers of the Church: The Proceedings of the Seventh International Patristic Conference, Maynooth, 2008*, edited by D. Vincent Twomey and Janet E. Rutherford, 57–72. Dublin: Four Courts, 2010.

Bakken, Kenneth L. "Holy Spirit and Theosis: Toward a Lutheran Theology of Healing." *St. Vladimir's Theological Quarterly* 38 (1994) 409–23.

Basil the Great [Basil of Caesarea]. *On the Holy Spirit*. Translated by Stephen Hildebrand. Yonkers, NY: St. Vladimir's Seminary Press, 2011.

Beintker, Michael, and Albrecht Philipps, eds. "Das Handeln Gottes in der Erfahrung des Glaubens" [The action of God in the experience of faith]. Ch. 2 in *Das Handeln Gottes in der Erfahrung des Glaubens: Ein Votum des Theologischen Ausschusses der Union Evangelischer Kirchen in der EKD (UEK)* [The action of God in the experience of faith: A statement by the Theological Committee of the Union of Evangelical Churches in the EKD (UEK)]. Berlin: De Gruyter Brill, 2021.

Bergin, Helen. "Feminist Pneumatology." *Colloquium* 42 (2010) 188–207.

Boff, Leonardo. *Come, Holy Spirit: Inner Fire, Giver of Life and Comforter of the Poor.* Maryknoll, NY: Orbis, 2015.

Boseto, Leslie. "Mission and Unity in United and Uniting Churches: A Pacific Perspective." *Ecumenical Review* 39 (1987) 282–90.

Budden, Chris. *Following Jesus in Invaded Space: Doing Theology on Aboriginal Land.* Eugene, OR: Wipf & Stock, 2009.

Bulgakov, Sergius. *The Bride of the Lamb.* Translated by Boris Jakim. London: T&T Clark, 2002.

Burnabas, D. "Theological Vision of the Church of South India." In *United to Unite: History of the Church of South India, 1947–1997*, edited by J. W. Gladstone, 47–60. Chennai: Church of South India, 1997.

Caltech Science Exchange. "What Is Entanglement and Why Is it Important?" California Institute of Technology, 2024. https://scienceexchange.caltech.edu/topics/quantum-science-explained/entanglement.

Calvin, John. *Institutes of the Christian Religion.* Edited by John T. McNeill. Translated by Ford Lewis Battles. Library of Christian Classics 20—21. Louisville: Westminster, 1960.

Cantalamessa, Raniero. *The Mystery of Pentecost.* Collegeville: Liturgical, 2001.

Chen Zemin. "Spirit, Please Come Upon Us" ["Shang Zhu Zhi Ling Ken Qiu Jiang Lin"]. In *Search and Witness* [*Qiu Suo Yü Jian Zheng*], 249–52. N.p.: Chinese Christian Society, 2007. [Privately translated by Chuan Xu, Sept. 27, 2024.]

China Christian Council. "Introduction to Doctrines: Important Q&A." https://en.ccctspm.org/answer/3?page=6.

Chung, Meehyun. "Inquiry of Pentecostalism Regarding Pneumatology: A Theological Suggestion of a Feminist Perspective." *International Review of Mission* 107 (2018) 49–63.

The Church of North India. *The Constitution of the Church of North India.* Delhi: ISPCK, 1987.

———. *Plan of Church Union in North India and Pakistan.* Madras: CLS, 1965.

The Church of South India. "Basis of Union." In *The Constitution of the Church of South India*, 68–89. Madras: Christian Literature Society, 1952.

Comblin, Joseph. *The Holy Spirit and Liberation.* Maryknoll, NY: Orbis, 1989.

Community of Protestant Churches in Europe. *Agreement Between Reformation Churches in Europe (The Leuenburg Agreement).* Mar. 16, 1973. https://www.leuenberg.eu/documents/.

Confessional Synod of the German Evangelical Church. "Barmen Theological Declaration." Creeds and Confessions. https://creedsandconfessions.org/barmen-declaration.html.

"Confession of the Reformed Churches of Piedmont (The Waldensian Confession of Faith of 1655)." Creeds and Confessions. https://creedsandconfessions.org/waldensian-confession.html.

Confessional Synod of the German Evangelical Church. "Barmen Theological Declaration [1934]." Creeds and Confessions. https://creedsandconfessions.org/barmen-declaration.html.

Congar, Yves. "The Motherhood in God and the Femininity of the Holy Spirit." Pages 155–64 in *The River of Life Flows in the East and in the West.* Vol. 3 of *I Believe in the Holy Spirit* Translated by David Smith. London: Geoffrey Chapman, 1983.

"The Creed of Nicaea—Agreed at the Council in 325." Early Church Texts. https://earlychurchtexts.com/public/creed_of_nicaea_325.htm.

Crisp, Oliver D., and Fred Sanders, eds. *The Third Person of the Trinity: Explorations in Constructive Dogmatics.* Grand Rapids: Zondervan, 2020.

Crittenden, Jeffrey Paul. *Leisure Resurrected: Rekindling the Fire of Early Christian Communities.* Eugene, OR: Pickwick, 2023.

Cyril of Jerusalem. *Catechetical Lectures.* In vol. 7 of *The Nicene and Post-Nicene Fathers,* Second Series. Edited by Philip Schaff and Henry Wace. Translated by Edwin Hamilton Gifford. New York: Christian Literature, 1893.

Daly, Mary. *Beyond God the Father: Toward a Philosophy of Women's Liberation.* Boston: Beacon, 1974.

Day, Juliette. "Cyril of Jerusalem on the Holy Spirit." In *The Holy Spirit in the Fathers of the Church: The Proceedings of the Seventh International Patristic Conference, Maynooth, 2008,* edited by D. Vincent Twomey and Janet E. Rutherford, 73–98. Dublin: Four Courts, 2010.

Dingayan, Luna L. *A Catechetical Guide on the UCCP [United Church of Christ in the Philippines] Statement of Faith.* https://uccpchurch.com/wp-content/uploads/2016/03/A-Catechetical-Guide-on-the-UCCP-SOF.pdf.

Djomhoue, Priscille. "Manifestations of Ecumenism in Africa Today: A Study of the Mainline and Pentecostal Churches in Cameroon." *International Journal for the Study of the Christian Church* 8 (2008) 355–68.

Dodson, Jacob, and Amos Yong. "Charismatic Gifts." St. Andrews Encyclopaedia of Theology. https://www.saet.ac.uk/Christianity/CharismaticGifts.

Dow, John. *This Is Our Faith: An Exposition of the Statement of Faith of the United Church of Canada.* Toronto: The United Church of Canada, 1943.

Eglise Protestante Unie de France [United Protestant Church of France]. "Nouvelle déclaration de foi 2017" ["New statement of faith 2017"]. https://epudf.org/convictions/declarations-de-foi-et-textes-doctrinaux/.

Ephrem the Syrian. *St. Ephrem the Syrian: The Hymns on Faith.* Translated by Jeffrey T. Wickes. The Fathers of the Church 130. Washington, DC: Catholic University of America Press, 2015.

Finnamore, Alice. "Holy, Holy, Holy." Unpublished hymn, 2025.

Florensky, Pavel. *The Pillar and Ground of the Truth.* Translated by Boris Jakim. Princeton: Princeton University Press, 1997.

Friends Peace House. "About Us." https://friendspeacehouse.com/index.php/about-us.

Gondarra, Djiniyini. "Pentecost for Australian Aborigines." *Renewal Journal* 1 (1993) 33–39.

Gregory of Nyssa. "On What it Means to Call Oneself a Christian." In *St. Gregory of Nyssa: Ascetical Works,* translated by Virginia Woods Callaghan, 79–92. The Fathers of the Church 58. Washington, DC: Catholic University of America Press, 2000.

Gregory Nazianzen. *Fifth Theological Oration.* In vol. 7 of *The Nicene and Post-Nicene Fathers,* Second Series. Edited by Philip Schaff and Henry Wace. Translated by Charles Gordon Browne and James Edward Swallow. New York: Christian Literature, 1894.

Hall, Douglas John. *Confessing the Faith*. Minneapolis: Fortress, 1996.

———. *Professing the Faith*. Minneapolis: Fortress, 1993.

———. *Thinking the Faith*. Minneapolis: Fortress, 1989.

Harris, Leon. "The Holy Spirit as Liberator: An Exploration of a Black American Pneumatology of Freedom." In *The Third Person of the Trinity: Explorations in Constructive Dogmatics*, edited by Oliver D. Crisp and Fred Sanders, 179–95. Grand Rapids: Zondervan, 2020.

Heatherington, Jessica. "Looking for the Light of Christ and Hope of the Holy Spirit at COP30: They Aren't Where You Might Expect. I Offer a Prayer at the End of This Reflection." Faith. Climate Crisis. Action., Nov. 14, 2025. https://jessicahetherington.substack.com/p/looking-for-the-light-of-christ-and.

"Heidelberg Catechism [1563]." Evangelische Kirche in Deutschland. https://www.ekd.de/en/Heidelberg-Catechism-302.htm.

Hill, Graham. "Contemporary Issues in Evangelism and Mission: Perspectives and Contributions from the Uniting Church in Australia." *Uniting Church Studies* 27 (2025) 30–44.

Igreja Presbiteriana Unida do Brasil [United Presbyterian Church of Brazil]. "Declaração de Atibaia" ["Atibaia Declaration"]. September 10, 1978. https://ipu.org.br/declaracao-atibaia/.

———. "Princípios de Fé e Ordem" ["Principles of faith and order"]. https://ipu.org.br/documentos/principio-de-fe-e-ordem/.

Inbody, Joel. "Sending God: Bodily Manifestations and Their Interpretation in Pentecostal Rituals and Everyday Life." *Sociology of Religion* 76 (2015) 337–55.

Irenaeus of Lyon. *Against Heresies*. In vol. 1 of *The Ante-Nicene Fathers*. Edited and translated by A. Cleveland Coxe. New York: Christian Literature, 1885.

———. *Proof of the Apostolic Preaching*. Translated by Joseph P. Smith. Westminster: Newman, 1952.

Jacobs, Adrian. "The Holy Spirit." In *The Theology of The United Church of Canada*, edited by Don Schweitzer et al., 153–72. Waterloo: Wilfrid Laurier University Press, 2019.

Jensen, David H. "Discerning the Spirit: A Historical Introduction." In *The Lord and Giver of Life: Perspectives on Constructive Pneumatology*, edited by David H. Jensen, 1–23. Louisville: Westminster John Knox, 2008.

———. "Introduction." In *The Lord and Giver of Life: Perspectives on Constructive Pneumatology*, edited by David H. Jensen, viii–xvii. Louisville: Westminster John Knox, 2008.

Johnson, Elizabeth. *She Who Is: The Mystery of God in Feminist Theological Discourse*. New York: Crossroad, 1993.

———. *Women, Earth, and Creator Spirit*. Mahwah, NJ: Paulist, 1993.

Johnson, James Weldon. "The Creation." In *God's Trombones*, 17–20. New York: Viking, 1927.

Joint National Conference of the China Christian Council and Chinese Christian Three-Self Patriotic Movement of Protestant Churches in China. "Church Order of Protestant Churches in China, 2018." *Chinese Theological Review* 30 (2020) 1–22.

Jones, Jeanette. "A Theological Interpretation of 'Viriditas' in Hildegard of Bingen and Gregory the Great." *Portfolio of the Department of Musicology and Ethnomusicology* 1 (2012). https://www.bu.edu/pdme/jeannette-jones/#_edn21.

Kärkkäinen, Veli-Matti. *The Holy Spirit: A Guide to Christian Theology*. Louisville: Westminster John Knox, 2012.

———. *One with God: Salvation as Deification and Justification*. Collegeville, MN: Liturgical, 2004.

———. *Pneumatology: The Holy Spirit in Ecumenical, International, and Contextual Perspective*. 2nd edition. Grand Rapids: Baker Academic, 2018.

———. *Spirit and Salvation*. Vol. 4 of *A Constructive Christian Theology for the Pluralistic World*. Grand Rapids: Eerdmans, 2016.

Kim, Kirsteen. *The Holy Spirit in the World: A Global Conversation*. Maryknoll, NY: Orbis, 2007.

———. *Mission in the Spirit: The Holy Spirit in Indian Christian Theologies*. Delhi: ISPCK, 2003.

Kukla, Elliott. "Terms for Gender Diversity in Classical Jewish Texts." Transtorah, 2006. http://www.transtorah.org/PDFs/Classical_Jewish_Terms_for_Gender_Diversity.pdf.

Lang, Andy. "Come, Holy Spirit." *Witness for Justice: United Church of Christ*, May 28 2020. https://www.ucc.org/come_holy_spirit_05282020/.

Leahy, Brendan. "'Hiding Behind the Works': The Holy Spirit in the Trinitarian Rhythm of Human Fulfillment in the Theology of Irenaeus." In *The Holy Spirit in the Fathers of the Church: The Proceedings of the Seventh International Patristic Conference, Maynooth, 2008*, edited by D. Vincent Twomey and Janet E. Rutherford, 11–31. Dublin: Four Courts, 2010.

LeSieur, Simon P. "Come, Holy Spirit: Towards a Pneumatologically-Recalibrated Mainline Ecclesiology at West Vancouver United Church." DMin Ministry Focus Paper, Fuller Seminary, 2022.

Long, Kimberly Bracken. *The Worshiping Body: The Art of Leading Worship*. Louisville: Westminster John Knox, 2009.

Luther, Martin. *The Large Catechism*. Translated by F. Bente and W. H. T. Dau. https://www.ccel.org/l/luther/large_cat/large_catechism.html.

———. *Lectures on Genesis 1–5*. Vol. 1 of *Luther's Works*. Edited by Jaroslav Pelikan. Translated by George V. Schick. St. Louis: Concordia, 1958.

———. *Sermon on the Mount and the Magnificat*. Vol. 21 of *Luther's Works*. Edited by Jaroslav Pelikan. Translated by A. T. W. Steinhaeuser. St. Louis: Concordia, 1956.

———. *Sermons on Epistle Texts for Epiphany, Easter, and Pentecost*. Vol. 7 of *Martin Luther: Sermons*. Edited by John Nicholas Lenker. Translated John Nicholas Lenker et al. 1909. https://sermons.martinluther.us/Luther_Lenker_Vol_7.pdf.

———. *The Small Catechism*. https://www.ccel.org/ccel/luther/smallcat.toc.html.

———. *Word and Sacrament III*. Vol. 37 of *Luther's Works*. Edited by Robert H. Fischer. Minneapolis: Fortress, 1976.

Macleod, Ennis. "On Not Losing the Way: The Holy Spirit in the Basis of Union." In *The Present and Future of the Basis of Union: Marking Fifty Years*, edited by Geoff Thompson and Ji Zhang, 95–104. Melbourne: Uniting Academic, 2024.

McFague, Sallie. *Models of God: Theology for an Ecological, Nuclear Age*. Minneapolis: Fortress, 1987.

Medina, Néstor. "Theological Musings Toward a Latina/o Pneumatology." In *The Wiley Blackwell Companion to Latino/a Theology*, edited by Orlando Espín, 174–89. Chichester: Wiley, 2015.

Meng Yanling. "An Approach to Biblical Exegesis for Evangelical Women: The Story of Dinah in Genesis 34." *Chinese Theological Review* 30 (2020) 171–95.

Moltmann, Jürgen. *The Church in the Power of the Spirit: A Contribution to Messianic Ecclesiology.* Translated by Margaret Kohl. New York: Harper and Row, 1977.

———. *God in Creation: A New Theology of Creation and the Spirit of God.* Translated by Margaret Kohl. Minneapolis: Fortress, 1993.

———. *Science and Wisdom.* Translated by Margaret Kohl. Minneapolis: Fortress, 2003.

———. *The Source of Life: The Holy Spirit and the Theology of Life.* Translated by Margaret Kohl. Minneapolis: Fortress, 1997.

———. *The Spirit of Life: A Universal Affirmation.* Translated by Margaret Kohl. Minneapolis: Fortress, 1992.

Moore, Clive, ed. "Boseto, Leslie (1933–)." Solomon Islands Historical Encyclopaedia, 1893–1978. https://www.solomonencyclopaedia.net/biogs/E000403b.htm.

Musuku, Tobias M. "Prophetic Mission of Faith Communities During Apartheid South Africa, 1948–1994: An Agenda for a Prophetic Mission Praxis in the Democratic SA." *Missionalia* 42 (2014) 151–67. https://missionalia.journals.ac.za/pub/article/view/66/pdf_30.

"Niceno-Constantinopolitan Creed." Creeds of Christendom. https://www.creeds.net/ancient/nicene.htm.

O'Loughlin, Thomas. "St Augustine's View of the Place of the Holy Spirit in the Formation of the Gospels." In *The Holy Spirit in the Fathers of the Church: The Proceedings of the Seventh International Patristic Conference, Maynooth, 2008*, edited by D. Vincent Twomey and Janet E. Rutherford, 86–95. Dublin: Four Courts, 2010.

Origen. *De Principiis.* In vol. 4 of *The Ante-Nicene Fathers.* Edited by Alexander Roberts and James Donaldson. New York: Christian Literature, 1885.

Oussoren, A. H. Harry. "The Scope of the Spirit's Life-Giving Work: Series Post 8." Pilgrim Praxis, May 8, 2020. https://www.minister.ca/the-scope-of-the-life-giving-spirit.

Outler, Albert C. "A Focus on the Holy Spirit: Spirit and Spirituality in John Wesley." *Quarterly Review* 8 (1988) 3–18.

———. "The Wesleyan Quadrilateral—In John Wesley." *Wesleyan Theological Journal* 20 (1985) 7–18.

Owen, Michael. "The Place and Nature of Doctrine in the Uniting Church." In *Marking Twenty Years: The Uniting Church in Australia 1977–1997*, edited by William W. Emilsen and Susan Emilsen, 287–97. North Parramatta: UTC, 1997.

Peterson, Cheryl M. *The Holy Spirit in the Christian Life.* Grand Rapids: Baker Academic, 2024.

Pinnock, Clark H. *Flame of Love: A Theology of the Holy Spirit.* Downer's Grove: InterVarsity, 1996.

Pitakaji, Armstrong. "A Theo-Cultural Exploration on the Sacredness of Land in Contemporary Lauru Context." MA dissertation, University of Kwazulu Natal, 2019.

Polkinghorne, John, and Michael Welker. *Faith in the Living God: A Dialogue.* London: SPCK, 2001.

Ramsey, Michael. *Holy Spirit: A Biblical Study.* London: SPCK, 1977.

Roberts, Richard. *The Spirit of God and the Faith of Today.* Chicago: Willett, Clark & Colby, 1930.

Rogers, Eugene. *After the Spirit: A Constructive Pneumatology from Resources Outside the Modern West.* Grand Rapids: Eerdmans, 2005.

Rowe, Keith. "The Wesleyan Heritage as Conversation Partner in a New Day." In *Marking Twenty Years: The Uniting Church in Australia 1977–1997*, edited by William W. Emilsen and Susan Emilsen, 47–56. North Parramatta: UTC, 1997.

Ruether, Rosemary Radford. *Sexism and God-Talk: Toward a Feminist Theology.* Boston: Beacon, 1983.

Ruthven, Jon. *On the Cessation of the Charismata: The Protestant Polemic on Postbiblical Miracles.* Sheffield: Sheffield Academic, 1993.

Sahu, Dhirendra Kumar. *The Church of North India: A Historical and Systematic Theological Inquiry into an Ecumenical Ecclesiology.* Frankfurt am Main: Peter Lang, 1994.

———. *United and Uniting: A Story of the Church of North India.* Delhi: ISPCK, 2001.

Samartha, Stanley J. "The Holy Spirit and People of Various Faiths, Cultures and Ideologies." In *The Holy Spirit*, edited by Dow Kirkpatrick, 20–39. Nashville: Tidings, 1974.

Sanders, Fred, and Scott Swain, eds. *Retrieving Eternal Generation.* Grand Rapids: Zondervan, 2017.

Schaab, Gloria L. "Liberation Pneumatology: On the Unfettered Work of the Holy Spirit in the World." *The Heythrop Journal* 64 (2023) 383–97.

Schleiermacher, Friedrich D. E. *The Christian Faith [1820–21].* Edited and translated by H. R. MacKintosh and J. S. Stewart. Minneapolis: Fortress, 1976.

Schweitzer, Don, and Ohwang Kwon. *Hope Peace Unrest: The Holy Spirit in the Korean Community in The United Church of Canada.* Gyeonggi-do: Story, 2023.

Schweitzer, Don, et al. "Conclusion." In *The Theology of The United Church of Canada*, edited by Don Schweitzer et al., 333–43. Waterloo: Wilfrid Laurier University Press, 2019.

Seppälä, Serafim. "The Holy Spirit in Isaac of Nineveh and East Syrian Mysticism." In *The Holy Spirit in the Fathers of the Church: The Proceedings of the Seventh International Patristic Conference, Maynooth, 2008*, edited by D. Vincent Twomey and Janet E. Rutherford, 127–50. Dublin: Four Courts, 2010.

Shaw, Sally. *Creating Space for an Encounter with the Holy: The Holy Spirit and Presiding in Public Worship.* DMin thesis, Emmanuel College/University of Toronto, 2014.

Shinn, Roger L. *Confessing Our Faith: An Interpretation of the Statement of Faith of the United Church of Christ.* Cleveland: Pilgrim, 1990.

Shinn, Roger Lincoln, and Daniel Day Williams. *We Believe: An Interpretation of the United Church Statement of Faith.* Cleveland: United Church, 1966.

Sitoy, T. Valentino Jr. *Several Springs, One Stream: United Church of Christ in the Philippines, Volume I: Heritage and Origins (1898–1948).* Quezon City: United Church of Christ in the Philippines, 1992.

Sterritt, Angela. "Indigenous Languages Recognize Gender States Not Even Named in English." *The Globe and Mail*, Mar. 11, 2016, L4.

Thayer, Anne T., and Douglas Jacobsen, eds. *Christ, Creeds and Life: Conversations About the Center of our Faith.* Cleveland: United Church, 2007.

Thompson, David M. "Earthen Vessels of God's Building? The Identity of United and Uniting Churches." In *"With a Demonstration of the Spirit and of Power": Seventh*

International Consultation of United and Uniting Churches, edited by Thomas F. Best, 76–98. Faith and Order Paper No. 195. Geneva: World Council of Churches, 2004.

Ting, K. H. "What the Spirit Is Saying to the Church in China." In *God Is Love: Collected Writings of Bishop K. H. Ting*, 390–97. Colorado Springs: Cook Communications, 2004.

Tootikian, Vahan H. *The Pastor's Manual for the Officers of the Armenian Evangelical Churches.* Paramus, NJ: Armenian Evangelical World Council, 2003.

Union of Protestant Churches of Alsace and Lorraine. "Dialogue interreligieux/ Dialogue œcuménique." https://www.uepal.fr/missions/dialogue-interreligieux/dialogue-oecumenique/.

———. "Ce que nous croyons: La foi seule." https://www.uepal.fr/wp-content/uploads/2019/01/CQNC-12-Reforme-Foi-seule-WEB.pdf .

United Church in Jamaica and the Cayman Islands. *Our Church.* Edited by Elaine Commissiong et al. Grand Cayman: United Church in Jamaica and the Cayman Islands, 2019.

United Church in Papua New Guinea and the Solomon Islands. *Basis for the Union, Constitution of the United Church in Papua, New Guinea and the Solomon Islands.* Port Moresby, Papua New Guinea: UFM, 1968.

"United Church of Canada." In *Churches Respond to BEM*, edited by Max Turian, 2:276–86. Faith and Order Paper 132. Geneva: World Council of Churches, 1986.

The United Church of Canada. *The Authority and Interpretation of Scripture.* Toronto: United Church of Canada, 1992.

———. *Baptism and Renewal of Baptismal Faith.* Toronto: United Church of Canada, 1986.

———. "Basis of Union: Twenty Article of Doctrine (1925)." https://united-church.ca/sites/default/files/2024-05/united-church-basis-of-union.pdf.

———. *Mending the World: An Ecumenical Vision for Healing and Reconciliation.* Toronto: United Church of Canada, 1997.

———. "A New Creed (1968)." https://united-church.ca/community-and-faith/welcome-united-church-canada/faith-statements/new-creed-1968.

———. "A Song of Faith (2006)." https://united-church.ca/community-and-faith/welcome-united-church-canada/faith-statements/song-faith-2006.

———. "A Statement of Faith (1940)." https://united-church.ca/community-and-faith/welcome-united-church-canada/faith-statements/statement-faith-1940.

———. *A Sunday Liturgy: For Optional Use in The United Church of Canada.* Toronto: United Church of Canada, 1984.

———. *That We May Know Each Other: United Church–Muslim Relations.* Toronto: United Church of Canada, 2004.

The United Church of Christ [USA]. "Statement of Faith—Adapted by Robert V. Moss." https://www.ucc.org/what-we-believe/worship/statement-of-faith/#Robert-V.-Moss-Version/.

The United Church of Christ [USA]. "Statement of Faith in the Form of a Doxology" https://www.ucc.org/what-we-believe/worship/statement-of-faith/#doxological-version.

The United Church of Christ in Japan. "The Constitution of the United Church of Christ in Japan." https://uccj.org/constitution.

United Church of Christ in the Philippines. "Statement of Faith." https://uccphilippines.wordpress.com/uccp-statement-of-faith/.

United Free Church of Scotland. "Statement of Faith." 1921. https://www.ufcos.org.uk/about-us/statement-of-faith/.

The United Methodist Church [USA]. "Korea: Peace, Justice, and Reunification: 2016 Book of Resolutions, #6135." Church and Society. https://www.umcjustice.org/who-we-are/resolutions-adopted-by-general-conference-charlotte/korea-peace-justice-and-reunification-6135.

The United Reformed Church [UK]. "A. The Basis of Union." In *The Manual*. https://urc.org.uk/wp-content/uploads/2022/08/The-Basis-of-the-Union.pdf.

———. "[Response of the] United Reformed Church in the United Kingdom." In *Churches Respond to BEM: Official Responses to the "Baptism, Eucharist and Ministry" text*, edited by Max Thurian, 1:101–109. Faith and Order Paper 129. Geneva: World Council of Churches, 1986.

———. "Statement Concerning the Nature, Faith, and Order of the URC." https://urc.org.uk/who-we-are/what-we-believe/statement-concerning-the-nature-faith-and-order-of-the-urc/.

———. *What Do We Believe About . . . Holy Spirit?* London: The United Reformed Church, 2021.

The Uniting Church in Australia. *Basis of Union*. Rev. ed., 1992. https://uniting.church/basisofunion.

———. "The Church: Its Nature, Function, and Ordering (1963)." In *Theology for Pilgrims: Selected Theological Documents of the Uniting Church in Australia*, edited by Rob Bos and Geoff Thompson, 69–186. North Parramatta, Australia: Uniting Church, 2008.

———. "Discerning the Work of the Holy Spirit." In *Building on the Basis: Papers from the Uniting Church in Australia Assembly Working Groups on Doctrine and Worship 2000–2011*, edited by Christopher C. Walker, 13–25. North Parramatta, Australia: Assembly of the UCA, 2012.

———. "Report on Ministry in the Uniting Church in Australia (1991)." In *Theology for Pilgrims: Selected Theological Documents of the Uniting Church in Australia*, edited by Rob Bos and Geoff Thompson, 233–321. North Parramatta, Australia: Uniting Church, 2008.

———. "Response to *Baptism, Eucharist and Ministry* by the Uniting Church in Australia (1985)." In *Theology for Pilgrims: Selected Theological Documents of the Uniting Church in Australia*, edited by Rob Bos and Geoff Thompson, 210–29. North Parramatta, Australia: Uniting Church, 2008.

———. "Revised Preamble to the Constitution." July 2009. https://ucaassembly.recollect.net.au/nodes/view/137.

———. "Understanding the Church's Teaching on Baptism (1988)." In *Theology for Pilgrims: Selected Theological Documents of the Uniting Church in Australia*, edited by Rob Bos and Geoff Thompson, 509–57. North Parramatta, Australia: Uniting Church, 2008.

Uniting Church in Sweden. "A Theological Foundation for the Uniting Church in Sweden." https://equmeniakyrkan.se/english/.

Uniting Church of Christ in the Philippines. *Confirmation Manual of the Uniting Church of Christ in the Philippines*. Manila: The United Church of Christ in the Philippines, 1993. https://uccpchurch.com/wp-content/uploads/2016/03/Confirmation-Manual.pdf.

Uniting Presbyterian Church in Southern Africa. *The Manual of Faith and Order*. Rev. ed. Kempton Park, South Africa: Uniting Presbyterian Church in Southern Africa, 2017.

Wallace, Mark I. "The Green Face of God: Christianity in an Age of Ecocide." *CrossCurrents* 50 (2000) 310–31.

Wang Weifen. "The Holy Spirit Gives and Nurtures Life" ["Sheng Ming Yun Yu Zhi Ling]. In *Chinese Theology and Its Cultural Origins* [*Zhong Guo Shen Xue Ji Qi Wen Hua Yuān Yuán*], 203–215. Nanjing: Nanjing Theological Seminary, 1997. [Privately translated by Chuan Xu, Oct. 18, 2024.]

Welker, Michael. "The Holy Spirit." *Theology Today* 46 (1989) 5–20.

———. *What Happens in Communion?* Grand Rapids: Eerdmans, 2000.

Wells, Harold G. "The Holy Spirit and Theology of the Cross: Significance for Dialogue." *Theological Studies* 53 (1992) 476–92.

———. "Resistance to Domination as a Charism of the Holy Spirit." In *Spirits of Globalization: The Growth of Pentecostalism and Experiential Spiritualities in a Global Age*, edited by Sturla J. Stålsett, 170–182. London: SCM, 2006.

Wells, Patricia. *Welcome to The United Church of Canada: A Newcomer's Introduction to a New Creed*. Toronto: United Church of Canada, 1986.

Wesley, Charles. "Come, Holy Ghost, Our Hearts Inspire." Hymnary, 1740. https://hymnary.org/text/come_holy_ghost_our_hearts_inspire_let_u.

Wesley, John. *Explanatory Notes on the New Testament*. New York: Carlton & Porter, 1860.

———. "The Circumcision of the Heart." Pages 398–414 of *Sermons I*. Edited by Albert Outler. Vol. 1 of *The Works of John Wesley, Bicentennial Edition*. Nashville: Abingdon, 1984.

———. "The Marks of New Birth." Pages 417–30 of *Sermons I*. Edited by Albert Outler. Vol. 1 of *The Works of John Wesley, Bicentennial Edition*. Nashville: Abingdon, 1984.

———. "The Means of Grace." Pages 375–97 of *Sermons I*. Edited by Albert Outler. Vol. 1 of *The Works of John Wesley, Bicentennial Edition*. Nashville: Abingdon, 1984.

———. "On the Trinity." Pages 373–86 of *Sermons II*. Edited by Albert Outler. Vol. 2 of *The Works of John Wesley, Bicentennial Edition*. Nashville: Abingdon, 1985.

Williams, Delores. *Sisters in the Wilderness: The Challenge of Womanist God-Talk*. Maryknoll, NY: Orbis, 1993.

Wordsworth, William. "Lines Written a Few Miles Above Tintern Abbey, on Revisiting the Banks of the Wye During a Tour, 13 July 1798." In *Lyrical Ballads*. London: J. and A. Arch, 1798. https://romantic-circles.org/sites/default/files/RCOldSite/www/rchs/reader/tabbey.html.

World Council of Churches. *Baptism, Eucharist and Ministry*. Faith and Order Paper No. 111. Geneva: World Council of Churches, 1982.

———. *Come Holy Spirit: Renew the Whole Creation: Six Bible Studies*. Geneva: World Council of Churches, 1989.

———. *The Nature and Purpose of the Church: A Stage on the Way to a Common Statement*. Faith and Order Paper No. 181. Geneva: World Council of Churches, 1998.

———. "United and Uniting Churches." https://www.oikoumene.org/church-families/united-and-uniting-churches.

Yong, Amos. *The Spirit Poured Out on All Flesh: Pentecostalism and the Possibility of Global Theology.* Grand Rapids: Baker Academic, 2005.

Zizioulas, John. *Being as Communion: Studies in Personhood and Church.* Yonkers: St. Vladimir's Seminary Press, 1985.

www.ingramcontent.com/pod-product-compliance
Lightning Source LLC
LaVergne TN
LVHW050626100826
845148LV00011B/1748
9798385265657